IN DEFENSE OF CIVILIZATION

IN DEFENSE OF CIVILIZATION

How Our Past Can Renew Our Present

MICHAEL R.J. BONNER

sh.
SUTHERLAND HOUSE
TORONTO, 2023

Sutherland House
416 Moore Ave., Suite 304
Toronto, ON M4G 1C9

First edition, February 2023

If you are interested in inviting one of our authors to a live event or media appearance, please contact sranasinghe@sutherlandhousebooks.com and visit our website at sutherlandhousebooks.com for more information about our authors and their schedules.

We acknowledge the support of the Government of Canada.

Manufactured in China
Cover designed by Lena Yang
Book composed by Karl Hunt

Library and Archives Canada Cataloguing in Publication
Title: In defense of civilization : how our past can renew our present / Michael R.J. Bonner.
Names: Bonner, Michael Richard Jackson, 1982- author.
Identifiers: Canadiana 20260126152 | ISBN 9781997701651 (softcover)
Subjects: LCSH: Civilization. | LCSH: World history. |
LCSH: Civilization—Forecasting.
Classification: LCC CB69 .B66 2026 | DDC 909—dc23

ISBN (hardcover) 978-1-990823-06-0
ISBN (paperback) 978-1-997701-65-1
eBook 978-1-990823-18-3

TABLE OF CONTENTS

ACKNOWLEDGEMENTS

I AM GRATEFUL TO Chris Szado, Henry Hopwood-Phillips, Lola Salem, Levi Roach, Ljiljiana Radenovic, Ian Hodder, Hélvio Vairinhos, Derek Ng, Ben Sharma, Caylan Ford, and Ashkan Etemadi, who all read drafts of this book at various stages of completion.

Special thanks to Chris Champion, editor-in-chief of the Dorchester Review, for encouraging me to write this book; to Ken Whyte of Sutherland House for publishing it; and to Beyon Miloyan and Trilby Kent for editing it.

Introduction

HUMAN HISTORY IS LARGELY a record of failure. Economic strife, inflation, military overstretch, foreign warfare, domestic unrest, famine, and disease have always conspired against us and usually defeated us. More often than not, we have to struggle through hard times, enduring a substantial reduction in living standards and state capacity, or the total collapse of institutions.

At the end of the twentieth century, people scoffed at such ideas. In the 1990s, nothing seemed quite so absurd as collapse—unless, of course, you were living in China, where collapse was widely feared, or in Russia, Rwanda, and the former Yugoslavia where it actually happened. Yet, even so, the threat of world war and nuclear annihilation suddenly seemed remote after the end of the Cold War, and advanced thinkers announced a new era of steady progress everywhere. The less-terrifying prospect of decline seemed simply implausible.

Then came 9/11 and the ever-looming threat of terrorism, warfare, natural disasters, climate change, financial collapse, anaemic recovery, a rising tide of civil unrest in Europe and America, demagoguery, populism, and all the insanities of the culture war. Next came pestilence in the form of the COVID-19 pandemic, bringing with it not only death, but also personal isolation, unemployment, and further social division. Repeated rounds of fiscal stimulus have devalued currencies and provoked shortages. International supply chains have broken down. And, as I write, a war rages in the borderlands of a defunct, but still heavily armed, superpower: the conflict threatens to spread throughout Europe; and we are faced, once again, with the spectre of global famine, an energy crisis, and nuclear destruction.

So current events are a vivid reminder of the fragility of civilization and the threat of collapse. But our reflections should not be confined to the melancholy contemplation of disaster and destruction. Human civilization has extraordinary powers of recovery; and, since its original appearance long ago, civilization has always been preferable to barbarism or anarchy. Renewal is possible even after a long interval, as is shown, for example, by the revival of Europe after the collapse of the Roman Empire, or the ebb and flow of civilization in China despite repeated foreign conquest.

The purpose of this book is threefold: to explain what makes civilization what it is, to show what we are in danger of losing in the event of collapse, and to point the way toward renewal.

The first chapter is a discussion of what civilization means in general. I contrast it with what came before it in the remote past, and with the state of anarchy and barbarism that follows its collapse. I venture an anthropological and historical explanation of what civilization is, how it arises, and what makes it fragile. I judge that there are three principal features or outcomes of civilized life. These are clarity, beauty, and order. Renewal is the subject of the second chapter. Despite its tendency to collapse, the history of civilization is one of frequent regeneration. However bleak things may seem, they can be improved. I argue that civilization spread and developed through the imitation of past examples—not necessarily or exclusively through innovation and not through future-orientation. The third chapter is an examination of our own time and the worrying threats to civilized life which can now be detected. No good will come from merely identifying problems, though, so I try to trace them to their roots and propose solutions in Chapters IV to VI. I present some examples of how we have shown ourselves to be rational, beautiful, and orderly, how we have failed to do so recently, and how we may do so again. The result is an exploration of some of mankind's greatest achievements and most catastrophic failures. For the sake of brevity, I focus on what I believe to be the best, most illustrative examples, not necessarily the most thorough or exhaustive. Then comes a reflection on what looking to past examples has meant in contemporary China and what it may mean in the West. Finally, an afterword offers a few final reflections to tie the book together.

A word about sources. I have tried to support what I say with academic-style references. For the most part, they are *only* references to authoritative texts: there is no additional argumentation in my notes, and they can safely be ignored unless you are interested in further reading about the topics that I raise. I cannot claim to be an expert in everything I discuss. My academic formation was in classical and oriental languages, meaning Graeco-Roman and Perso-Arabic literature. I read widely in late-antique and Islamic historiography, and eventually wrote two theses and three books on the history of the Sasanian dynasty: the rulers of Iran between the third and seventh centuries. Studying Late Antiquity took me deep into Byzantine, Armenian, and Chinese history also. So, I feel that I am on solid ground when it comes to history and literature. As for the artistic and mathematical matters that I raise, they are well beyond my expertise, and so I have always tried to cite the best authorities that I could find. Experts will surely find things to criticize, but the overall picture should, I hope, be sound.

Speaking of the big picture, I am a fan of 'big history'—the sort of historiography in which the particular and the minute are dissolved within deep currents and long-term trends. I want to draw attention here to the main sources that have shaped my understanding of those trends. First of all, something should be said about Kenneth Clark's 1969 documentary series and book *Civilisation*.[1] This series traced the history of Western art from the fall of the Roman Empire to the twentieth century. It is perhaps the most engaging thirteen hours of television ever, and it is a superb introduction to the history of western European art. But it has a narrow geographic and cultural focus, and at least one another flaw. Clark poses the question as to what civilization is, but does not really arrive at an answer. I refer to Clark's *Civilisation* from time to time, but my views are rather different from his, and I have tried to go deeper into the *origin* of civilization and what it actually is. My views here are rooted mostly in the work of Jacques Cauvin, whose book *The Birth of the Gods and the Origins of Agriculture* posits that settled life, agriculture, and what I am calling civilization were caused by a fundamental change in outlook, inspired in large part by religion.[2] Felipe Fernández-Armesto's *Out of Our Minds* is the best and most accessible account of intellectual history that I have yet read, and it helped me to make sense of the main trends of twentieth-century thought, though the author covers the entirety of human history also.[3] Peter Conrad's *Modern Times, Modern Places* focuses on the twentieth century and is probably the best guide to the upheavals and disruptions of that time, though it makes for slow

1 Kenneth Clark published the text of his documentary, with minor modifications, as Clark, K., *Civilisation: A Personal View*, Harper and Row Publishers, New York, Hagerstown, San Francisco, London, 1969, and this is how I refer to the documentary throughout this book.

2 Cauvin, J., *Naissance des divinités; naissance de l'agriculture*, CNRS editions, Paris, 1994, published in English as *The Birth of the Gods and the Origins of Agriculture*, Cambridge University Press, Cambridge, 2000.

3 Fernández-Armesto, F., *Out of Our Minds: What We Think and How We Came to Think It*, One World Books, London, 2019.

and dense reading.[4] Finally my entire chapter on Order is practically a recapitulation of Robert Nisbet's classic of American sociology *The Quest for Community*.[5] I have followed Nisbet's arguments closely, and have tried to bring them up to date in light of contemporary scholarship. I believe that the overall point of Nisbet's book has held up well since it was published in 1953, but many of his historical arguments could be improved. Those are the greatest influences on my thinking in this book, and I encourage others to read them also.

Apart from those, there are simply too many books, ideas, events, writers, and so on for me to take account of them all. Some people will surely be upset that I have downplayed or omitted whatever seems most important to them. Others may believe that I have exaggerated things of small significance. I apologize in advance. I wanted this book to be short, and I wanted its arguments to be like medicine administered in the minimum effective dose. Sextus Empiricus, a second-century philosopher who was especially influential during the Reformation, compared philosophical arguments to cures or therapeutics administered in the right dosage.[6] Though I am not a philosopher, I am inclined to agree with Sextus; and I am mindful that the difference between medicine and poison is often a matter of *quantity*. So, what I have presented here is an *outline* of the big picture—a sketch only, but a useful one, I hope.

MRJB

4 Conrad, P., *Modern Times, Modern Places: How Life and Art Were Transformed in a Century of Revolution, Innovation and Radical Change*, New York, Alfred A. Knopf, 1999.

5 Nisbet, R., *The Quest for Community: A Study in the Ethics of Order and Freedom*, with an introduction by Ross Douthat, Wilmington, Delaware, ISI Books, 2019 (originally published 1953).

6 Sextus Empiricus, III.xxxii.

CHAPTER I

What Is Civilization?

Well-wrought this wall: Weirds broke it.
The stronghold burst . . .

Snapped rooftrees, towers fallen,
the work of Giants, the stonesmiths,
mouldereth.
                                        Rime scoureth gatetowers
                                        rime on mortar.

Shattered the showershields, roofs ruined,
age under-ate them.
                                        And the wielders & wrights?
Earthgrip holds them—gone, long gone,
fast in gravesgrasp while fifty fathers
and sons have passed.

The Ruin, an Anglo-Saxon poem
of the eighth or ninth century

FOR THE FIRST two-and-a-half million years of their existence, our most ancient hominid ancestors produced only utilitarian objects. A rudimentary aesthetic sense is suggested by an emphasis on the symmetry of hand axes, for instance, but *function* is to the fore in stone tools that have survived.[1] This changed about forty thousand years ago. The period known as the Upper Palaeolithic, at the end of the last Ice Age, was the first and longest period of creativity that our species has yet experienced. Painted, sculpted, and carved images appeared along with personal adornments, jewellery, and musical instruments. New kinds of tools were devised, sometimes made of bone, ivory, and wood. Weaving of bast fibres was developed, and in what is now China a rudimentary pottery was invented.

The art of Palaeolithic man suggests a new attitude to life. His paintings (most famously found in caves at Lascaux, Altamira, and Ardèche) are some of the finest artworks ever produced. They have no connection whatever with any high culture; and so, even though they were hidden away deep underground, when they appear in books or are seen in person, they are immediately accessible to everyone. The artists have carefully observed and depicted naturalistic animal forms, and their arrangement conveys feelings of energy, vitality, and movement, which an observer can still feel today.

But much is missing. There is no sense of order, much less of narrative. Images are often superimposed upon one another haphazardly, like the lions and bison at Chauvet cave in Ardèche

1 White, R., *Prehistoric Art: The Symbolic Journey of Mankind*, H. N. Abrams, New York, 2003, pp. 7–18; Mithen, S., *The Prehistory of the Mind: A Search for the Origins of Art, Religion and Science*, Thames and Hudson, London, 1996, pp. 105–128.

or the incongruous jumble of deer and salmon carved on a reindeer antler found in the Lorthet cave in the Pyrenees.[2] Animals are depicted quite accurately, but their hooves are sometimes deliberately omitted. No Palaeolithic art has yet been found depicting the sun, the moon, the stars, or a landscape, which must tell us something about our ancestors' perception of time. Very few figures of men and women appear. When Palaeolithic artists bothered to draw them, they depicted amalgams of human and animal forms, and confined them to the most remote parts of their caves.[3] In the so-called Shaft, deep within the Lascaux cave, we find a stick figure of a man with an apparent erection and the head of a bird: he is prostrate beside a disembowelled bison, a spear, and what appears to be a staff with a bird on it. In the End Chamber of the Chauvet cave, there is a somewhat natural-looking female pubic triangle flanked by the legs of a woman but without feet; and directly above we find the head of a bison, not the rest of the woman. The famous figure of the 'sorcerer' found in the Cave of the Trois-Frères in Arriège seems to show a figure with an upright posture, human legs and hands, the back, ears, and antlers of a reindeer, the tail of a horse, and the phallus of a cat.[4] Notably, this blending of human and animal forms was not confined to the walls of caves, as shown by the ivory figurine of the lion-headed man found at Hohlenstein-Stadel in Germany.

Scholars in the late twentieth century assumed that the world of the Upper Palaeolithic was probably much the same as that

2 Bahn, P. G. / Vertut, J., *Images of the Ice Age*, Facts on File, New York, 1988, p. 80; 124; 190.

3 Clottes, J., *What Is Palaeolithic Art: Cave Painting and the Dawn of Human Creativity*, originally published in 2011 in French as *Pourquoi l'art préhistorique?* by Éditions Gallimard, translated by Oliver Y. Martin and Robert D. Martin, University of Chicago Press, Chicago, 2016, pp. 147–152; Leroi-Gourhan, A., *Treasures of Prehistoric Art*, H. N. Abrams, New York, 1967, pp. 121–136; 172–182.

4 Bahn, P. G. / Vertut, J., *Images of the Ice Age*, Facts on File, New York, 1988, p. 144.

of contemporary hunter-gatherers.[5] There was certainly some long-distance exchange of flint and chert for stone tools, but it was otherwise a world of immediate, brief relationships with the environment, with other people, and with gods or spirits.[6] Social life would have been dominated by giving, sharing, and immediate reciprocity within a small group because there were few long-term commitments among people, places, and things.[7] Perhaps this can explain somewhat why we find no pictures of groups of Palaeolithic people, nor any symbols of the passage of time. This is odd, to say the least, because Palaeolithic people must have been as competent observers of animals, nature, and even the weather, as any other hunters. But this does not come across in their images.

Palaeolithic art was not 'art for art's sake', but probably bound up with religious, perhaps shamanic, practices.[8] The images of anthropomorphic animals or theriomorphic people may reflect a lost mythological world, as elaborate and complex perhaps as that of

5 Woodburn, J., 'Hunters and Gatherers Today and Reconstruction of the Past' in Gellner, E. (ed.), *Soviet and Western Anthropology*, Duckworth, London, 1980, pp. 95–117.

6 Ingold, T., *The Perception of the Environment: Essays on Livelihood, Dwelling, and Skill*, Routledge, London, 2000, pp. 40–61; Bird-David, N. *et al.*, '"Animism" Revisited: Personhood, Environment, and Relational Epistemology', *Current Anthropology*, 40, Supplement, 1999, pp. 67–90; Ingold, T., 'Building, Dwelling, Living: How Animals and People Make Themselves at Home in the World' in Strathern, M. (ed.), *Shifting Contexts: Transformations in Anthropological Knowledge*, Routledge, London, 1995, pp. 57–80.

7 Bird-David, N., 'The Giving Environment: Another Perspective on the Economic System of Hunter-Gatherers', *Current Anthropology*, 31(2), 1990, pp. 189–196.

8 The main theories of the purpose of prehistoric art are summarized and analysed in Lewis-Williams, D., *The Mind in the Cave: Consciousness and the Origin of Art*, Thames and Hudson, London, 2002, pp. 41–68; Bahn, P. G., *The Cambridge Illustrated History of Prehistoric Art*. Cambridge University Press, Cambridge, 1998, pp. 218–254; Bandi, H.-G. *et al.*, *The Art of the Stone Age: Forty Thousand Years of Rock Art*, Crown Publishers Inc., New York, 1961, pp. 26–28.

the San peoples of Southern Africa, or the 'Dreamtime' of Australian Aborigines.[9] However this may be, the blending of human and animal forms suggests that there was no rigid distinction between man and beast, and our sense of place in the world was unstable.

That sense of our place in the world, when fully developed, was the main impetus for settled life and what I am calling civilization. The adoption of agriculture is often construed as the *cause* of these things, but this is a misunderstanding. The so-called Agricultural Revolution, the domestication of animals, urban life, the development of states, and so forth, had many causes. Climate change, population growth, happenstance—these and other social, economic, and environmental explanations have been ventured over the years.[10] No model has escaped criticism. None suffices on its own. But surely before any energy could have been devoted to agriculture and so forth, people must have developed the idea that they had their proper place in the world where they might settle permanently, plan for the future, and contemplate the past. The archaeological record bears this out, since we find evidence of settlement around communal ritual centres throughout the Near East *before* the full development of agriculture and the domestication of animals.[11]

9 Lewis-Williams, D., *The Mind in the Cave: Consciousness and the Origin of Art*, Thames and Hudson, London, 2002, pp. 136–162; Clottes, J., *What Is Palaeolithic Art: Cave Painting and the Dawn of Human Creativity*, originally published in 2011 in French as *Pourquoi l'art préhistorique?* by Éditions Gallimard, translated by Oliver Y. Martin and Robert D. Martin, University of Chicago Press, Chicago, 2016, pp. 39–85.

10 These are summarized in Simmons, A. H., *The Neolithic Revolution in the Near East: Transforming the Human Landscape*, University of Arizona Press, Tucson, 2007, pp. 10–29.

11 Cauvin, J., *Naissance des divinités; naissance de l'agriculture*, CNRS editions, Paris, 1994, published in English as *The Birth of the Gods and the Origins of Agriculture*, Cambridge University Press, Cambridge, 2000; Hodder, I., *The Leopard's Tale: Revealing the Mysteries of Çatalhöyük*, Thames and Hudson, London, 2006, pp. 233–258.

In other words, about twelve thousand years ago, the old economic model of hunting and gathering persisted but people had settled down around public religious sites. They developed historical ties to place and to shared ancestors long before they began farming. And so ultimately it was a change of attitude or outlook that gave us civilization. In his famous documentary, Kenneth Clark expressed that point like this:

> Civilisation means something more than energy and will and creative power . . . How can I define it? Well, very shortly, a sense of permanence . . . Civilised man, or so it seems to me, must feel that he belongs somewhere in space and time; that he consciously looks forward and looks back.[12]

This attitude, it should be emphasized, has nothing to do with any peculiar technological system. It does not even depend upon reading and writing, as may be popularly imagined, since the written word appeared long after civilization. Few of us probably realize how old it really is.

The civilized attitude first took shape in the material culture of the Neolithic period, about twelve thousand years ago. At the site of Çatalhöyük in southern Turkey, for instance, houses were built and rebuilt according to a uniform pattern; and ancestors were buried under the floors of dwellings—signs of stability and a shared past.[13]

12 Clark, K., *Civilisation*, 1969, pp. 14; 17.

13 Goring-Morris, N. / Belfer-Cohen, A., 'Long-term Memory and the Community in the Later Prehistory of the Levant' in Hodder, I. (ed.), *Religion, History, and Place in the Origin of Settled Life*, Boulder, University Press of Colorado, 2018, pp. 99–114; Benz, M., *et al.*, 'Re-presenting the Past: Evidence from Daily Ritual Practices and Rituals at Körtik Tepe' in Hodder, I. (ed.), *Religion, History, and Place in the Origin of Settled Life*, Boulder, University Press of Colorado, 2018, pp. 137–161.

It is also visible in art. In contrast to the swirling, vagrant motion of Palaeolithic cave paintings, the wall art at Çatalhöyük begins to convey a sense of purpose and direction. Modern observers will find the images crude in comparison with those of the Upper Palaeolithic, and probably less beautiful. But this is not the point. At Çatalhöyük we find paintings with clear narrative content, such as the image of several human figures hunting and baiting a stag and a wild boar, among other similar energetic scenes.[14] These images speak for the first time of human organization, common purpose, and social cooperation, as well as stability and rootedness.

Those features reach maturity quite suddenly in the art of ancient Egypt. The carved reliefs, statuary, and figurines of the Old Kingdom, which appeared nearly five thousand years ago, are a vision of a harmonious society, guided by a wise king, well-counselled by his ministers, who rules in cooperation with the gods, and whose authority is that of a benevolent hero, not a tyrant.[15] Man's purpose in life is no longer uncertain. We behold an ideal state of the world in which confident and cheerful people go about their affairs rationally. We find sympathy for the tasks of ordinary people—the sort of work, which in the later Graeco-Roman world would have been performed by slaves and either ignored or ridiculed, is respectfully portrayed in the figures of people grinding grain, washing a jar, and brewing beer.[16] Their faces are intelligent and no less dignified and serene than the more aristocratic images of kings, priests, and bureaucrats. The ancient Egyptian religion obviously maintained an attachment to half-human, half-animal

14 For the wall painting at Çatalhöyük in general, see Mellaart, J., *Çatal Hüyük: A Neolithic Town in Anatolia*, New York, McGraw-Hill Book Company, 1967, pp. 131–177.

15 Aldred, C., *Egyptian Art in the Days of the Pharaohs 3100–320 BC*, Thames and Hudson, London, 1980, pp. 11–18.

16 See the Reader's Digest documentary by Clark, K. *In the Beginning*, 1975.

divinities, and this must remind us of certain Palaeolithic images. But we have come a long way from the abstract figure of a man with a bird's head hidden away in a remote recess of a cave to the elegant exposition of men and women and all their activities.

How would I describe this transformation? Civilization produced three main outcomes, and they are discernible first in the material culture of the Egyptian Old Kingdom. The first is a sense of *clarity*, expressing the idea that the world is a coherent whole which human beings can perceive and understand. It gives rise to the use of language to describe the world and our experience of it, and becomes visible in the elegant presentation of hieroglyphs in which words and ideas were recorded for thousands of years. The second is a sense of *beauty*, expressed with seemingly mathematical rigour in the harmonious proportions of Egyptian art and architecture. The third, less obvious, but more profound than the first two outcomes, is a sense of *order*. It is founded on the belief that there is some principle of organization in the world in which all things animate and inanimate have their proper place and purpose. We can see this in the sympathetic depiction of nature and in symbols of political and religious authority. Clarity, beauty, and order—they appear together first in Egypt; but they are the main results of civilization everywhere.

Despite the achievements of Egyptian civilization, civilized man, as a fully developed person, does not find his prototype there. Egypt of the Old Kingdom clearly produced men and women of genius: its artists, scribes, and administrators were obviously capable of distinguishing themselves, otherwise their images would never have been preserved. But we know practically nothing about them as persons. Even the great architect Imhotep is little more than a name to us, though he was highly regarded as the first person to build in stone, as a skilled physician, and in a later age as a god. To judge by Egyptian art, depicting personal characteristics was far less important than representing what is eternal in man and his place in the order of things. Accordingly, the art of Egypt reached a state of perfection early, and became stereotyped and static.

The civilizations of ancient Mesopotamia were somewhat better acquainted with variety and personal characteristics. We can see this in the early art of Sumer and Akkad, which is less idealized and more various than that of Egypt, but it is more obvious in Mesopotamian literature. Very often, as in the Sumerian *Epic of Gilgamesh*, we encounter a certain pessimism about the world's constant state of flux and vicissitude. Yet we also perceive a delight in the variety of human experience and in the full exercise of all man's faculties. Many centuries' worth of royal inscriptions bear this out, but perhaps most vividly in the hymns of praise addressed to the Sumerian king Shulgi of Ur (d. c. 1999 BC). Shulgi's first and greatest boast was his mastery of writing and mathematics in early youth. He was similarly skilled in all the religious lore of his age, and was adept at interpreting omens. He was a mighty warrior and hunter who intimidated his human and animal adversaries. He had extraordinary endurance when running over long distances. And yet he was also a great lover of music with a skilful and delicate touch upon stringed instruments and reed pipes alike. Not only could he play the lute and the lyre, but he could also tune them properly. Just as he was musical, he was also eloquent and intelligent: he spoke clearly and articulately; he delighted in rational debate, which he encouraged among his governors. He grasped all the subtleties of the legal system; and he pronounced his verdicts in five languages. He could understand and correct the rough speech of a mountain man, and no one could switch between languages faster than Shulgi.[17]

17 I am paraphrasing and condensing the hymns found in Klein, J., *Three Šulgi hymns: Sumerian royal hymns glorifying King Šulgi of Ur*, Bar-Ilan University Press, Ramat Gan, 1981. For analysis see Klein, J., 'The Royal Hymns of Shulgi King of Ur: Man's Quest for Immortal Fame', *Transactions of the American Philosophical Society*, 71 (7), 1981, pp. 1–48.

What a portrait of a confident, intelligent, and civilized man! Shulgi's boasts would fit in well with our own notions of a well-balanced lifestyle right down to a love of music and physical fitness. More importantly, though, we must understand Shulgi's accomplishments as representing an ancient ideal of a full and complete life in which all human faculties form a whole and are exercised accordingly. They are not a series of discrete experiences or unrelated adventures, as we might think of them now. Those hymns of praise were written about four thousand years ago, but the sense of confidence in all human faculties has remained a feature of every civilizing epoch in our history.

Civilization is all the more remarkable for having lasted at all. The earliest states were generally not long-lived—especially so in Mesopotamia where several small states rose and fell, while Egypt remained a unit. Our friend Shulgi's dynasty, the so-called Third Dynasty of Ur, enjoyed slightly more than a hundred years of relative stability and then collapsed. The Egyptian Old Kingdom, which lasted about seven centuries, must have seemed indestructible in comparison, but it too disintegrated. The civilization of the Indus River valley lasted even longer between 3300 and 1300 BC, but its cities were gradually abandoned over that period before the final collapse came. The problems faced by early states were often overwhelming. No one could have foreseen the dangers of environmental degradation, political turmoil, and (perhaps worst of all) disease. Our own experience of a novel virus shows that enormous disruption can occur even without a huge death toll. There are good reasons to think that zoonotic diseases were rife in the early days of settled life, as people and animals crowded into cities where sanitation left much to be desired.[18] When we add to

18 Scott, J. C., *Against the Grain: A Deep History of the Earliest States*, Yale University Press, New Haven, 2017.

this the threat of drought, salinization, crop failure, climate change, warfare, civil strife, and other troubles, we are all the more surprised that civilized life managed to pull through at all.

But long after settled life had become a habit, and after many of those early challenges were resolved, the collapse of civilization was the rule and not the exception. This is true even in the absence of violence or other calamities. The end of the Egyptian Old Kingdom seems to have been caused by regional separatism to the detriment of central authority, not civil war or foreign invasion.[19] This has led some people to assume that something so delicate as civilization could only have been held together by the coercive and tyrannical power of the state. James C. Scott has accordingly urged us to think of the breakdown of early states as a welcome relief from oppressive taxation, the rigours of law and order, military service, and so forth.[20] But I find this argument hard to credit. It would be wrong to confound the state with civilization itself, but stable and reliable institutions are essential to civilization; nor can we expect to enjoy any of civilization's benefits without making at least some of the sacrifices which Scott deplores. Moreover, the collapse of a central authority, even an oppressive one, can create instability, uncertainty, and sometimes anarchy. The recent collapse of the Soviet Union, for instance, was relief to many; but the instability and confusion caused by it led to the rise of a kleptocracy and the near-lawless rule of oligarchs and strongmen.

Furthermore, the coercive power of civilized states, and their capacity for violence, pale in comparison with those of tribal or

19 Seidlmayer, S., 'The First Intermediate Period (c. 2160–2055 BC)' in Shaw, I. (ed.), *The Oxford History of Ancient Egypt*, Oxford University Press, Oxford, 2003, pp. 108–136.

20 Scott, J. C., *Against the Grain: A Deep History of the Earliest States*, Yale University Press, New Haven, 2017.

pre-state societies. The idea that there was no war or violence before the appearance of civilization originated with Rousseau and became fashionable in the mid-twentieth century, but it is quite wrong. Warfare is in fact much older than civilization, as attested by late-Palaeolithic and early-Neolithic mass graves at Jebel Sahaba in Egypt and the so-called 'Talheim Death Pit' in Germany. Both sites show that ancient warfare was significantly more violent and destructive than in later times, since it involved regular indiscriminate massacres of entire communities of both sexes and all ages. To judge by evidence of traumas in ancient skeletons, the prehistoric homicide rate in what is now Illinois has been estimated at 70 times higher than that of the Unites States in 1980 and 1,400 times higher than that of 1980s Britain. Ancient and modern non-state conflicts tend to produce an average death rate of about 10 percent of the total population. To put this in perspective, a little more than a million Americans died in the Second World War, or 0.39 percent of the population at the time. If the figure had been 10 percent, as in non-civilized warfare, total American deaths would have amounted to about thirteen million. Those are just some of the examples presented in Lawrence H. Keeley's study *War Before Civilization*.[21] Some may well question prehistoric statistics, of course. And yet, whatever the failures of civilized states throughout history, civilization has always been preferable to what came before it.

Still, no matter how desirable, secure, and deeply rooted civilization may seem, it is actually quite fragile. This idea seemed so self-evident to our ancient ancestors that it found universal expression in the myth of decline from an ancient golden age. The lineaments of this story are a scheme of ages classified with

21 Keeley, L. H., *War Before Civilization: The Myth of the Peaceful Savage*, Oxford University Press, Oxford, 1996.

reference to gold, silver, bronze, and iron; and as the value of the metal decreases, so do the conditions of human life and the moral worth of the people then living. The first appearance of this myth in European literature is found in the *Works and Days* attributed to the Greek poet Hesiod who lived in the eighth century BC.[22] But it is far more ancient and it appears in much the same form in Zoroastrian, Jewish, and Hindu scripture, as well as in Norse mythology.[23] But a long decline was not the worst possible fate. The myth of a sudden and violent collapse of a high civilization takes shape in the Mesopotamian, Chinese, and Biblical stories of a great flood, the destruction of Atlantis, the apocalyptic destruction at the end of the world familiar from Christianity and Islam, and the Norse myth of Ragnarök.

The real event behind the myth of a golden age and catastrophic destruction is the so-called Late Bronze Age collapse. In about 1200 BC, the interconnected world of Egypt, the Aegean, the Levant, and Mesopotamia suddenly came crashing down.[24] The kingdoms of Mycenae in Greece, the Kassites in Babylon, the Hittite empire in Anatolia, the Egyptian New Kingdom, Ugarit, and the Amorites in the Levant—these all collapsed, many of them violently.[25] Nearly every important city of western Eurasia was destroyed and abandoned. Scholars have blamed earthquakes, internal rebellion,

22 Hesiod, WD, l. 109–201.

23 West, M. L., *The East Face of Helicon: West Asiatic Elements in Greek Poetry and Myth*, Oxford University Press, Oxford, 1997, pp. 312–319; Heinberg, R., *Memories & Visions of Paradise: Exploring the Universal Myth of a Lost Golden Age*, J. P. Tarcher, Los Angeles, 1989.

24 Cline, E. H., *1177 B.C.: The Year Civilization Collapsed*, Princeton University Press, Princeton, revised edition, 2021.

25 The violence of this period is the main subject of Drews, R., *The End of the Bronze Age: Changes in Warfare and the Catastrophe ca. 1200 B.C.*, Princeton University Press, Princeton, 1995.

invasion by marauding 'Sea Peoples', collapse of trade, the dissolution of marriage alliances, plague, climate change, drought, famine, and volcanic eruption. Eric Cline calls it a 'perfect storm' of calamities, accelerated and worsened by the international connections and interdependence.[26] In the disarray that followed, we can contrast the so-called Egyptian Third Intermediate Period with the Greek Dark Ages. Egypt was badly weakened, but managed to hobble on, despite civil war and political fragmentation. We notice a decline in material culture in the form of haphazard and slovenly construction of tombs out of recycled materials.[27] But the Greek Dark Ages were far worse. All monumental stone architecture ceased, as did wall painting; the human population diminished considerably; some sites such as Pylos remained uninhabited for a thousand years; and the former Mycenaean state vanished and gave way to disunity and regionalism. Art was confined to unimaginative geometric patterns on pottery, often of clumsy execution.[28] Most surprising of all, writing seems to have been entirely forgotten not only in Greece but in the Levant also. Even the Greek oral tradition, as reflected by Herodotus, Thucydides, and the Homeric poems, shows that very little was remembered of the Mycenaean Age.[29]

The Dark Age was almost unspeakably barbarous. This comes across forcefully in the poems that are conventionally attributed to Homer but really the products of countless, anonymous bards who

26 Cline, E. H., *1177 B.C.: The Year Civilization Collapsed*, Princeton University Press, Princeton, revised edition, 2021, pp. 134–166.

27 I am judging from the evidence presented in Taylor, J., 'The Third Intermediate Period' in Shaw, I. (ed.), *The Oxford History of Ancient Egypt*, Oxford University Press, Oxford, 2003, pp. 324–363, but Taylor disagrees with my conclusions.

28 See the clear, concise exposition of sub-Mycenaean pottery in Desborough, V. R. d'A., *The Greek Dark Ages*, St Martin's Press, New York, 1972, pp. 29–63.

29 Desborough, V. R. d'A., *The Greek Dark Ages*, St Martin's Press, New York, 1972, pp. 321–325.

had recorded and augmented an older oral tradition. The fact that this oral tradition was developed in the first place is sometimes taken as evidence that the early Iron Age did not represent a precipitous decline. After all, the verses of the *Iliad* and the *Odyssey* seem to preserve some recollections of the old aristocratic culture. Agamemnon is 'king of rich Mycenae' which is said to have a 'well-built citadel' with 'wide ways', even though that city was a ruin when the *Iliad* was composed.[30] We may also catch a reminiscence of the old civilization in the episode of the Trojan prince Hector's brief return to his city as the war rages before its walls. Troy would likewise have been a heap of rubble in the early Iron Age. But in the *Iliad* the palace of Priam, king of Troy, is a vision of orderly, civilized family life: 'fifty chambers of polished stone adjoin one another where Priam's sons sleep beside their wives', and within the court there are 'twelve well-roofed chambers of polished stone for his noble daughters and sons-in-law', and so forth.[31] And we cannot fail to be touched by the scene of Hector saying goodbye to his infant son before returning to the battlefield as his tearful wife Andromache implores him to stay—an expression of courage, which is undoubtedly a virtue in any epoch.[32]

But the *Iliad* is otherwise preoccupied with the brutality of warfare, personal honour, prowess in battle, and public signs of approval. Though Aristotle and others admired these principles, it was obvious to them that they did not by themselves make a civilization. Achilles, Ajax, and the other heroes are essentially brutes, and their world is as barbarous and violent as that depicted in the Biblical Book of Joshua, which (though largely fictional) refers to the same period. Likewise, the opening paragraphs of Thucydides'

30 *Iliad* VII.180; II.569; IV.52.
31 *Iliad* VI.237–250.
32 *Iliad* VI.467–475.

history depict this era as one of interminable marauding and piracy, when all men went about armed 'like barbarians', when trade was unknown, and farming not worth the trouble.[33] Aeschylus' cycle of dramas harking back to that time is a horrific tale of murder, blood-guilt, human sacrifice, and revenge; and the ruling family of Mycenae, the House of Atreus, is the embodiment of savagery.[34] And we should not forget that the main theme of the *Iliad* is that Achilles and Agamemnon quarrelled over possession of the sex-slave Briseis—a topic which has grown increasingly distasteful with time.

The world of the *Odyssey* is less remote than that of the *Iliad*, but only slightly. Odysseus stands out among the heroes of the Trojan War, and he comes nearer to our idea of a civilized man than they do. Odysseus had visited many cities and 'he knew the thinking of many men'.[35] Guile and cunning, not brawn alone, are his attributes; it was he that famously devised the stratagem of the Trojan Horse. He is an intelligent and persuasive speaker sent to remonstrate with the sulking Achilles, and he is the trickster who outwits the Cyclops. But he is a long way from our confident friend Shulgi of Ur and his command of all human faculties. The story of Odysseus' longing for hearth and home and his rightful place as king of Ithaca must tell us *something* about the gradual return of civilization after the collapse of the Bronze Age—so too must the love of poetry, song, and feasting which we meet in the *Odyssey*, as well as the charming description of life at the palace of Alcinous whom Odysseus visits. But civilization still had a long way to go,

33 Thucydides I.1–6.

34 See the introduction to Aeschylus, *The Oresteia: Agamemnon, The Libation Bearers, the Eumenides*, translated by Robert Fagles with an introductory essay, notes, and glossary by Robert Fagles and W. B. Stanford, Penguin Books, New York, 1979, pp. 13–97.

35 *Odyssey* I.4

and the world of Odysseus, like that of Aeschylus' tragedies, is still one of cannibals, monsters, blood-drinking ghosts, witches, sorcery, magical plants, and journeys to the underworld.

The sudden and total collapse of an entire world system is not otherwise attested in history. It may, however, be paralleled by other violent calamities on a smaller scale. The complete disappearance of civilization in Mesoamerica at the end of the first millennium AD and the Roman destruction of Carthage in 146 BC come to mind.[36] And we should not forget that our own experience of attritional and mechanized warfare, as well as nuclear bombs, forced us to contemplate total destruction throughout the twentieth century. Perhaps the nearest parallel is the collapse of the Roman Empire in western Europe. In the first century after the fall of Rome, Goths, Alans, Vandals, and Huns swarmed across Europe and North Africa spreading rape, pillage, and anarchy. Literacy almost disappeared, building in stone ceased, and long-distance trade collapsed. A vivid portrait of decline after the collapse of Roman power is afforded by that Anglo-Saxon poem *The Ruin* which I quoted in this chapter's epigraph.[37] But the most startling scientific evidence of decline is that the level of pollution captured in polar icecaps fell back to that of prehistoric times—an indication that industrial activity had basically disappeared.[38] But after the Bronze Age collapse, this sort of total disaster was unusual.

36 Culbert, T. P., 'The Collapse of Classic Maya Civilization' in Yoffee, N. / Cowgill, G. L. (eds), *The Collapse of Ancient States and Civilizations*, The University of Arizona Press, Tucson, 1988, pp. 69–101; Million, R., 'The Last Years of Teotihuacan Dominance' in Yoffee, N. / Cowgill, G. L. (eds), *The Collapse of Ancient States and Civilizations*, The University of Arizona Press, Tucson, 1988, pp. 102–164.

37 *The Earliest English Poems*, translated and introduced by Michael Alexander, second edition, Penguin Books, 1986 (originally published in 1966), pp. 28–29.

38 Ward-Perkins, B., *The Fall of Rome and the End of Civilization*, Oxford University Press, Oxford, 2006.

The example of states in Mesopotamia is more typical. Whereas the Egyptian state and its civilization ebbed and flowed together over the ages, Mesopotamia shows that many city-states and empires can rise and fall while a common civilization carries on beneath. Much the same can be said for the rise and fall of kingdoms and dynasties in Mediaeval Europe and imperial China, all animated by a common spirit of civilization. This may tempt some people to think not of decline, or disappearance, but rather of constant change and evolution.

Yet the longer the time scale, the less tenable this observation seems. No one would say that a distinctly Mesopotamian, ancient Egyptian, or Roman civilization has survived anywhere on earth. There had been no indigenous Mesopotamian political order since the Persian conquest of Babylon in 539 BC. The latest possible evidence for the existence of a distinct Mesopotamian civilization is from AD 75, when the last cuneiform tablet was written. That form of writing had been confined to learned use hundreds of years before, and had already been obliterated from most of the Levant in the Bronze Age collapse. Not long after the first century AD, cuneiform finally disappeared altogether; and the civilizations of Sumer and Akkad were forgotten, remaining totally unknown until the nineteenth century when they were rediscovered.[39] The last relic of ancient Egypt is a disorderly hieroglyphic inscription made in the year AD 394, carved into the wall of the temple of Isis at Philae. It is pitifully crude in comparison with the beauty and confidence of the Old Kingdom. And it was not long after that date in the late fourth century, after many centuries of slow decay, that the extinction of the old Egyptian civilization was complete.

39 Yoffee, N., 'The Collapse of Ancient Mesopotamian States and Civilization' in Yoffee, N. / Cowgill, G. L. (eds), *The Collapse of Ancient States and Civilizations*, The University of Arizona Press, Tucson, 1988, pp. 44–68.

To judge by the grumblings of Rome's own historians, there was no period of Roman history that was not considered decadent; nor was the Roman state ever really stable. Polybius and Sallust believed that the decline of Rome had begun immediately after the final destruction of Carthage.[40] Livy and Tacitus beheld in their own days a long descent from virtue and freedom, and Tacitus was sure that nothing was left of the old Roman morality.[41] Two centuries later we find the historian Ammianus Marcellinus rehearsing similar criticisms about luxury, greed, idleness, pretence, and exaggerated devotion to the circus.[42] Commentary on Roman decadence may have become something of a literary cliché, which was carried on even by later Byzantine authors like Procopius of Caesarea and his followers. There are so many low points, and so many apparent recoveries, between the founding of Rome in 753 BC and the fall of Constantinople in 1453 that determining the height of Roman power from which it declined, and the moment of its collapse, will always be subject to debate.

There must also be some doubt about what we mean by 'Roman' and by 'decline and fall', as Edward Gibbon famously put it. The hated Etruscan kings of Rome were banished in favour of a republican constitution, which gradually gave way first to a dictatorship and later to an autocracy. The Roman administrative state was reorganized many times under the successors to Augustus and Diocletian. Foreigners were integrated into the state so thoroughly that, with time, even the emperors were Roman only in name. The empire was divided, reunited, and divided again; and the capital was shifted from Rome to Constantinople. Moreover, there is no policy which

40 Polybius, VI.57; Sallust, Cat., 10.1–5.

41 Livy, *Ab Urbe Condita*, Pr. 9–10; Tacitus, *Annales*, I.ii–iv, for instance.

42 Ammianus, *Res Gestae*, XVI.4; XXVIII.4.

accelerated decline in one age which cannot also be said to have arrested it in another.[43] The western half of the empire collapsed long before its eastern counterpart was conquered, the city of Rome having been sacked repeatedly before the conventional date of extinction in AD 476. The east carried on from its capital at Constantinople, surviving the Frankish conquest in AD 1204, until the end came in the middle of the fifteenth century.[44] Roman culture belonged to a common Mediterranean civilization which both predated and outlived the empire. The Latin language, the Christian religion, and some aspects of Roman law have obviously carried on. But even if we are less confident than Polybius and his followers in determining the moment of decline or collapse, we must admit that the civilizations of western Europe and the Mediterranean have long ceased to be Roman and that formerly Roman features have been appropriated and assimilated by new peoples unknown to the ancient world.

Here we arrive at another truth. A long-lived civilization gradually transforming itself over many centuries, weathering many troubles before a final collapse, and leaving behind traces of itself tells us that civilization, although fragile, can be renewed. And the eventual recovery after the collapse of the Bronze Age shows that revival can happen even after a long interval of darkness and barbarism. I take up this theme in the next chapter.

43 Bowersock, G. W., 'The Dissolution of the Roman Empire' in Yoffee, N. / Cowgill, G. L. (eds), *The Collapse of Ancient States and Civilizations*, The University of Arizona Press, Tucson, 1988, pp. 165–175.

44 Explanations for the long survival of East Rome are discussed in Wickham, C., *The Inheritance of Rome: Illuminating the Dark Ages 400–1000*, Penguin Books, London, 2009, pp. 255–278; 298–317.

CHAPTER II

Rebirth

The thing that hath been, it is that which shall be; and that which is done is that which shall be done: and there is no new thing under the sun.

Ecclesiastes 1.9

The Zhou gazes down upon the two dynasties that preceded it. How brilliant in culture it is! I follow the Zhou.

Confucius, *Analects*, 8.20

EVERY GREAT REVIVAL of civilization has been inspired by the past. Rebirth comes not as the result of random experiments that happened to turn out well, but the deliberate imitation of what had worked before: the 'future possibilities which the past makes available to the present'.[1] This

1 MacIntyre, A., *After Virtue: A Study in Moral Theory*, third edition, Notre Dame, University of Notre Dame, 2007, p. 223.

would seem to go against everything we are told nowadays about the importance of innovation and novelty. But it is historically irrefutable. To understand this, we must return to the darkness of the early Iron Age and trace the regrowth and spread of civilization from Mesopotamia outward.

Assyria and Phoenicia

After the Bronze Age collapse, the Hittite and the Aegean civilizations were over. Babylonia was partially occupied and regularly plundered by marauders. Egypt would never again be a great power. Only one great civilization with any connection to the old world of the Bronze Age was left standing. The so-called Neo-Assyrian Empire had weathered about two centuries of disorder and had returned to prominence in northern Mesopotamia in about 911 BC. There, civilized life managed to pull through and carry on much as before. Nearly everywhere else it was a dark age.

The isolation and barbarism of that time were broken by the merchants of the Levant. The Greeks called them Phoenicians, though they called themselves Canaanites in their own language. They had been the traders and middlemen of the former globalized world of the Bronze Age. At the opening of the Iron Age, they were vassals to the Neo-Assyrian Empire, and it was in the service of that state that the Phoenicians set out and established colonies and trading hubs throughout the Mediterranean. These adventures connected the old world with the new. The Phoenicians and the wares that they traded inspired the iconography, artisanal techniques, and religious practices of Archaic Greece.[2] Ecstatic divination, reading the entrails

2 The latest word on the Phoenicians is López-Ruiz, C., *Phoenicians and the Making of the Mediterranean*, Harvard University Press, Cambridge, 2021.

of sacrificial animals, and the idea of temples came from the old world also, and eastern gods joined the Greek pantheon. The Greeks borrowed from the Phoenicians a large vocabulary pertaining to craftsmanship and luxury goods,[3] as well as the practices of lending money at interest, insurance, joint financing of business ventures, and deposit banking.[4] But no oriental export was more important in the long run than the Phoenician alphabet. It was adapted to the Greek language no earlier than 800 BC, long after the loss of the old syllabic script. Scholars tend to think that this was the work of a single person.[5] Who it was, we shall never know; but it should remind us never to underestimate the effect that individuals of genius may have on civilization.

Rome

Of course, it was neither Phoenicia nor Greece that came to rule the Mediterranean world, but Rome. In the early Iron Age, that damp cluster of huts along the banks of the Tiber would have seemed an unlikely candidate for world domination, much less for a repository and conduit of civilization. Yet this is exactly what happened for many complex reasons—not the least of which was good fortune, as the ancient historian Polybius constantly reminds us. But, in my opinion, two reasons were overwhelmingly more important than all others.

The first is that the supremacy of Rome would have been unthinkable without the unity of the Mediterranean first achieved

3 Burkert, W., *The Orientalizing Revolution: Near Eastern Influence on Greek Culture in the Early Archaic Age*, Harvard University Press, Cambridge, 1998, pp. 33–40.

4 Miles, R., *Carthage Must Be Destroyed: The Rise and Fall of an Ancient Civilization*, Penguin Books, New York, 2010.

5 Powell, B. B., *Homer and the Origin of the Greek Alphabet*, Cambridge University Press, Cambridge, 1991, pp. 10–12.

by the merchants of Phoenicia. Their North African trading colony at Carthage (in modern Tunisia) soon eclipsed the Levantine homeland and formed trading and military alliances with the other powers of the day. When Rome overcame Carthage, and finally destroyed it in 146 BC, she inherited the Mediterranean as a cultural and economic whole. The second is that Rome had long been influenced, and in the sixth century BC was ruled by, the first great civilization in northern Italy: the Etruscans. It was through them that the Romans became acquainted with the prestigious wares, iconography, and the technologies of Egypt, Syria, Urartu, and Assyria. The origin of the Etruscans is mysterious and has been debated since the days of Herodotus. But wherever they originated, there is hardly an element of Etruscan culture that is not based on an oriental model, brought across the sea by Phoenician merchants and craftsmen. The Phoenician alphabet, which the Etruscans received from the Greeks, was soon used to write Latin. Etruscan hydraulic technology, derived from that employed in the east, was used to drain the swamp where the Roman forum stands, and was the basis for the concept of the Roman aqueduct. Characteristically Roman cultural models, such as eating while reclined on couches, the ritualized consumption of wine, divination by inspecting an animal's liver, and so forth, were inherited from Etruscan imitation of the pomp and splendour of the Assyrian court.[6] And because the Etruscans had been in contact with the Greeks for many centuries, Etruscan heritage predisposed the Romans to imitate Greek examples. Nevertheless, after the expulsion of the last Etruscan king from the city of Rome in 509 BC, and after the final defeat

6 Haynes, S., *Etruscan Civilization: A Cultural History*, The J. Paul Getty Trust, Los Angeles, 2000, pp. 47–133. Sannibale, M., 'Orientalizing Etruria', in Turfa, J. M. (ed.), *The Etruscan World*, Routledge, Oxford, 2018, pp. 99–133.

of Carthage, Romans would rarely acknowledge their debt to the Etruscans and never to Carthage.[7]

Europe After Rome

In contrast, when Rome fell in AD 476, the old empire was never belittled or forgotten. For the barbarians of Europe, Rome was what Assyria had been for the Greeks and Etruscans, and what they and the Phoenicians had been to Rome. Although we should not dismiss the contribution of the Huns and Germans to European art and customs, we should also not forget that the new Europeans were haunted by the ghost of the old civilization. Theoderic, king of the Ostrogoths, emerged from the anarchy of the fifth century, revived the old imperial court ceremonial, conducted his administration and correspondence in Latin, and was a legitimate emperor of Rome in all but name.[8] In the ninth century, Charlemagne, king of the Franks, attempted a full restoration of the imperial office under the aegis of the papacy. The success of these political efforts is debatable, since neither revival long outlived its author.

But the goal of restoring the old civilization was never abandoned. The Greek language had been forgotten in most of the west; but manuscripts of the Latin authors were copied ceaselessly in monasteries. In the ninth century, they were gathered and corrected by Alcuin of York and his fellow scribes at the behest of Charlemagne—an effort to bring clarity and order to the relics of

7 Livy I.viii.3 mentions a few customs borrowed from the Etruscans by Romulus in the mythical past. Of course, there was some antiquarian interest in Etruscan matters, best exemplified by the writings of Varro and the emperor Claudius; but their works have been lost.

8 Heather, P., *The Restoration of Rome: Barbarian Popes and Imperial Pretenders*, Oxford University Press, Oxford, 2013, pp. 3–102.

Antiquity.[9] And all churchmen were required to adhere to a high standard of written and spoken Classical (not Vulgar) Latin. When it was time to write Charlemagne's biography, the writer Einhard deliberately imitated not a saint's life or some other recent text but Suetonius' *Lives of the Caesars* which was some seven hundred years old by that point. We now call all these developments the Carolingian Renaissance.

Like the Phoenicians after the Bronze Age collapse, the church was the one western Roman institution to emerge from the rubble of the fifth century stronger than before. The church had only been sanctioned by the Roman government for about two hundred years, since about the time of the conversion of Constantine I, so it might well have perished along with the Roman government. This did not happen. Despite St Augustine's doubts about the value of classical learning,[10] it was churchmen who copied, disseminated, and stored the relics of ancient literature. Many of the civilizing functions of the old government were taken over by ecclesiastics also. The early-mediaeval local bishop, for instance, sat in his cathedral dispensing judgement like a civil magistrate in an urban basilica, and barbarian princes measured their progress toward civilization by conversion to the old Roman religion.[11]

Unsurprisingly, the legacy of Roman imperial authority came to be disputed between the papacy and the successors to Charlemagne. Every European monarch who has adopted the title of emperor has likewise associated himself with the trappings of Roman imperial

9 On Frankish intellectual life at the time, see Wickham, C., *The Inheritance of Rome: Illuminating the Dark Ages 400–1000*, Penguin Books, London, 2009, pp. 405–423.

10 Augustine, *Confessions*, III.iv; IV.xvi; V.iv; X.xxxv.

11 These reflections were brought home to me in correspondence with Henry Hopwood-Phillips.

power, perhaps no one more notoriously than Napoleon. The mantle of Romanism has passed to America, but America's model is the pagan Roman republic, not the Christian empire. Now the Roman imperial legacy belongs exclusively to the papacy, where the theory of 'an empire without end' is still dominant, and where the office of *pontifex maximus*, instituted by Numa Pompilius in the mythical past, is now held by the successor to St Peter.[12] The emperors of Eastern Rome would have laughed at such pretences; since, as far as they were concerned, they and their subjects were and had always been Romans, nor had they ever lost contact with their Greek heritage, or so they thought. Even so, the Eastern Emperor Justinian I felt obliged to conquer Italy and North Africa in the sixth century AD, and to renew Roman authority in the west—so strong was the myth of the old empire.[13] This conquest lasted only a short time, and in the end the brief political union of east and west faded away. Reunion and revival, when they finally came, took an intellectual, not a political, form in the European Renaissance when the scholars of Italy united the literary heritage of Rome with that of ancient Greece.

Charlemagne's vision of a renewed Christian and Roman civilization had been inspired in part by the mosaics of the old Byzantine court at Ravenna which he had visited and despoiled to decorate his court at Aachen. There he had seen images of the emperor Justinian and his retinue, and the Frankish king copied what he saw. Charlemagne's octagonal chapel, an imposing mass of marble and gold, arose amidst huts of timber and mud, and is a respectable example of eastern Roman architecture.[14] Yet the

12 Heather, P., *The Restoration of Rome: Barbarian Popes and Imperial Pretenders*, Oxford University Press, Oxford, 2013, pp. 349–414.

13 Heather, P., *The Restoration of Rome: Barbarian Popes and Imperial Pretenders*, Oxford University Press, Oxford, 2013, pp. 105–204.

14 The deliberate imitation of Roman forms is covered in Wickham, C., *The Inheritance*

all-consuming imitation of Antiquity was still a long way off, and Charlemagne's vision would not take shape until the connection with the past was fully restored some six centuries later. Latin translations of Arabic versions of Greek texts circulating in the late Middle Ages could not compete with the original manuscripts; when these had gradually made their way westward out of Byzantium between the thirteenth and fifteenth centuries, the effect was transformative.

Rebirth in the East

But before we discuss the revival of Europe, we should observe that similar rebirths had already occurred several times in the East. The Neo-Assyrian state which had arisen out of the rubble of the Bronze Age collapse was overthrown by what we call the Second Babylonian Empire in 626 BC. That state was an ostensible revival of the ancient patrimony of Sumer and Akkad in its heyday under the rule of Hammurabi more than a thousand years earlier. A renaissance followed, as ancient forms of art, architecture, and the old religion were revived.[15] Notably, the inscriptions of the new Babylonian kings revived the grammar and orthography of the Old Akkadian language—a transformation not unlike the Carolingian insistence upon correct Classical Latin. The new Babylonian Empire might have carried on for some time, but in less than a century it was subsumed within the world's first great international state.

The first Persian Empire, also called the Achaemenid Empire, began to rule over the Near East when the armies of the Persian king Cyrus the Great marched into Babylon in 539 BC. This was

of Rome: Illuminating the Dark Ages 400–1000, Penguin Books, London, 2009, pp. 232–251.

15 Beaulieu, P.-A., *A History of Babylon*, Wiley Blackwell, 2018, pp. 219–245.

the end of Mesopotamia's political independence, but not her civilization. Though Cyrus had conquered Babylon, he portrayed himself as the restorer of an ancient order, and he surrounded himself with the trappings of the Sumerian, the Assyrian, and the Babylonian monarchies. Just as we saw Theoderic and Charlemagne appropriating the language of Roman power and religion, Cyrus's propaganda adopted ideas and expressions from the Babylonian *Epic of Creation* and the ancient *Esagil Chronicle* composed about a millennium and a half earlier.[16] Cyrus thereby portrayed himself and his empire as the fulfilment, not the end, of Mesopotamian monarchy and civilization. The Achaemenid state notably adopted the use of Aramaic, the prestigious Neo-Assyrian language, and carried on the practice of writing it with Phoenician letters. When Egypt was added to the Persian Empire, that state united the two oldest civilizations within a single polity. In Egypt, the Persian monarch ruled as Pharaoh. Everywhere else he was the 'King of Kings'—a revival of the old Assyrian royal title.

The Persian conception of civilized order is most clearly visible in the ruins of the ceremonial capital built originally by Darius I. It was known to the Greeks as 'The Persian City' or Persepolis, but the Persians called it Parsa. The architecture of the throne room would have been an obvious expression of royal power, based on earlier Near Eastern models designed to overawe the visitor. But in place of images of a tyrant destroying his enemies or hunting wild beasts, the relief of the Persian king, his heir, and his courtiers is a vision of hierarchy, stability, order, dignity, and peace.[17] The king sits calmly upon his

16 Schaudig, H., 'The Magnanimous Heart of Cyrus: The Cyrus Cylinder and Its Literary Models' in Shayegan, R., *Cyrus the Great: Life and Lore*, Ilex Foundation, Boston, 2018, pp. 16–25.

17 Brosius, M., *A History of Ancient Persia: The Achaemenid Empire*, Wiley Blackwell, 2021, pp. 85–87.

throne as advisers approach confidently and respectfully. They are not grovelling or abasing themselves. Likewise, reliefs adorning the staircases leading to the audience hall show courtiers and officials moving in relaxed attitudes. Their faces are calm and cheerful. They are shown conversing with one another, they shake hands, and they touch shoulders as they wait to meet the king. Reliefs of the various subject peoples displaying individual characteristics, their peculiar clothing, and local animals evince a love of variety which could be mistaken for modern multiculturalism. These images of a benevolent and orderly government are obviously idealized. But they give the lie to the hostile caricature of the Persian Empire as an oppressive despotism which we find in certain Graeco-Roman authors. And so, it was undoubtedly a bad day for civilization when Alexander the Great burned down Persepolis in 330 BC.

The conquest of the Persian Empire by Alexander followed a series of conflicts with the Greek-speaking world. One of these wars saw the destruction of Athens in 479 BC: a mixed blessing since the rebuilding of the acropolis gave us the Parthenon and the Erechtheum. But in Iran an indigenous political order did not recover for some 500 years, nor did the unity and centralisation achieved under the Achaemenids. Nevertheless, Alexander and his successors never escaped the gravitational pull of the old empire. Just as Cyrus had appeared as the rightful successor to the kings of Babylon and Assyria, Alexander portrayed himself as the continuator of the Persian monarchy. Alexander courted Iranian support, he advertised himself as the avenger of Darius III who had been killed in a plot, he adopted Iranian customs and clothing, he married an Iranian princess, and included Iranian aristocrats within his government.[18] His successors shared Alexander's vision

18 Wiesehöfer, J., *Ancient Persia*, I.B. Tauris, London, 2001, pp. 105–114.

of a union of the Hellenic and Iranian worlds. The Hellenistic kingdoms that arose from the ruins of Alexander's empire imitated indigenous models of kingship and transmitted them westward to the Graeco-Roman world where Alexander remained an object of emulation for centuries. But the Iranian attitude to Alexander was ambivalent, remembering him both as the last of the Achaemenids and as the destroyer of the old empire.

India

Despite Alexander's conquests, the Achaemenid state was influential far beyond its borders—notably so in what is now India. The old view that the Aryan invaders had destroyed the civilization of the Indus valley and started again from scratch cannot be true. The invaders, whose language formed the basis of Sanskrit, borrowed from their subjects the words for plough, furrow, writing, record, scribe, letter, and so forth. If they borrowed the word, they surely acquired the thing also. And so, the Aryans learnt the arts of civilization from the peoples whom they conquered, not the reverse.

But it was the drive to imitate the Achaemenid Empire that set the standard for Indian civilization up to the present moment. It began with the Aramaic alphabet, derived from the Phoenician, which the scribes of India learnt from the Achaemenid bureaucracy, and which in many modified forms is still used to write all the languages of the subcontinent. The Mauryan Empire, founded by Chandragupta in 320 BC, was the most successful attempt at a pan-Indian state before the modern era.[19] It was heavily influenced by

19 Keay, J., *India. A History: From the Earliest Civilisations to the Boom of the Twenty-First Century*, Harper Press, London, 2000, pp. 78–100.

the centralizing Achaemenid example, even down the patronage of the Buddhist religion in imitation of the Iranian kings' Zoroastrianism. No Indian buildings made of stone are attested before the Maurya epoch, when the practice was imported from Iran along with Persian styles and decorative motifs. The Mauryan palace at Pataliputra reveals the blending of Indian building techniques with Iranian styles, notably in the design of capitals and the use of peristyle halls recalling the splendour of Persepolis. Long after the fall of the Persian Empire, the public inscriptions of Ashoka (272–232 BC), Chandragupta's grandson, mimicked the structure and phraseology of Achaemenid royal inscriptions (themselves based on far older Mesopotamian models). Some of Ashoka's edicts were even published in Aramaic, so as to carry on the practice of the old Iranian administrative state.[20]

China

One wonders whether the theory of centralization on the Achaemenid model also influenced the consolidation of the Chinese states by the first emperor Qin Shihuang (259–210 BC). Or were they following the example of the Mauryan empire? Either way, the importance of unity and stability in Chinese philosophy and political thought long predates the Qin dynasty. The age of constant conflict that came before Chinese unification is known as the Warring States period (471–221 BC), and before that came the so-called Spring and Autumn period beginning in 771 BC. These were times of rivalry between different Chinese states, and they were distinguished by

20 De Casparis, J. G. / Fussman, G. / Skjærvø, P. O., 'AŚOKA', *Encyclopaedia Iranica*, Vol. II, Fasc. 7–8, 1987, pp. 779–785.

an intellectual dynamism that shaped all Chinese thought for more than two thousand years.[21]

Master Kong, known in the West as Confucius (551–479 BC), appeared at the very end of the Spring and Autumn period. He had not attained much success as a bureaucrat, but he and the ethical system he taught had attracted a considerable following. Confucius believed that the political fragmentation and moral chaos of his own time could be halted only by looking to the early days of the most stable and long-lived kingdom in Chinese history: the Zhou state, which lasted between 1046 and 256 BC. Tradition held that the Zhou king Wu overthrew the ancient Shang dynasty: the first Chinese civilization for which we have archaeological and written evidence. Wu then posthumously declared his late father, king Wen, as the first king of the Zhou dynasty. Wu's heir, King Cheng, was not old enough to ascend the throne when his father died, and so Wu's brother was regent until Cheng came of age. This brother was the famous Duke of Zhou, whom Confucius especially admired for having presided over a golden age. And so, the traditions, administrative structures, and ritual system of the early Zhou, and the manners of its rulers, were to be preserved and renewed forever. This necessitated special literary and liturgical instruction of the sort required for a career as a civil servant. Some sought out such training in the hopes of lucrative jobs; but Confucius encouraged it for its own sake. Loyal disciples followed the example of the Venerable Sage (as Confucius came to be called under the Han dynasty), and the Zhou were held up and imitated as a model of civilized order right up to the twentieth century.

21 Pines, Y., *The Everlasting Empire: The Political Culture of Ancient China and Its Imperial Legacy*, Princeton University Press, Princeton and Oxford, 2012, pp. 11–43.

The survival of Confucius' ideas looked doubtful at first. Qin Shihuang and his advisers established what later ages regarded as a tyranny. Shang Yang, a senior adviser to Qin Shihuang, was responsible for devising a framework of the so-called 'legalist' state: a standardized system of weights and measures, heavy taxes on trade, registration of the entire population, and universal conscription, along with an elaborate system of ranks, privileges, and rewards for various acts deemed meritorious. But most notoriously, there was also a ferocious system of tortures and punishments even for small infractions. The contemporary Confucian philosopher Xunzi deplored this depressing state of affairs, but his pupil Han Fei gave legalism a seemingly rational basis.[22] None of this was remotely agreeable to China's older Confucian tradition. The antipathy, however, was mutual, since the first emperor and his chief minister Li Si wanted a total break with the Confucian past. So, in 213 BC, an order went out that all Confucian texts were to be burnt, and some 460 Confucian scholars were buried alive, or otherwise executed. Sima Qian (c. 145 to c. 86 BC), the great historian of the early Han dynasty (202 BC to AD 220), explained all this as an effort to keep ordinary people ignorant and to ensure that no one could use the past to criticize the present.[23]

But the Duke of Zhou and his admirer Master Kong had the last laugh. The Qin state collapsed after a mere fifteen years; and subsequent scholars wanted to make up for suspected losses. And so, the tendency to look to the past, scrutinizing old texts ever more carefully, was ironically strengthened. The *Analects*, the book of Confucius' sayings, became required reading for any educated

22 Keay, J., *China: A History*, Basic Books, New York, 2011, pp. 75–77.

23 Watson, B. (trans.), *The Records of the Grand Historian of China Translation from the Shih Chi of Ssu-ma Ch'ien*, vol. 1, Columbia University Press, New York, 1961, p. 185.

Chinese person from the Han dynasty onward.[24] Until the twentieth century, no other religion or philosophy ever displaced it, although Buddhism and to a lesser extent Daoism became almost equally influential under the Sui and Tang dynasties. But their ascendancy was brief, and Confucianism effectively absorbed them, evolving into an amalgam of an ethical philosophy and civil religion. The Song emperors encouraged a neo-Confucian revival beginning in the late tenth century, and from the Ming dynasty onward the *Analects* and other Confucian texts formed the basis of the Chinese civil service examination until 1910—a practice imitated in Japan, Korea, and Vietnam.

The history of imperial China is a cycle of dissolution and reintegration of basically the same territory, the same administrative structures, and the same philosophy over the course of two millennia, no matter where the ruling dynasty came from. Indigenous rulers' attitudes occasionally bordered on a kind of Confucian fundamentalism, as in the case of the short-lived Xin dynasty (AD 9–23), when the project of a Confucian utopia failed. When China was ruled by foreigners (as was the case more often than not), the pull of the Confucian ideal was so great that no conquerors ever escaped being absorbed into it. A telling example of this is the Western Wei dynasty (AD 535–557), whose emperors originated among the non-Chinese nomads called Xianbei.[25] They became more Chinese than the Chinese, peppering official documents with allusions to the ancient Zhou state, and lifting phrases from speeches attributed to its illustrious duke for use in bureaucratic documents. Ancient official titles and nomenclature

24 *Confucius, Analects, with Selections from Traditional Commentaries*, translated by Edward Slingerland, Hackett Publishing, Inc., Indianapolis / Cambridge, 2003, pp. xx–xv.

25 Keay, J., *China: A History*, Basic Books, New York, 2011, pp. 219–220.

were revived, and decrees were issued in archaic Chinese, which bureaucrats were forced to learn. This example held good right up to the twentieth century. The Qing, the last imperial dynasty which fell in 1911, were of Manchurian origin, and its emperors were vehement defenders of the Confucian ideal.

'I am not someone who was born with knowledge', Confucius said, 'I simply love antiquity, and diligently look there for knowledge'.[26] He transmitted and did not innovate. And the quintessentially Confucian notion of *zhengming*, or the 'rectification of names', meant not redefinition of concepts according to modern usage, but the *recovery* of their true and original meanings.[27] The idea of looking to the past has never been presented more straightforwardly, and nowhere else has it been more diligently and consistently observed than in China.

Iran

Iran, however, is a close second. Despite Alexander's conquests, the memory of the old Achaemenid state remained vivid in Fars in southwestern Iran. There the ruins of Persepolis and the tombs of the ancient kings gave the governor of that region a level of prestige which the monarch of the day lacked. This was true when Iran was ruled by Alexander's Macedonian successors and when they were replaced by the loose, decentralized rule of the nomadic Parthians in about 250 BC. So, it is no surprise that the last pre-Islamic, indigenous Iranian empire was founded by a governor of Fars in the 220s AD.[28] The propaganda of the Sasanian Empire (as the new empire came to be called) held that the reigning house was

26 Confucius, *Analects*, 7.20.

27 Confucius, *Analects*, 13.3; Keay, J., *China: A History*, Basic Books, New York, 2011, pp. 70–71.

28 Jackson Bonner, M. R., *The Last Empire of Iran,* Gorgias Press, Piscataway, 2020.

descended from Darius III, and that the new state was a revival of the old. The mythical origin of Ardashir, the founder of the dynasty, narrated his abandonment at birth and his adoption by a shepherd—exactly the same foundation story first told about Sargon of Akkad in about 2334 BC, and later appropriated by Cyrus the Great. The monuments of the Achaemenid age were likewise co-opted and reused for Sasanian royal inscriptions; and the Sasanian kings revived much of the imagery and symbolism of Near Eastern and Achaemenid monarchy.

At the end of Antiquity, Iran and Rome were the two great powers of western Eurasia, and it was not long before most of the small, independent kingdoms between them were subsumed within either empire. Armenia was a notable anomaly, being culturally Iranian but nevertheless staunchly Christian, and therefore caught up within the constant cycle of warfare between the two powers. But despite bouts of hostility, Rome and Persia viewed themselves as the two co-equal pillars of civilized order on earth, holding out against the hostile, chaotic world of the desert and the steppe. Contrary to all expectation, in the seventh century AD, when the two powers had exhausted themselves in their most violent war yet, rule of most of Eurasia passed to the Arabs who managed to overpower them.[29] The old Sasanian Empire fell apart under attack and was swallowed whole in AD 651. The Romans were forced to give up Egypt, Syria, and the Levant at about the same time. The Arabs found themselves at the head of an empire whose extent was basically the same as that of the old Achaemenid state at its height, and it was soon expanded across North Africa into the Iberian peninsula and eastward into Central Asia.

29 Howard-Johnston, J., *Witnesses to a World Crisis: Historians and Histories of the Middle East in the Seventh Century*, Oxford University Press, Oxford, 2010.

Early attempts to fill the void left by the Roman and Iranian governments were not entirely successful. Despite a millennium or so of contact with Mesopotamia, the Arabs had little experience of statecraft. The Arab Umayyad clan was the first dynasty to rule the new empire. They maintained their power through a policy of Arab supremacy and rigid separation from their subject peoples, while local administrators were left to carry on as best they could—a far cry from the internationalism and flexibility of the Achaemenid and Sasanian states. That rigidity provoked a strong reaction. Fifty-thousand Arabs stationed at the garrison city of Marv in eastern Iran mixed with the local population, adopted their culture, and took Iranian wives just as Alexander's troops had done about a thousand years earlier. It was they who overthrew the ruling Umayyad clan in AD 750 and did away with the system of ethnic separatism. This was the beginning of the so-called Abbasid dynasty, and it ushered in what we have come to call the Golden Age of Islam.

The main impetus for this golden age was the deliberate imitation of Sasanian models of politics and statecraft.[30] The Arab capital at Damascus was restored to Mesopotamia, not far from the ancient site of Babylon and the old Sasanian capital at Ctesiphon upon the Tigris. The practices of the Sasanian bureaucracy, especially the office of the Grand Vizier, were revived. Coins were minted according to Sasanian models, art and architecture followed where the old empire had left off, and Muslim Caliphs were instructed in ancient Iranian courtly manners and wisdom literature. Imitation of the Sasanians was so deeply ingrained that the practice was continued by the smaller states

30 Gutas, D., *Greek Thought, Arabic Culture: The Greco-Arabic Translation Movement in Baghdad in Early Abbasid Society (2nd–4th / 8th–10th centuries)*, Routledge, London, 1998; Jackson Bonner, M. R., *The Last Empire of Iran*, Gorgias Press, Piscataway, 2020, pp. 343–347; Katouzian, H., *The Persians: Ancient, Mediaeval, and Modern Iran*, Yale University Press, New Haven, 2009, pp. 73–79.

which arose amidst the decline and eventual collapse of the Abbasid Empire in AD 1258. But the intellectual revival sponsored by the Abbasid Caliphs also had a Sasanian precedent. The sixth-century Sasanian king Khusro I (a contemporary of Justinian) is said to have welcomed Greek philosophers at his court and to have collected and studied the scientific and religious texts of all countries and peoples.[31] Al-Mansur (r. AD 754–775) and his successors imitated this example and sponsored the translation into Arabic of Greek, Middle Persian, and Sanskrit scientific, medical, and philosophical texts.[32] This translation movement took shape on a gigantic scale, dwarfing the near-contemporary efforts of Charlemagne and Alcuin. Moreover, it lasted much longer and its effects were far greater.

Interest in ancient Greek philosophy and science was the most important part of this movement. Translators in service to the Caliphs got their texts from two sources: Syriac translations of the original Greek works and Greek manuscripts directly from Byzantium. This meant that the entire corpus of Aristotle, Euclid, Ptolemy, Galen, and so on became accessible to scholars throughout the Islamic world. This is usually contrasted with contemporary intellectual conditions in Europe, where scholars either had to do without those texts altogether or depend on inferior Latin summaries or digests, but the truth is that the intellectual foundation of mediaeval Arabic scholarship was broader and denser than that of any other civilization, including India and China, at the same time. So, it is no surprise that so many extraordinary polymaths, such as al-Kindi, al-Farabi, Averroes, Avicenna, and others, flourished for some two centuries as a direct result of Abbasid interest in ancient learning.

31 Jackson Bonner, M. R., *The Last Empire of Iran,* Gorgias Press, Piscataway, 2020, pp. 233–235.

32 Bennison, A. K., *The Great Caliphs: The Golden Age of the 'Abbasid Empire*, Yale University Press, New Haven, 2009, pp. 175–202.

But the translation movement had two other knock-on effects which rarely get the emphasis that they deserve.[33] The first is that Abbasid attention paid to the Greek heritage helped to revive interest in ancient scholarship at Byzantium itself, thereby reviving the East Roman state from something of a dark age between the seventh and ninth centuries AD. The second is that Arabic scholarship inspired the European interest in the past that led to what we call the Renaissance. Until the revival of Greek in western Europe, the science and philosophy of Antiquity was accessible almost exclusively through Arabic translations and the scholarship of eastern savants. And so, toward the end of the Middle Ages, the Arabic versions of classical texts, especially the works of Aristotle and the Neoplatonists, became the focus of another translation movement. From the eleventh to the thirteenth century, Adelard of Bath, Robert Ketton, Hermann of Carinthia, Gerard of Cremona, and Michael Scot brought nearly the whole of Arabic learning into Latin along with commentaries and other scholarship.

The originality of Abbasid scholarship is often unfairly forgotten. The process of translation was not slavishly literal, mechanical, or performed only once.[34] Translations were often redone and updated so as to ensure that everything had been understood properly, and that process often served to resolve problems or to correct errors. For instance, Ptolemy's mathematical and astronomical treatise known as the *Almagest* was translated twice by al-Hajjaj and Ishaq ibn Hunayn, respectively, and the two scholars brought its mathematical

33 Bennison, A. K., *The Great Caliphs: The Golden Age of the 'Abbasid Empire*, Yale University Press, New Haven, 2009, pp. 203–214; Lyons, J., *The House of Wisdom: How the Arabs Transformed Western Civilization*, Bloomsbury Publishing, New York, 2009.

34 Saliba, G., *Islamic Science and the Making of the European Renaissance*, The MIT Press, Cambridge, Mass., 2007, pp. 73–129.

calculations into line with the current state of that science and corrected its mistakes. Ibn al-Haytham and al-Biruni wrote up critiques of Ptolemy, trying to square his model of the universe with that of Aristotle, and these would inspire later advances by al-Tusi (AD 1201–1274) and al-Shatir (AD 1304–1375). Similarly, Abu Bakr al-Razi (AD 854–925) and Ibn al-Nafis (AD 1212–1288) published criticisms of Galen's medical system, correcting it according to their own observations. But the astronomical work was more influential.

The flourishing of civilization under Abbasid patronage lasted only about two hundred years. The empire was too large and could not be held together for very long. It began its slow disintegration in the late ninth century AD, as native Iranian and Turkic dynasties asserted their independence from Baghdad, purporting to revive the splendour of the Sasanian world in their turn, and patronizing their own scholars. When the Mongol invasions snuffed out the Caliphate once and for all in AD 1258, the Abbasid empire had long been a shadow of its former self. The carnage wrought by the Mongols is astounding even by the standards of the twentieth century, though we cannot be certain of the death toll.[35] Millions may not have been massacred in *each* of the cities of Khurasan, as contemporary chroniclers claim, but the huge figures can be taken as evidence that the body-count was quite unlike anything that anyone had experienced before,[36] and after the destruction of Baghdad, Mesopotamia would never again be the centre of a great civilization. This was not the end of Islamic science, but philosophical speculation began to be diverted into either non-rational dogmatism or Sufi

35 Morgan, D., *Mediaeval Persia 1040–1797,* second edition, Routledge, London and New York, 2016, pp. 53–62; Saunders, J. J., *The History of the Mongol Conquests*, The University of Pennsylvania Press, Philadelphia, 1971, pp. 54–63; 109–112; 177–178.

36 Morgan, D., *Mediaeval Persia 1040–1797,* second edition, Routledge, London and New York, 2016, pp. 79–81.

mysticism. No one could have predicted that Averroes, Avicenna, and al-Farabi would eventually fall out of favour in the East and find their largest audience in Europe, or that their greatest intellectual descendant would be St Thomas Aquinas. Nor could anyone have foreseen that doubts about Aristotelian and Ptolemaic astronomy originally raised by al-Hajjaj would inspire what we have come to call the Scientific Revolution, but this is what happened.

Before we leave the Islamic Golden Age, there are three other examples of the regenerative power of Iranian civilization that should be noted. First, we have the mere fact that the Persian language survived the Arab conquest of Iran. In every other part of the Arab empire, the indigenous language ceased to be spoken. A possible exception to this is the Coptic language of ancient Egypt which survives to this day as the liturgical language of Egyptian Christians. But Persian not only remained in use throughout Iran and Central Asia, but also *increased* in prestige. Second, this prestige quickly came to be embodied in the tradition of Persian poetry which took root in the various regional courts that arose amidst the fragmentation of the Abbasid Caliphate. The greatest of these poets was Abolqasem Ferdowsi who served the sultan Mahmud of Ghazna in what is now Afghanistan. Ferdowsi collected and versified as much of the ancient heritage of Iran as he could find. The result was the *Shahnameh*, the Iranian national epic, completed in AD 1010.[37] It inspired an entire genre of epic poetry, best exemplified by Nezami (d. 1209) and Attar (d. 1221). But the *Shahnameh* has pride of place and has been a touchstone of Iranian civilization from the very beginning. Third comes the great tradition of Iranian

37 Rypka, J., *History of Iranian Literature*, written in collaboration with Otakar Klíma *et al.*, edited by Karl Jahn, D. Reidel Publishing Company, Dordrecht, 1968, pp. 154–166.

administrators and bureaucrats who served Iran's conquerors while absorbing them into indigenous traditions of statecraft. Al-Jahiz, the ninth-century Arabic prose stylist, satirized such men as reflexively hearkening back to Sasanian examples;[38] but the bureaucrats had the last laugh. There were obviously a great many such people, but three stand out. Nezam al-Molk (AD 1018–1092) served the Seljuk conquerors Alp Arslan and Malik Shah, and wrote his *Book of Government* (or *Siyasat-nameh* as it is called in Persian) as a manual of political advice, full of episodes drawn from the Sasanian past, and which is still influential in the East.[39] Two centuries later, Ata-Malik Juvaini (AD 1226–1283) and Rashid al-Din Hamadani (AD 1247–1318) served their Mongol rulers and inducted them into Iranian civilization—almost literally, since those two men were the foremost historians of their time as well as able administrators and political advisers.[40]

The European Renaissance

Iranian civilization and Arabic scholarship were influential far beyond the Islamic world. They contributed enormously, in fact, to the European Renaissance. The *Oration on the Dignity of Man*, for instance, the great manifesto of the Renaissance by Pico della Mirandola (AD 1463–1494), opens with an invocation of 'Abdallah ibn al-Muqaffa' (AD 724–759), the famed translator of Sasanian

38 Pellat, C. (trans.), *The Life and Works of Al Jahiz*, Routledge & Kegan Paul, London, 1969, pp. 273–275.

39 Darke, H. (trans.), *The Book of Government or Rules for Kings*: the Siyar al-Muluk *or* Siyasat-nama *of Nizam al-Mulk*, Routledge, London and New York, third edition, 2002; Katouzian, H., *The Persians: Ancient, Mediaeval, and Modern Iran*, Yale University Press, New Haven, 2009, pp. 92–98.

40 Katouzian, H., *The Persians: Ancient, Mediaeval, and Modern Iran*, Yale University Press, New Haven, 2009, p. 100.

texts into Arabic.[41] In his painting *The School of Athens*, Raphael depicted Averroes reading over the shoulder of Pythagoras. Such examples should remind us that, until well into the seventeenth century, self-respecting European scholars could be expected to know at least some Arabic as well as Latin and Greek.[42] This interest eventually inspired the creation of the Medici Oriental Press which produced the first printed editions of Arabic medical and astronomical scholarship for an eager European audience.[43] Arabic (the Latin of the Islamic world) had been taught for some time at the universities of Padua and Bologna, and with time other great universities imitated that example; but many scholars, such as Andrea Alpago, travelled to Damascus to learn it first-hand. Technology and scientific instruments came from 'the Arabs' also. And prototypes of astrolabes, sextants, quadrants, and other astronomical devices were ordered from the East and reproduced at home. Absorption and imitation of Arabic scholarship had been so thorough that the physician and anatomist Andreas Vesalius could refer to 'those Arabs who are now rightly as familiar to us as are the Greeks'.[44]

But the familiarity was not always openly admitted, as in the work of Nicolaus Copernicus (AD 1473–1543). His earliest astronomical

41 Pico della Mirandola, G., *Oration of the Dignity of Man: A New Translation and Commentary*, edited by Francesco Borghesi, Michael Papio, and Massimo Riva, Cambridge, Cambridge University Press, 2012.

42 Saliba, G., *Islamic Science and the Making of the European Renaissance*, The MIT Press, Cambridge, Mass., 2007, pp. 226–232.

43 Jones, R., 'The Medici Oriental Press (Rome 1584-1614) and the Impact of Its Arabic Publications on Northern Europe' in Russell, G. A., *The 'Arabick' Interest of the Natural Philosophers in Seventeenth-Century England*, Brill, Leiden, 1993, pp. 88–108.

44 This is found in the preface of Vesalius' *On the Fabric of the Human Body* addressed to emperor Charles V, which can be found online at https://www.nlm.nih.gov/exhibition/historicalanatomies/vesalius_home.html.

opinions rested on citations of al-Battani, al-Bitruji, al-Zarqallu, Averroes, and Thabit ibn Qurra. Yet the later Copernican theories of planetary motion are lifted from the models and theorems of al-Tusi, al-'Urdi, al-Shirazi, Ibn al-Shatir, and al-Khafri—without acknowledgement.[45] Copernicus' placement of the sun at the centre of the solar system made greater sense of those older mathematical models, formed over the course of some five centuries of engagement with the texts of Aristotle and Ptolemy. Copernicus, who did not know Arabic, may have seen summaries of those earlier models and theorems in translation, or he may have been briefed on them by an interpreter. However this may be, perhaps we should think of Copernicus not as a new type of European scientist but as the last of the old Persian astronomers whom he had imitated.[46]

Despite the influence of Arabic scholarship upon the Renaissance, the effect of the Graeco-Roman heritage has proven more memorable. Here I think we can see the same process of awakening interest in the past as in every earlier revival, but in the Renaissance it is more explicitly documented—especially the contemplation of ruins. Petrarch, Dante, and Poggio attributed their fascination with Roman antiquity to the ruins of the city of Rome itself, which they explored at various times in the fourteenth and fifteenth centuries. But others, such as Boccaccio and Ciriaco of Ancona, examined the ancient ruins up and down the countryside of Italy, copying inscriptions and making sketches. When Ciriaco was asked why

45 Saliba, G., *Islamic Science and the Making of the European Renaissance*, The MIT Press, Cambridge, Mass., 2007, pp. 193–232; Ragep, F. J., 'Copernicus and His Islamic Predecessors: Some Historical Remarks', *Filozofski vestnik*, XXV (2), 2004, pp. 125–142.

46 *Cf.* Falk, S., *The Light Ages: The Surprising Story of Mediaeval Science*, W. W. Norton and Company, New York, 2020, pp. 284–285.

he did this, he replied 'to wake the dead'.[47] The antiquarian popes Nicholas V and Pius II began to embellish the city of Rome with new monuments in a classical style, and excavations uncovered wall paintings, as well as such statues as the Apollo of the Belvedere, the Laocoön, the Venus of the Vatican, and Cleopatra's torso. These and other similar discoveries inspired the movement to imitate Antiquity which culminated in the rebuilding of St Peter's Basilica according to classical plans by Bramante, Maderno, Bernini, and Michelangelo.

The revival of classical literature happened at the same time. It resembled, albeit on a larger scale, the older achievements of Alcuin of York and his associates. Popes and aristocrats offered huge sums for manuscripts of ancient authors. Texts were hunted down all over Europe. They were copied, and fresh editions of many newly discovered Latin writers began to circulate. Knowledge of Greek had eluded Dante and Petrarch, but not Poggio; and refugees from Byzantium appeared in Italy with their companions Homer and Plato.[48] Manuel Chrysoloras, the most important of them, was recruited to teach Greek in Florence. It was he and his superior grammar book that touched off the revival of Greek and that continues to this day, though the classics are now regularly put into modern vernacular languages, not Renaissance Latin.

And so, to paraphrase Jacob Burckhardt, Europeans learnt to think as the ancients thought, to write as they wrote, and to feel as

47 Belozerskaya, M., *To Wake the Dead: A Renaissance Merchant and the Birth of Archaeology*, W. W. Norton and Company, New York, 2009.

48 Reynolds, L. D. / Wilson, N. G., *Scribes and Scholars: A Guide to the Transmission of Greek and Latin Literature*, fourth edition (originally published in 1968), Oxford University Press, Oxford, 2013, pp. 123–164; Wilson, N. G., *From Byzantium to Italy: Greek Studies in the Italian Renaissance*, second edition, Bloomsbury, London, 2017.

they felt.[49] This was the last such revival in the West. Later writers would think of it as a radical break with the past, but this far from the truth. The humanism of the Renaissance was no less Christian than its mediaeval antecedents, and the Carolingian revival had already prepared the way for a deeper and a more durable imitation of Antiquity. Thus, Cicero became the supreme model of clear prose, but some scholars even began to speak in the conversational Latin of Plautus and Terence. Children were given Classical names again; Graeco-Roman mythology, side by side with Christian themes, inspired popular literature; and Antiquity became the chief interest of life in every Italian court before spreading northward to the rest of Europe. The imitation of the remote past was an enormous boost to self-confidence which issued both in the discovery of the New World, and renewed confidence in all human faculties. This sense of confidence was shared by all the great scholars of the Renaissance, but is typified by Leon Battista Alberti (AD 1404–1472).[50]

Alberti's achievements, like those of other 'Renaissance men', represent a full and unitary life, not dilettantism or a mass of unconnected experiences. Alberti was an adviser to popes Eugene IV and Nicholas V, but this service was no impediment to his success in painting and architecture, both practical and theoretical. His manuals of perspective and the construction of buildings are not only instructive, but also fine works of literature, revelling in classical allusions and steeped in Ibn al-Haytham's science of optics.[51] Alberti's Latin was so good that some of his compositions were mistaken for lost classical works. Physics and mathematics he mastered at the age of twenty-four, and he found out everything

49 Burckhardt, J., *The Civilization of the Italian Renaissance*, pp. 104–170.

50 Burckhardt, J., *The Civilization of the Italian Renaissance*, pp. 85–87.

51 Onians, J., *Neuroarthistory: from Aristotle and Pliny to Baxandall and Zeki*, Yale University Press, New Haven and London, 2007, pp. 42–46.

he could about every sort of skill by questioning artists, artisans, and scholars about their work. He delighted in cryptography, as well as inventions and gadgets, and he even attempted to build a flying machine. Like Shulgi of Ur, Alberti also boasted of extraordinary athletic and musical achievements: he could jump over a standing man's head with his feet together, he could throw an apple over the highest buildings, and strike the vault of the cathedral of Florence with a coin. The strongest horses trembled beneath him, and he was an avid climber of mountains. He had taught himself music and his compositions were praised by discerning listeners. Cynics will accuse Alberti of exaggeration, since those are his own boasts, but there is no arguing with his designs of the Church of St Mark the Evangelist in Rome or the Basilica di Sant'Andrea in Mantua; and his literary works may still be read for pleasure.

The Paradoxical Outcome of the Renaissance

As much as I admire Alberti and his ilk, I feel a certain ambivalence about the Renaissance. There is much to be said for the cooperative and social attitude represented by Alberti's interest in the work of craftsmen and scholars. This is the spirit of civic humanism and the fleeting glory of Florence, Ferrara, Mantua, Urbino, and Milan—fleeting because it was already fading away when Baldassare Castiglione published his *Book of the Courtier* in 1528. This book is not primarily a guide to manners and behaviour, as is often thought, but rather a lament for a world long past: the melancholy reflections of old men on a better time before the French invasion of 1494 and the Italian Wars that followed.[52] This spirit of nostalgia and

52 Bartlett, K. R. / Bartlett, G. C., *The Renaissance in Italy: A History*, Hackett Publishing Company, Indianapolis, 2019, pp. 177–181.

interior brooding had always been part of the Renaissance, though. It began with Petrarch himself, the wandering, rootless scholar who had never been comfortable in civic life, and who was ultimately disappointed to discover that Cicero (whom he so greatly admired) had been a man of action as well as a contemplative writer. Petrarch loathed his own epoch and professed to worship Antiquity. But one can hardly imagine him fitting in among the ancients, because so solitary and aloof a man would not fit in anywhere. What Petrarch idolised was really a fantasy, and with him we encounter for the first time, as it seems, a new kind of man: a wholly autonomous individual preoccupied mostly by his own private thoughts and his own quest for self-knowledge. Such a person would soon come to feel that he owed nothing to Antiquity, since his vision of the past was not grounded in truth. And so, it is possible to say that the example of Petrarch inspired others both to imitate the past and to turn away from it.

The self-confidence that came from that imitation is long gone, but it did not disappear in a single moment. It faded away gradually amidst the ravages of the Black Death, the gradual monetization of the European economy, the Great Western Schism, the Reformation, and the Wars of Religion, among other factors. But nothing made forgetfulness of the past more attractive than the European expansion into new lands, the redrawing of maps, and encounters with new peoples. The idea of a new world of progress, discovery, and unlimited wealth seemed irresistible from the end of the fifteenth century onward. Everyone must have been tempted to believe it, but it had no intellectual foundation until Francis Bacon (1561–1626) produced one.

Bacon knew and respected the legacy of Antiquity, and yet he viewed the authority of its authors as an impediment to the advancement of science. In 1620, his treatise *Novum Organum* appeared, its title page fittingly adorned by the image of a galleon setting out from the Pillars of Hercules toward the New World beyond the ocean—a new theory of knowledge for a new age of exploration and discovery.[53] The purpose of knowledge, he argued in his treatise, was to increase the happiness of mankind, and nothing more; and science could therefore be judged by its usefulness.[54] Accordingly, Bacon had a dim view of the inventors, philosophers, and scientists of all former ages because they had failed to provide mankind with 'new discoveries and resources'.[55] Bacon furthermore attacked and undermined the very idea of Antiquity. Comparing the course of history to the life of a man, he argued that 'antiquity was the youth of the world', and his own time was its old age; and just as wisdom and knowledge are found among the old and not the young, they must be sought in the present age and not in the past, especially not in the remote past.[56] By avoiding old errors, Bacon continued, the future would be one of steady progress. This was the seed that germinated in the Age of Reason, and Bacon's view is basically the same as modern notions of progress.

Bacon had a point, but only a small one. There is something to be said for the idea of human happiness as an end in itself, but whether science and technology can bring it about is quite another matter. Yet Bacon was wrong about the debt owed to former ages. Without the intellectual strength that came from imitation and mastery of the past, the sense of clarity and reason that belong to all civilizing epochs would never have been emphasized in the period that we

53 Bacon, F., *The New Organon*, edited by Lisa Jardine and Michael Silverthorne, Cambridge University Press, Cambridge, 2000.

54 Bury, J. B., *The Idea of Progress: An Enquiry into Its Origin and Growth*, MacMillan and Company, London, 1921, pp. 50–59.

55 Bacon, F., *The New Organon*, edited by Lisa Jardine and Michael Silverthorne, Cambridge University Press, Cambridge, 2000, I.lxxxi, p. 66.

56 Bacon, F., *The New Organon*, edited by Lisa Jardine and Michael Silverthorne, Cambridge University Press, Cambridge, 2000, I.lxxxiv, pp. 68–69.

call the Enlightenment. Though we may have misgivings about the triumph of science and the failed revolutionary spirit of that age, its emphasis on empiricism and objectivity has added something to civilization. We might have continued the confident imitation of past achievements while also trusting reason and experience. But this is not what happened. Contrary to what anyone might have expected toward the close of the eighteenth century, there would be no break with the past without enormous misery. The age that followed was one of disillusionment, soured by political and intellectual revolutions betrayed or exposed as corrupt, by new ideologies, by warfare on a gigantic scale, by huge massacres and genocide.[57] We shall examine this depressing state of affairs in the next chapter.

57 Conrad, P., *Modern Times, Modern Places: How Life and Art Were Transformed in a Century of Revolution, Innovation and Radical Change*, New York, Alfred A. Knopf, 1999, p. 711.

CHAPTER III

What Went Wrong

> Let each of my readers direct his attention to these matters: the life and morals of the community, and the men and qualities by which through policies at home and abroad the empire was born and enlarged. Then as the standard of morality gradually slips, let him note how, with the relaxation of discipline, morals first gave way, as it were, then sank lower and lower, and then began to decline precipitously until we come to our own time when we can bear neither our vices nor their remedies.
>
> Livy, *Ab Urbe Condita*, Pr. 9

CONTEMPLATING THE STATE of our own civilization gives me an uneasy feeling. Something is wrong and we can all sense it. At the end of Kenneth Clark's *Civilisation*, he passes judgement on his own time, and what he says still feels relevant now. No society had ever been better nourished, or better educated. No generation of men and women had ever benefitted more from science and technology. But the long decline of Christianity and the moral and intellectual failures of Marxism had left Western civilization without a centre. Good, well-meaning people had plenty of strong convictions, but something was still missing. Clark felt optimistic but could not be joyful about the future.[1] Since the late 1960s, when *Civilisation* was made and broadcast, an astonishing number of people have risen out of poverty. Lifespans have grown longer. The world is now more closely connected than ever before. All the world's knowledge, from the earliest days of our species to the present moment, is readily available to anyone with an Internet connection. Yet the problem hinted at by Kenneth Clark is now worse.

Clark was not the first to attempt to diagnose the problem, of course. An earlier phase of it was described by Alexis de Tocqueville, who recognized that the freedom promised by an egalitarian society, such as we now live in, would effectively degrade social ties and leave people personally, politically, and socially isolated.[2] In an aristocratic society, de Tocqueville observed, families would remain in more or less the same position and very often in the same place. An individual man would always have reason to be mindful of his ancestors and descendants; and he would readily sacrifice personal pleasure for the sake of others, whether his present neighbours or those who had gone before or who were yet to be born. But in an egalitarian society, it would be possible to gain enough wealth to look after one's own needs, so as to owe nothing to anybody and to require nothing from others. People in such circumstances would come to feel themselves isolated and yet also capable of moulding their destinies however they wished. Each man would be cut off from his ancestors, and would be 'shut up entirely within the solitude of his own heart', wholly indifferent to the fate of others. This state of affairs prefigures Clark's notion of a civilization without a centre.

1 This is found at the end of episode 13 of the BBC series and in Clark, K., *Civilisation*, 1969, p. 347.

2 De la Démocratie en Amérique, vol. II.i.2.

De Tocqueville also predicted that a society of isolated persons, without common interests, would easily succumb to tyranny and would be unable to unite against it.[3] This was prescient, since twentieth-century totalitarianism was indeed founded on great masses of isolated individuals, or as Hannah Arendt put it, 'atomization'. This problem is still with us, even in places that have so far avoided tyranny. The proof is that a kind of loneliness grew over the course of the twentieth century in the West, and worsened toward its end. Participation in clubs or civic societies declined.[4] The number of men with no close friends at all has increased fivefold since 1990.[5] Suicides have been increasing in America since the end of the twentieth century,[6] and in 2016 Europe was found to be the most suicidal region in the world by gross rate.[7] Now hopelessness, despondency, and a sort of 'flatness' have been invoked to describe the dominant feeling of our time.[8] I suspect that the COVID-19 pandemic worsened this sense of despondency. Finally, even before the riot at the American Capitol on January 6, and the triumph of identity politics, advanced thinkers had begun to believe that we in the West were once again on the road to tyranny, or at least to the dissolution of liberal democracy.[9]

3 De la Démocratie en Amérique, vol. II.iv.6.
4 Putnam, R., *Bowling Alone: The Collapse and Revival of American Community*, 2000.
5 Cox, D. A., 'Men's Social Circles Are Shrinking', *Survey Center on American Life,* June 29, 2021 (retrieved from https://www.americansurveycenter.org/why-mens-social-circles-are-shrinking/).
6 Hedegaard H. / Curtin, S. C. / Warner, M., 'Increase in Suicide Mortality in the United States, 1999–2018', NCHS Data Brief, no 362. Hyattsville, MD, National Center for Health Statistics, 2020.
7 https://www.who.int/data/gho/data/themes/mental-health.
8 Newhouse, A., 'Everything Is Broken', *Tablet*, January, 2021 (retrieved from https://www.tabletmag.com/sections/news/articles/everything-is-broken).
9 Applebaum, A., *Twilight of Democracy: The Seductive Lure of Authoritarianism*, 2020; Mair, P. *Ruling the Void: The Hollowing Out of Western Democracy*, 2013; Eatwell, R. / Goodwin, M., *National Populism: The Revolt Against Liberal Democracy*, 2020; Brennan, J., *Against Democracy*, 2017.

Yet de Tocqueville mistook cause for effect. Forgetfulness of ancestors and an indifference to future descendants are not caused by atomization. Those factors could easily become a negative feedback loop or a vicious circle, of course, but the chain of causation goes the other way. The desire to make a radical break with the past is the cause of all forms of forgetfulness, indifference, dissolution of social ties, and at length atomization. Long ago, we developed the urge to create a new and different world, and we have uprooted ourselves from the old one. In so doing we have badly disrupted our sense of place and purpose. Apart from the malaise that I have described, many horrific disasters have arisen from this.

The Root of the Problem

The idea that mankind could be improved, renewed, and enlightened finds its origin in the writings of St Paul. 'Put off', he wrote, '. . . the old man, which is corrupt according to the deceitful lusts; and be renewed in the spirit of your mind; and . . . put on the new man, which after God is created in righteousness and true holiness'.[10] This message is one of spiritual transformation made possible by the life and death of Jesus Christ who came, as he himself said, 'not to destroy but to fulfil'.[11] The lusts and sin which do not belong to the original human nature had indeed been overcome, but posterity would inherit Adam's punishment and our bodies would forever be doomed to die. Death would not be the end, though, and the New Testament concept of a 'new creation' meant the restoration of the pristine human nature, not its cancellation, after the resurrection of

10 Ephesians 4:22–24.

11 Matthew 5:17.

the body.[12] The radical break with the past, the apocalyptic vision of 'a new heaven and a new earth', would come at the end of the world.[13] And the full renewal of humanity would be achieved only in heaven with God.

But this did not always stop people from trying to accomplish that future, spiritual transformation here on earth. Charlemagne's campaigns of terror and destruction in Saxony in the late eighth century were to bring the indigenous pagans out of darkness and into light by force. The same urge inspired the Crusades to 'liberate' Jerusalem and to convert the infidel occupiers of the Holy Land.[14] The Reformation is an even better example, with longer-lasting consequences. Its goal (laudable in principle) was to recover the pristine state of an ancient faith; but this is not what ended up happening. What Luther and the other reformers really achieved was a break with the past. Scripture was supposed to be the only foundation for right belief. The problem was that, without the authority of tradition, there were as many interpretations of scripture as there were people. Nothing could be done to reconcile the large array of antithetical opinions. Unsurprisingly, the sixteenth and seventeenth centuries were an epoch of nearly constant conflict, both intellectual and military. Some scholars, like Erasmus, refused to involve themselves in the contests of the day, but still maintained social relations as much as possible. Others, like Michel de Montaigne, withdrew from society altogether. Badly distraught by the violence around him, Montaigne shut himself up in a tower in Bordeaux, alone with all his books and classical quotations. There, he churned out a large collection of essays, exploring his private

12 Galatians 6:12–16, 2 Corinthians 5:14–19, Ephesians 2:11–22, Ephesians 4:17–24, and Colossians 3:1–11.

13 Revelation 21:1.

14 Jordan, W. C., *Europe in the High Middle Ages,* Penguin Books, 2001, pp. 102–103.

sense of scepticism, the problem of antithetical religious beliefs, and moral relativism.

The seed that Petrarch had planted had begun to germinate, and the plant would soon attain gigantic proportions.[15] Like Montaigne, René Descartes, who had been a soldier in the early part of the Thirty Years War, also withdrew into seclusion. Descartes aimed to remove himself from the influence of all contemporary and ancient authorities. This was the only way, he thought, to certain knowledge. Descartes was therefore determined to forget everything that he had formerly known and 'to begin again from the first foundations', as he describes in his *Meditations*, published in 1641.[16] Similarly, Thomas Hobbes, who was no stranger to warfare and upheaval, thought it better to remain ignorant than to trust anyone else, and so he condemned all those who took instruction 'from the authority of books, and not from their own meditation'.[17] Baruch Spinoza agreed, and placed enormous emphasis on the power of private reason, unaided by ancient authorities.[18] Much the same idea was expressed by David Hume and Jean-Jacques Rousseau, who exalted the interior perceptions of the mind above any other sort of knowledge.[19] Rousseau was especially keen on

15 I am following the perspective of Gregory, B. S., *The Unintended Reformation: How a Religious Revolution Secularized Society*, The Belknap Press of Harvard University Press, Cambridge, Mass., and London, 2014, pp. 114–122.

16 René Descartes, *Meditations on First Philosophy*, translated from Latin by Donald A. Cress, third edition, Hackett Publishing Company, Indianapolis/Cambridge, 1993 (originally published 1641), p. 13.

17 Thomas Hobbes, *Leviathan*, edited by Richard Tuck, Cambridge University Press, Cambridge, 1991 (originally published 1651), p. 28.

18 Baruch Spinoza, *Ethics: Proved in Geometrical Order*, edited by Matthew J. Kisner, translated by Michael Silverthorne and Matthew J. Kisner, Cambridge University Press, Cambridge, 2018 (originally published 1677).

19 David Hume, A *Treatise of Human Nature*, edited by L. A. Selby-Bigge, second edition, revised by P. H. Nidditch, Oxford University Press, Oxford, 1978

personal seclusion also, and trusted nothing but his own opinions. This was the thread picked up by Immanuel Kant, for whom the essence of enlightenment was unguided, private reason.[20] Next came Hegel, who believed that his own epoch was 'a birth-time and a period of transition to a new era', since 'Spirit has broken with the world it has hitherto inhabited and imagined'.[21] In other, more intelligible words, it would soon be time to start over from nothing in all branches of knowledge—a mode of thought that reached a new level of madness in the writings of Karl Marx. Hegel merely expected a break with the past and a revolution in knowledge, but Marx wanted to force it to happen.

Like Hegelianism and Marxism, the philosophy of utilitarian liberalism, best associated with John Stuart Mill and Jeremy Bentham, also required a break with the past and personal enlightenment. It sounds silly now, but in the nineteenth century, Mill could say with a straight face that 'speculation on the most important subjects' was in 'a backward state', and that 'little progress' had been made in moral philosophy throughout all human history.[22] Such an outlook could only seem plausible to someone who ignored or who had discarded all mankind's former achievements. Meanwhile, in

(originally published 1739–1740); Jean-Jacques Rousseau, *Les reveries du promeneur solitaire*, édition augmentée des *Lettres à Malesherbes,* texte établi avec introduction, chronologie, notes, et relevé de variantes par Henri Roddier, Classiques Garnier, Paris, 1998 (originally published 1782).

20 Immanuel Kant, 'An Answer to the Question: What Is Enlightenment?' in Schmidt, J. (ed. / trans.), *What Is Enlightenment?: Eighteenth-Century Answers and Twentieth-Century Questions*, University of California Press, Berkeley, 1996 (originally published 1784), pp. 58–64.

21 Hegel, G. W. F., *Phenomenology of Spirit*, translated by A. V. Miller with Analysis of the Text and Foreword by J. N. Findlay, Oxford University Press, Oxford, 1977 (originally published 1807), p. 6.

22 Mill, J. S., *Utilitarianism*, edited by Oskar Piest, Prentice Hall, Upper Saddle River, New Jersey, 1957 (originally published 1861), p. 3.

America, where rejection of old things was ironically something of a venerable institution, the urge to turn away from the past attained new vehemence in the writing of Ralph Waldo Emerson: 'the way, the thought, the good', he said, 'shall be wholly strange and new'.[23]

The Failure of Enlightenment Utopianism and the Darkness of the Nineteenth Century

There is a revolutionary spirit in the development of Western philosophy since the Reformation, and it began to take shape in the concept of a New World across the sea whose native peoples could be improved and enlightened and where settlers, uprooted from their ancestral lands, could live better lives. Hence, utopian literature proliferated from the sixteenth century onward.[24] Thomas More's *Utopia* (1516) is surely the most famous example since it gave its name to the genre, but there were others: Ludovico Agostino's *Dialogues on the Infinite* (1580), Tommaso Campanella's *City of the Sun* (1602), Ludovico Zuccolo's *Dialogues* (1625), John Valentino Andreae's *Christianopolis* (1619), and Francis Bacon's *New Atlantis* (1624), to name a few. Such works were supposedly inspired by the Spanish transatlantic empire. Long before the Puritan separatists arrived in New England, the idea of a religious utopia across the sea had already been advanced by the Jesuits of Paraguay.[25] A less overtly spiritual utopianism was inaugurated, once again, in the

23 This is from Emerson's essay entitled 'Self-Reliance', originally published in 1841 and can be found in Emerson, R. W., *Essays and Journals*, Selected with and Introduction by Lewis Mumford, Doubleday and Company, Garden City, New York, 1968, pp. 89–111; and the quotation is on p. 101.

24 Greengrass, M., *Christendom Destroyed: Europe 1517–1648,* Penguin Books, London, 2014, pp. 178–180.

25 Greengrass, M., *Christendom Destroyed: Europe 1517–1648,* Penguin Books, London, 2014, pp. 162–163.

writings of Francis Bacon, who argued that his special method of inductive reasoning would extend the power of the human race over nature.[26] Descartes also claimed to have developed a technique by which anyone could understand all truths by force of human reason alone.[27] Later, Nicolas de Caritat, the Marquis de Condorcet (1743–1794), argued that no bounds had been set upon the improvement of all human faculties, provided that everyone adhered to reason and facts, and that 'the perfectibility of man is absolutely infinite'[28]—a phrase which may as well have been the motto of Enlightenment utopianism.

Of course, it seemed that the colonial Americans had actually achieved the utopian dream, albeit with considerable support from the French.[29] Their revolutionary spirit swiftly returned to Europe where it had originated. But things did not work out quite how Condorcet and the other luminaries of the Enlightenment had expected, of course. The horrors of the French Revolution, the Terror, and the eventual defeat of Napoleon gave way to nearly a century of gathering darkness and pessimism. Disappointment following the liberal revolutions of 1848 added to the malaise. Technology continued to advance as the Industrial Revolution proceeded, but the vision of a world remade according to reason and democracy was a failure. Or was it? Perhaps it was man who had failed to live up to his own vision. Many people decided that there was therefore no point

26 Bacon, F., *The New Organon*, edited by Lisa Jardine and Michael Silverthorne, Cambridge University Press, Cambridge, 2000, I.cxxix, pp. 99–101.

27 René Descartes, *Discourse on the Method of Correctly Conducting One's Reason and Seeking the Truth in the Sciences*, translated with an Introduction and Notes, Oxford University Press, Oxford, 2006 (originally published 1637).

28 Condorcet, Jean-Antoine-Nicolas de Caritat marquis de, *Esquisse d'un tableau historique des progress de l'esprit humain*, Chez Agasse, Paris, 1794, p. 4.

29 Robertson, R., *The Enlightenment: The Pursuit of Happiness 1680–1790*, Penguin Books, 2020, pp. 706–735.

in trying to go on living any more. Others concluded that it was man who needed to be taken apart, studied, analysed, treated, and finally cured and readjusted. The light of reason accordingly gave way to darkness and various occult obsessions: spiritualism, seances, table turning, automatic writing, theosophy, and so on would purge man of his defects and adapt him for a new, utopian society. Or so thought the likes of Éliphas Lévi, Allan Kardec, Papus, and Helena Blavatsky.[30]

Weariness, disillusionment, and bitterness are represented in the quintessentially nineteenth-century theme of the 'twilight of the gods'—the *Götterdämmerung* which inspired Heine, Wagner, and Nietzsche—the imminent moment when the gods who had created and sustained the world would finally disappear. Darwinian evolution seemed to refute the idea that a divine intelligence had created the world, and the science of geology proved that the earth was far older than what the chronology of the Bible suggested. The world was old and senile; and imaginary aesthetes like Huysman's character Des Esseintes, and real ones like Oscar Wilde and Walter Pater, were bored by life.[31] 'Live? Our servants shall do that for us', wrote the French playwright Auguste Villiers de l'Isle-Adam in his play *Axël*.[32] An extraordinary number of European intellectuals committed suicide between 1860 and 1938.[33] Some observers felt, however, that something new and exciting was still on its way. Nietzsche thought that the old Christian morality which had long been sickening would soon give way to the 'revaluation of all

30 Muray, P., *Le XIXe Siècle à travers les âges*, Éditions Denoël, Paris, 1999.
31 Conrad, P., *Modern Times, Modern Places: How Life and Art Were Transformed in a Century of Revolution, Innovation and Radical Change*, New York, Alfred A. Knopf, 1999, pp. 13–39.
32 De l'Isle-Adam, A. V., *Axël*, Maison Quantin, Paris, 1890, p. 283.
33 Johnston, W. M., *The Austrian Mind: An Intellectual and History 1848–1938*, University of Chicago Press, Chicago, 1983, pp. 174–180.

values';[34] and Henry Adams and H. G. Wells foresaw a new religion in the dynamo and the hydroelectric turbine since they were more worthy of veneration than the God and saints of Christianity.

Meanwhile, the demons set loose by the Terror and the Napoleonic wars haunted the nineteenth century. We can still feel this in the disturbing paintings of Goya, the gloomy poetry of Baudelaire and Edgar Allen Poe, and the grim woodcuts of Gustav Doré.[35] Like reminiscences of the Greek Dark Age, it is all witches, cannibalism, tortures, assassinations, and gigantic monsters. Artists like Fuseli and Goya revived such frightening themes as Theseus and the Minotaur, Odysseus' confrontation with the cyclops, and Saturn devouring his children. Mary Wollstonecraft's *Frankenstein* bears the subtitle *The Modern Prometheus*: an allusion to the eponymous tragedy by Aeschylus. It has given us the horrific image of a monstrous amalgam of body parts stolen from churchyards and charnel houses, reassembled, and reanimated by a secret method known only to Victor Frankenstein—a grim perversion of the Christian vision of resurrection and eternal life, and a literal representation of breaking down the old man and building a new one.

The Art Nouveau styles of the late nineteenth and early twentieth centuries fittingly exude 'corruption, swooning, weariness, and languor'.[36] Gustav Klimt's *Death and Life* and *Hope I*, for example, juxtapose sexuality and fertility with grim images of death and

34 This expectation is the main subject of Nietzsche's *Anti-Christ*, and was something of an obsession in his declining years (Nietzsche, F., *The Anti-Christ, Ecce Homo, Twilight of the Idols, and Other Writings*, edited by Aaron Ridley and Judith Norman, translated by Judith Norman, Cambridge University Press, Cambridge, 2005 (originally published 1888), pp. 11; 64; 66; 74; 76; 120–121; 134; 136–138; 144; 155; 177; 185; 229).

35 Clark, K., *The Romantic Rebellion: Romantic versus Classic Art*, Longman Canada, Don Mills, 1973, pp. 45–95.

36 Eco, U., *On Beauty*, MacLehose Press, London, 2010, p. 346.

darkness. Such work prefigures the unsettling introspection in the paintings of Egon Schiele and Oskar Kokoschka. They aimed to represent an inner life, with Kokoschka attempting to grasp the psychology of many different subjects, and Schiele focusing mostly on his own neurotic anxieties and sexuality in numerous self-portraits.[37] It was a sign of the times, and it is not merely a coincidence that the same culture that gave rise to Klimt, Schiele, and Kokoschka also produced psychoanalysis. Freud's publication of *The Interpretation of Dreams* in 1900 set a seal on a whole century's worth of interior brooding typified by the attempts of Hegel and Marx to grasp the inner logic of history itself.

Confusion and Subjectivity

But for all that, the orderly universe of Copernicus, Galileo, and Kepler, governed by Newton's laws of gravity and motion, was still there. Man's place in it still seemed secure, despite his boredom, disillusionment, and self-preoccupation. But this began to change under the influence of Henri Poincaré and Henri Bergson.[38]

Poincaré, a French mathematician, began to expose the apparent inadequacies of Newton's assumptions. He had been in search of a model for the movements of more than two interdependent celestial bodies, and postulated a double wave bending back upon itself and intersecting infinitely—an early prefiguration of chaos theory. He was the first to propose gravitational waves, and his

37 Kandel, E. R., *The Age of Insight: The Quest to Understand the Unconscious in Art, Mind, and Brain, from Vienna 1900 to the Present*, Random House, New York, 2012, pp. 124–181.

38 I am following the analysis of Fernández-Armesto, F., *Out of Our Minds: What We Think and How We Came to Think It*, London, One World Books, 2019, pp. 332–338.

work on relativistic velocity transformations was taken up by Einstein. Poincaré then questioned the link between hypothesis and evidence. Any number of hypotheses, he said, could be suited to an experimental result. Superficially this seemed to be a repudiation of the scientific method; and it was construed to mean that scientific facts were created by scientists, and that science was nothing more than a series of conventions unrelated to the truth.

Next came Bergson, a French philosopher who had been influenced by Darwin. In his book *Creative Evolution,* he reimagined evolution as the motive force governing the universe, something akin to God or the World Soul.[39] He called it *élan vital*, or vital impetus, and described it as a spiritual force with the power to re-order matter. Change, Bergson said, was the expression of a creative will, and animals and plants evolved because they *wanted* to do so. His theory of 'duration' was even weirder, almost unintelligible. Duration meant 'the form which the succession of our conscious states assumes when our ego lets itself *live*'.[40] Bergson refused to think of time as divisible into a series of moments or in any way analogous to space: according to him, it was only a mental construct. Others at various times may have tried to re-imagine objective reality as a mental construct, or to impute will to inanimate objects, but Bergson's ideas proved most influential.

The ideas of Poincaré and Bergson were largely misunderstood and over-interpreted by those who heard them. Those who felt constrained by the determinism of nineteenth-century science

39 Bergson, H., *Creative Evolution*, authorized translation by Arthur Mitchell, PhD, Macmillan and Company, London, 1922 (originally published 1911).

40 Bergson, H., *Time and Free Will: An Essay on the Immediate Data of Consciousness*, authorized translation by F. L. Pogson, M.A., Dover Publications, Inc., Mineola, New York, 2001 (originally published in 1913 by George Allen & Company, Ltd., London), p. 100.

found what they were looking for and took those ideas for a radical assertion of free will and subjectivity. Poincaré's work prepared the way for Albert Einstein, but Bergson preconditioned how Einstein would be interpreted by a non-scientific public. Special and general relativity, published in 1905 and 1915, respectively, changed the way everyone perceived the universe. Einstein showed us that the speed of light does not and cannot vary, and time and distance are relative to it. They had seemed absolute to us, because we had never gone fast enough to know otherwise. Mass and energy could be converted into one another. Parallel lines eventually intersected, and a twin who went on a journey at a speed approaching that of light would return younger than his twin who had stayed home. It was actually an orderly, deterministic universe; but, to many who heard about it, relativity meant relativism.

In 1911, Ernest Rutherford published his work on the atom. He seemed to reveal a chaotic inner world of a nucleus surrounded by empty space in which electrons moved about in patterns that could not be followed or predicted. Meanwhile physicists were struggling to understand why light seemed to behave as both a particle and wave. This was the beginning of quantum mechanics: the study of the universe at and below the level of molecules and atoms. Most disconcertingly, though, both relativity theory and quantum mechanics seemed to be true, but they contradicted one another. The problem with special relativity was resolved by Paul Dirac in 1928. But the conflict between quantum mechanics and general relativity remains to this day, and the quest for a grand Theory of Everything to explain all physical aspects of the universe continues. Niels Bohr and Werner Heisenberg added more weirdness in 1927, when they discovered that the position and the velocity of sub-atomic particles could not be measured exactly at the same time: you can either know where they are or where they are going, but not both. Heisenberg called this phenomenon 'uncertainty'. Since everything in the universe was made of sub-atomic particles, uncertainty was construed to mean that no observations at any level could be considered objective. This was not an accurate understanding of the 'uncertainty principle', but it was influential nonetheless.

Altogether these developments in the early twentieth century were interpreted to mean that there was no fixed space or time, science was untrue and unreliable; and the building blocks of the universe behaved in an unpredictable and unintelligible manner, and they consisted of mostly empty space. Religion was false. The result was that we forgot where we were and why. Throw in the Freudian unconscious, the pragmatism of William James, and Ferdinand de Saussure's claim that language cannot describe reality, and all you have left is a kind of relativism: whatever works for me in this disorderly, unintelligible world is true.[41] Bergsonian *élan vital* meant that every man could construct his own personal utopia if he wanted to, or at least transform himself through willpower alone. This agglomeration of ideas may have helped people deal with the increasingly frenetic pace of technological change and the forces of chaos set loose by the First World War and the collapse of empires and institutions that followed. But their more durable effects have been wholly pernicious.

Futurism: The Matrix of Fascism, Bolshevism, and Nazism

The chaos and confusion of the early twentieth century forced people to look for certainty wherever they thought they could find it. But they made the mistake of looking to the future and seeking to embrace and accelerate the pace of change. This is what Italian poet

41 Fernández-Armesto, F., *Out of Our Minds: What We Think and How We Came to Think It*, London, One World Books, 2019, pp. 335, 344–347.

and art theorist Filippo Tommaso Marinetti called for in his *Futurist Manifesto* published in 1909.[42] The legacy of the past, Marinetti said, must not be superseded, but wholly repudiated and destroyed.

In place of the past, Marinetti wished to 'exalt aggressive action, a feverish insomnia, the racer's stride, the mortal leap, the punch and the slap'. Beauty exists only in struggle, he said, and Marinetti especially preferred the alleged beauty of speed: 'a racing car whose hood is adorned with great pipes, like serpents of explosive breath—a roaring car that seems to ride on grapeshot is more beautiful than the Victory of Samothrace'. Poetry, he went on, must be a violent assault on the forces of the unknown, to force them to bow before man. He glorified war as 'the world's only hygiene', and exalted 'militarism, patriotism, the destructive gesture of freedom-bringers, beautiful ideas worth dying for, and scorn for woman'. Museums were cemeteries. They, along with libraries, were to be demolished. Books should all be burnt. Admiring old artwork was to pour 'our sensibility into a funerary urn instead of hurtling it far off, in violent spasms of action and creation'. The admiration of the past was useless, and was nothing more than 'a solace for the ills of the moribund, the sickly, the prisoner'. 'Why should we look back', Marinetti asked, 'when what we want is to break down the mysterious doors of the Impossible? Time and Space died yesterday'. 'Take up your pickaxes, your axes and hammers and wreck, wreck the venerable cities, pitilessly!'

Most of that manifesto was obtuse nonsense. And it strikes a frightening, apocalyptic tone when it speaks of the present moment as 'the very first dawn' on earth with its 'red sword, slashing for the

42 Brain, R. *et al.* (trans.), 'The Founding and Manifesto of Futurism by F. T. Marinetti' in Apollonio, U. (ed.), *Documents of 20th Century Art: Futurist Manifestos*, Viking Press, New York, 1973, 19–24.

first time through our millennial gloom'. But Marinetti won many adherents determined to destroy the past, and who were obsessed by the excitement of progress and of speeding automobiles, steamships, and locomotives. Futurism, as an artistic movement, petered out by 1944, when Marinetti died. But the great significance of the manifesto is that it precisely reflected the ideas and trends that were to dominate the twentieth century.[43] The worship of technology and speed are still with us, and Elon Musk and Jeff Bezos could be considered contemporary futurist prophets of fast cars, rocket ships, and near-instantaneous deliveries. Tech companies and CEOs still speak of accelerating change, and Marinetti's visions of constant action and insomnia are the virtues of the modern office-worker.

Marinetti was alarmingly prescient about politics also. In Italy, the Futurists turned Fascist. They were Bolsheviks in Russia, and Nazis elsewhere.[44] Fascists and Nazis hated Communists and they fought infantile street fights before first forming a cynical non-aggression pact and then going to war in earnest. Yet they agreed with Marinetti's vision of the future: progress meant rejecting, repudiating, destroying the past. That was all that mattered. Thus, the most destructive ideologies and the totalitarian systems they spawned have a common origin not in the veneration of the past, but in a utopian vision of the future. In the Fascist utopia, the state would serve the strong. Communism would triumph upon the ruins of capitalism and usher in the dictatorship of the proletariat. Nazism reimagined the Marxist class struggle as a conflict among races, and envisioned the end point of history as the thousand-year Reich. These Golden Ages all lay ahead, owing nothing to

43 Fernández-Armesto, F., *Out of Our Minds: What We Think and How We Came to Think It*, London, One World Books, 2019, pp. 350–354.

44 Ohana, D., *The Futurist Syndrome, Volume III of the Nihilist Order*, Sussex Academic Press, Brighton, Portland, Toronto, 2010.

history; and, as Marinetti seemed to foresee, they would be ushered in amidst obscene destruction and insensate cruelty.

W. H. Auden called the 1930s a 'low, dishonest decade'—a significant understatement in retrospect, since the period from 1930 to the end of the Second World War was perhaps the lowest point that mankind had reached since the appearance of civilization. But the assertion of atavistic savagery abetted by science, machines, and technology had begun before the thirties and lasted throughout the twentieth century. The obvious corollary to nineteenth-century theories of progress and hygiene was a theory of degeneracy, whereby moral failure, crime, alcoholism, and so forth were caused by the excessive reproduction of the least desirable members of society.[45] Evolutionary theory accordingly became the excuse for purging them.

When it came to the idea of killing undesirable people, the Nazi and Soviet regimes were in full agreement.[46] Though they were almost always officially opposed, and eventually locked in a military struggle in Eastern Europe, it was as though Germany and the USSR cooperated in a single project of mass murder. It started in the 1930s with Soviet collectivized agriculture, the failure of which was blamed on Ukrainians. Stalin resolved to starve to death as many of them as possible, and at least four million died in what we now call the Holodomor. Other national minorities (mostly Poles) were identified as enemies of the Soviet leadership in the late 1930s, and those who survived famine and the Gulag were simply shot. When Germany and Russia partitioned and invaded Poland in 1939, both regimes sought to eliminate the entire Polish intelligentsia out of fear that they might mount a resistance. Two campaigns of murder and

45 Pick, D., *Faces of Degeneration: A European Disorder, c. 1848–1918*, Cambridge University Press, Cambridge, 1996 (first printed in 1989).

46 I am following Snyder, T., *Bloodlands: Europe Between Hitler and Stalin*, Basic Books, New York, 2010.

deportation began in parallel. The Germans also singled out Polish Jews for ghettos and labour camps. When, in 1941, Hitler turned against the Soviet Union and invaded, killing reached unheard of levels. The Soviets encouraged partisan resistance in Belarus, and the Germans reacted by killing hundreds of thousands of innocent people, including women and children, and taking the men as slaves. The Soviets invited an uprising in Warsaw, and the Germans murdered more than a hundred thousand Poles and levelled the city. The Soviets looked on such atrocities with indifference.

To quote historian Timothy Snyder, 'living space for Germans was to be dying space for others'.[47] Hitler's project of conquering the USSR had five components: a swift victory; a Hunger Plan whereby thirty million people would be starved to death in the winter of 1941–1942; the extermination of all Jews in a Final Solution; the deportation, murder, enslavement, or assimilation of whoever remained according to the so-called Generalplan Ost; and finally the settlement of the vacant lands by German colonists.[48] The whole diabolical project could not be carried out, as the German war effort ran up against Russian opposition and began to fail. Everything but the Final Solution was scaled back. Instead of murdering political enemies, German death squads began to shoot Jews. This was not especially fast or efficient, and so a new technique was found. It was a ghastly relic of the Age of Reason. At the height of the French revolutionary Terror, public burials could not keep pace with the high speed of the guillotine; and so, in 1799 a French architect proposed a more efficient alternative. His recommendation was, as he said, capable of finishing off 'an entire nation if necessary'

47 Snyder, T., *Bloodlands: Europe Between Hitler and Stalin*, Basic Books, New York, 2010, p. 416.
48 For a clear, accessible summary of these developments, see Frankopan, P. *Silk Roads: A New History of the World*, Vintage Books, 2017, pp. 350–384.

by chemical poisoning and incineration.[49] The idea was ignored for about a hundred and fifty years until the Nazis actually did it, employing asphyxiation by carbon monoxide or hydrogen cyanide at the death camps in occupied Poland to which the Jews had been deported from their ghettos. No other racial murder of the twentieth century matched the Holocaust, but not for want of trying. Such horror recalls the kill-rates of non-civilized warfare and its aim of total elimination; and it reminds us of the fragility of civilization and how swiftly we can descend into savagery when given the chance. The earlier precedent of the Greek and Armenian genocides and the later examples of Cambodia, Bosnia, and Rwanda point to the same conclusion.

Many of the Futurists' most violent fantasies were fulfilled in the Third Reich, including the burning of books, the destruction of museums, and the demolition of entire cities.[50] Looking far into the future, the Führer saw a world remade with Germany at its centre. Germans would colonize lands emptied of Slavs and Jews; the Crimea would be the Reich's Riviera; and the Volga would be its Mississippi. In fact, the Reich would replace America as the new land of limitless opportunity; and, after cities like Manhattan had perished in flames, even Americans themselves would settle there. Hitler's gaze extended so far that he loved imagining the eventual *ruins* of his empire. He wanted them to be beautiful, and commissioned his architect Albert Speer to design his new capital

49 Michelet, J., *Histoire de la revolution française*, tome sixième, originally published in 1847, deuxième edition, Librairie International, Paris, 1869, p. 320; Muray, P., *Le XIXe Siècle à travers les âges*, Éditions Denoël, Paris, 1999, pp. 47–48; Évard, J.-L., 'Guerre et revolution: la crise charismatique', *Lignes*, 36 (1), 1999, pp. 138–159.

50 Conrad, P., *Modern Times, Modern Places: How Life and Art Were Transformed in a Century of Revolution, Innovation and Radical Change*, New York, Alfred A. Knopf, 1999, pp. 417–499; pp. 716–717.

Germania with future destruction in mind.[51] The Nazis wanted to think of themselves as revivers of folksy Germanness, but they achieved only its ruin. Eugenicist policies were supposed to purify mankind and restore his proper place in the natural order, but what they amounted to was an assault on humanity and nature. Hence, the perversity of referring to industrial slaughter at the death camps as 'productivity' and the transport, murder, and incineration of human beings as 'processing'. When the Allied victory was certain, and Berlin was a heap of rubble, Hitler ordered the total destruction of Germany and all its infrastructure: 'a final demonstration of technology's power over nature'.[52] This was the so-called *Nero Decree*, but it was never carried out.

Soviet mythmaking emphasized the Red Army's liberation of Auschwitz and contemporary Russian propaganda sometimes tries to give the USSR credit for ending the Nazi mass murders. But there is little truth to this. The worst of the mass murders had already happened by the end of the war, and many death camps (such as those at Treblinka and Sobibor) had already been shut down and demolished. Explicit reports of Nazi atrocities had circulated throughout the USSR from the beginning. Stalin himself received intelligence briefings about the murder of Jews which he recorded in his personal diary. But when it came to the destruction of Soviet Jews, Soviet newspapers and radio broadcasts tended to obscure who the victims really were and why they were murdered, claiming that the killing was motivated by hatred of

51 Conrad, P., *Modern Times, Modern Places: How Life and Art Were Transformed in a Century of Revolution, Innovation and Radical Change*, New York, Alfred A. Knopf, 1999, p. 488.

52 Conrad, P., *Modern Times, Modern Places: How Life and Art Were Transformed in a Century of Revolution, Innovation and Radical Change*, New York, Alfred A. Knopf, 1999, p. 491.

Soviet citizens *in general.*[53] The Soviet leadership, perhaps catering to Stalin's own anti-Semitism, were mostly indifferent to the plight of the Jews, and the myth of Russian national suffering left no room for them. After 1945, the number of Soviet Jews murdered by the Nazis with Soviet connivance was a state secret, and the Holocaust was deliberately excluded from the Soviet experience of the war.[54] Consider, for instance, the horrific massacre in the ravine called Babyn Yar at Nazi-occupied Kiev in 1941. The Soviets had investigated and documented the murders there for the Nuremberg trials, but the report was doctored, so as to conceal the fact that the victims were Jewish and that it was the beginning of what we now call the Holocaust.[55]

The world was surely glad to see the end of Hitler and the fall of the Third Reich, but the Allied victory did not make the world appreciably better. The horrors of Communism became apparent little by little, embarrassing Western intellectuals who still wished to think of it as a viable alternative to democratic capitalism. Nietzsche's prediction that socialism would lead to death on a massive scale came true.[56] But Western powers and the United Nations were slow to take note. They famously ignored the Soviet invasion of Hungary in 1956. Some left-wing intellectuals, such as Eric Hobsbawm, refused to denounce the invasion, because he thought that doing so would cede the moral high ground. Others, however, thought the invasion was the last straw—which is odd to say the least, since

53 Berkhoff, K., 'Total Annihilation of the Jewish Population: The Holocaust in the Soviet Media, 1941-45', *Kritika: Explorations in Russian and Eurasian History*, 2009, 10 (1), pp. 61–105.

54 Snyder, T., *Bloodlands: Europe Between Hitler and Stalin*, Basic Books, New York, 2010, pp. 339–377.

55 Plokhy, S., *The Last Empire: The Final Days of the Soviet Union*, updated with a new foreword, Basic Books, New York, 2014, p. 66.

56 Nietzsche, F., *The Will to Power*, section 125.

they had apparently not minded the horrors described above and the cynical non-aggression pact between Stalin and Hitler. Similarly, Mao Zedong's Great Leap Forward accidentally killed forty-five million people by murder and starvation, and Pol Pot killed one quarter of the Cambodian population; but not even these failures seemed enough to discredit Communism. Its proponents were only forced to admit they were wrong when the Soviet Union finally collapsed between 1988 and 1991 after a long period of internal decay.

The End of Ideology

The Futurists were no more, the great ideologies had been exposed as murderous and corrupt, but the idea of repudiating the past lingered. In Europe and the Americas, the years after the Second World War were spent in search of new alternatives to the ideas and systems that were supposed to have caused conflict.[57] J. Robert Oppenheimer, who had led the efforts that culminated in the atomic bomb, turned to Hindu mysticism. This would culminate in the hippie movement of the 1960s, The Beatles' association with the Maharishi Mahesh Yogi, and latterly the faux-spirituality of yoga and celebrity Buddhism. Jimmy Page revived the occultism of Aleister Crowley. Alone among his generation, Pete Townshend broke the mould and embraced Sufism for a while, which at least showed some originality, but it had no public appeal. When it came to philosophy, the ideas of Martin Heidegger and those of the so-called Frankfurt School never caught on outside academia, but existentialism did. The rejection of ideology seemed to inaugurate

57 Fernández-Armesto, F., *Out of Our Minds: What We Think and How We Came to Think It*, London, One World Books, 2019, pp. 362–368.

a return to the relativism of the early twentieth century, and Jean-Paul Sartre was its prophet. He said that the first principle of existentialism was that 'man is nothing else but that which he makes of himself'.[58] God does not exist, there is no determinism, man is entirely free, nor is there a fixed human nature. Western intellectuals of the 1950s and 1960s accepted this doctrine, and, to quote Fernández-Armesto, they 'barricaded themselves in self-contemplation'.[59] Outside academia, existentialism justified the most embarrassing pseudo-intellectualism of the beatniks and self-indulgence of the hippies. All their sexual licence, violence, deliberate rudeness, drug abuse, uncleanliness, and defiance of authority were justified as part of a project of 'becoming oneself'.

But what is disturbing about existentialism is not so much that it presupposes that life has no purpose. Far worse is the idea that life is a jumble of discrete experiences that do not form a coherent whole, much less a *narrative*. Breaking up human life into a series of unrelated episodes or moments means that there can be no connection with the past, especially a shared past. Nor can there really be any sense of a future either, since there is only an inchoate accumulation of present moments. This view is articulated in Sartre's novel *La Nausée* which (ironically, perhaps) is structured as a *biography* of the main character Antoine Roquentin.[60] Viewing life as a series of unconnected moments would obviously appeal to people who are convinced that the past is evil and should be forgotten, and this is why existentialism caught on.

58 Kaufmann, W., *Existentialism: From Dostoevsky to Sartre*, twelfth edition, New York, Meridian Books, 1960, p. 291.

59 Fernández-Armesto, F., *Out of Our Minds: What We Think and How We Came to Think It*, London, One World Books, 2019, p. 363.

60 MacIntyre, A., *After Virtue: A Study in Moral Theory*, third edition, Notre Dame, University of Notre Dame, 2007, p. 214.

Decolonization

Apart from Nazism, and to a lesser extent Marxism, few things have seemed more worthy of oblivion after the Second World War than the evils of colonialism. In the early twentieth century, there was a certain ambivalence about the peoples over whom European powers ruled. It was still easy to claim that they needed enlightening by superior masters. But there was also a belief that a decrepit Europe could be regenerated by supposedly primitive or even savage cultures.[61] Hence, Picasso and his ilk were inspired by statues and masks from the Congo and the Ivory Coast. Prokofiev's *Scythian Suite* (1915) paid homage to an ancient people of the Asiatic steppe renowned for their bloodlust. Igor Stravinsky's ballet *The Rite of Spring* (1913) glorified the savagery of Russian paganism. European interest in jazz and the appearance of Josephine Baker as a sex symbol connected the supposed primitiveness of black American culture with energy and vitality. This mode of thought must seem embarrassing now, and its racist undertones seem all the more sinister when we remember that the Nazi obsession with 'rebarbarisation' belongs to the same trend.[62]

The age of empires may have begun amidst all the confident exuberance of the Renaissance, but it ended in humiliation, guilt, cruelty, and violence. Yet the European talent for uprooting people from their ancestral customs and reshaping their societies has continued. Europeans and Americans just do it to themselves

61 Conrad, P., *Modern Times, Modern Places: How Life and Art Were Transformed in a Century of Revolution, Innovation and Radical Change*, New York, Alfred A. Knopf, 1999, pp. 345–399.

62 The phrase 'rebarbarisation of Europe' was coined by Thomas Mann in his 1947 play *Doktor Faustus*, but the idea itself goes back to Nietzsche (Asscheim, S. E., *The Nietzsche Legacy in Germany 1890–1990,* University of California Press, Berkeley, 1992, pp. 299–300).

now.[63] Americans have always claimed somewhat hypocritically to hate empire, and contemporary American wokeism advertises itself as the enemy of neo-conservatism and colonialism alike. And yet the three are so similar that they may not be distinct phenomena at all, but rather three expressions of a single impulse.[64] The insistence on altering, abolishing, or defunding institutions, renaming everything, and pulling down statues was once achieved abroad by European colonial powers, and eventually by American military and foreign policy. Now they happen spontaneously within America in an effort to dismantle an old and to establish a new society. Many Americans are paradoxically dismayed by this, and so are many foreigners. French President Émmanuel Macron, for instance, denounced woke culture, and his diversity minister Élisabeth Moreno singled it out as 'something very dangerous'.[65] This strikes me as extremely ironic, coming from the land of Robespierre, Saint-Just, and Napoleon. Irony aside, the history of the West since the Enlightenment is already littered with the wreckage of ruined institutions and forgotten ideas; and one may well wonder how much is left to tear down at this point.

The Western Obsession with Novelty Spreads

Much has also been torn down elsewhere, since the European obsession with novelty has spread abroad. This was true even for

63 Del Noce, A., *The Crisis of Modernity*, edited by Lancellotti, C., McGill-Queen's University Press, Montréal and Kingston, 2015, p. 134.

64 Gray, J., 'American Unreality', *The New Statesman*, October 28, 2020 (https://www.newstatesman.com/uncategorized/2020/10/american-unreality).

65 Nussbaum, A., 'Macron Minister Slams 'Wokeness,' Wants to Keep It Out of France', *Bloomberg*, May 18, 2021 (retrieved from https://www.bloomberg.com/news/articles/2021-05-18/macron-minister-slams-wokeness-wants-to-keep-it-out-of-france).

those two ancient pillars of civilization which European powers never totally subjugated or colonized: China and Iran. No two civilizations had been more regularly attacked, conquered, and ruled by foreigners throughout history; and yet both had always absorbed their invaders into indigenous streams of culture and civilization—but not, alas, in the nineteenth and twentieth centuries.

The Qing dynasty, established by Manchu invaders in 1644, gave rise to some of China's most competent and intelligent emperors. In the eighteenth century they brought China to a peak of prosperity and stability, and the empire reached its largest territorial extent. But in the following century, European powers inflicted repeated humiliations, the most conspicuous of which were the Opium Wars and the seizure of ports and spheres of influence. It looked and felt like the dismemberment of China, and confidence in the ruling Manchus was shaken. Reaction came in the form a series of violent uprisings. One of these was the bloodiest civil war in history: the so-called Taiping Rebellion which lasted from 1850 to 1864, and in which as many as thirty million people died.[66] It was both a nativist revolt and a messianic movement influenced by Christianity. Hong Xiuquan, the rebel leader, believed himself to be the brother of Jesus Christ, and began by destroying Buddhist and Confucian shrines, but soon launched into a genocidal slaughter of Manchus. The emperors Xianfeng and Tongzhi faced down the uprising (albeit with British assistance), and the Manchu dynasty managed to hold together. But the strength and prestige of the ruling house were gone, and further humiliations came in the form of a military defeat by Britain, France, and Japan, and renewed diplomatic meddling by European powers.

66 Spence, J. D., *God's Chinese Son: The Taiping Heavenly Kingdon of Hong Xiuquan*, W. W. Norton & Company, New York, 1996.

The Manchu court embarked on various projects of reform at the end of the nineteenth century. Among these were investments in European-style armaments, as well as naval and army units, a steamship company, textile mills, mining, foreign language schools, scientific and technological schools, and programmes for sending Chinese students to Europe and America.[67] These activities were known as the Self-Strengthening Movement and encouraged belief that ancestral Chinese culture had to be radically reconstructed. The scholar Kang Youwei (1858–1927) reimagined Confucius himself as a reformer, and argued that the original Confucian classics were forgeries. The so-called New Text of the classics (supposedly reproduced from memory in the Later Han dynasty) was, in Kang's opinion, authentic. Scholars now reject this interpretation, but at the time it allowed Kang and his followers to reinterpret history in conformity with liberal principles of progress; and thus the door was open to restructuring all Chinese institutions.

Reform of the old civil service examination system provoked vigorous resistance from conservatives. As a result, Kang sought Anglo-American and Japanese support for a coup, but the effort failed and he went into exile. Reform was on hold for the moment, but Western ideas began to pour into China rapidly. In the late 1890s, Lin Shu, Yan Fu, and Liang Qichao translated occidental texts into Chinese and disseminated their ideas.[68] Darwin's works on evolution, the lectures of Thomas Huxley on 'Evolution and Ethics', Adam Smith's *Wealth of Nations*, John Stuart Mill's treatise

67 Tanner, H. M., *China: A History*, v. 2: *From the Great Qing Empire through the People's Republic of China*, 1644–2009, Hackett Publishing Company, Indianapolis / Cambridge, 2010, pp. 87–92.

68 Tanner, H. M., *China: A History*, v. 2: *From the Great Qing Empire through the People's Republic of China*, 1644–2009, Hackett Publishing Company, Indianapolis / Cambridge, 2010, pp. 94–95.

On Liberty, and Montesquieu's *Spirit of the Laws* were the most prominent of them. The result was that intellectuals imbibed a noxious blend of social Darwinian thought and liberalism. One conclusion seemed inescapable: China had fainted in the struggle for survival of the fittest, and recovery meant assimilating Western theories of education and liberty. Liang Qichao came to the depressing conclusion that the people of China had not been educated enough for democracy. He founded a newspaper in exile in Japan and ensured that copies of it were regularly smuggled into China.

Further calamities came in 1900 with flooding, drought, and widespread unemployment. The Boxer Rebellion, another nativist, anti-Manchu uprising, threatened to overturn the Qing throne yet again. Its anti-Manchu sentiment was obviously repugnant to the Qing. But the dowager empress Cixi sought to exploit its hatred of foreigners and Christianity, by declaring war on all European and Japanese powers whose fleets were massing at Tianjin harbour, intending to intervene in the chaos. The plan miscarried, and the foreigners captured Tianjin and Beijing, forcing the Qing court to flee to Xi'an. Peace was restored in the end, but the foreigners had done enormous damage. No more proof was needed that the Qing were corrupt and incompetent. The dowager empress reacted by instructing officials to study Western and Chinese systems of government and to present recommendations for reform and abolition of various practices and institutions. The result was the so-called New Policies: a long series of innovations lasting right up to the collapse of the Qing in 1911.

During that period the Manchu court lost control over Chinese society. The likes of Kang Youwei and Liang Qichao were still advocating patiently for reform while in exile in Japan. But young radicals at home talked of a total break with the past, the extermination of the Manchus, anarchy, liberal democracy, and rejection of China's patriarchal family structure. In 1903, Zou Rong (1885–1905) published a tract called *The Revolutionary Army*, blending a call for American-style independence with his visions of racial struggles between Han and Manchu and 'yellow and white'. 'Sweep away millennia of despotism in all its forms', he wrote, 'throw off millennia of slavishness, annihilate the five million and more of the furry and horned Manchu race, cleanse ourselves of 260 years of harsh and unremitting pain, so that the soil of the Chinese subcontinent is made immaculate, and the descendants of the Yellow Emperor will all become Washingtons'.[69] This spirit of remaking China continued long into the twentieth century.

The collapse of the Chinese imperial system in 1911 was almost instantaneous. The fall of the Qing gave way first to a republic and then to regional separatism and rule by warlords. Amidst the confusion of that time, Chinese intellectuals of the so-called New Culture movement attempted to discern the causes of China's poverty, weakness, and failure in comparison with Western success. One of the principle influences on New Culture was Futurism, and the translations of futurist plays prepared by the intellectual Song Chunfang brought the ideas of Marinetti and his followers into China.[70] Those ideas were diametrically opposed the spirit of Confucianism, whose founder is supposed to have said: 'if you crave speed, then you will never arrive'.[71] And so it was in the futurist spirit of destruction that Chen Duxiu, a professor at Peking University and eventual co-founder of the Chinese Communist Party, blamed Chinese culture for all recent failures: Confucianism, respect for elders, the old family

69 Zou Rong, 'The Revolutionary Army', translated by John Lust, *The Revolutionary Army: A Chinese National Tract of 1903*, Mouton, Paris, 1968.

70 Brezzi, A., 'Four Foolish Pieces: the First Translations of the Italian Futurist Avant-garde', *Italian Association for Chinese Studies, Selected Papers*, v. 1, 2016, pp. 9–28.

71 Confucius, *Analects*, 13.17.

system, hierarchy, and so on—these were all for the ash heap of history because they had restrained China's progress and made it unfit for survival. For Chen and his associates, the evolution of civilization meant 'constantly replacing the old with the new', and he encouraged young China, as he put it, to 'smash the Confucian family shop'.[72]

Such an intellectual climate favoured experiments in every form of revolutionary innovation, from parliamentary democracy to military dictatorship, theocracy, Leninism, Stalinism, Fascism, anarchism, and so on. Yan Xishan, the warlord of Shanxi immediately after the fall of the empire, notably announced that the perfect ideology was a combination of 'militarism, nationalism, anarchism, democracy, capitalism, communism, individualism, imperialism, universalism, paternalism, and utopianism', and he ran his province accordingly.[73] No mention of Confucian, Daoist, or Buddhist doctrines, though. Such experiments issued in another civil war beginning in 1927, the eventual triumph of Mao Zedong in 1949, and the horrors of the Great Leap Forward and the Great Proletarian Cultural Revolution from the late 1950s to Mao's death in 1976. These were efforts to industrialize China rapidly and to purge all lingering features of traditional Chinese culture. Local shrines and temples were destroyed, priests and scholars were murdered, and the grave of Confucius was desecrated.[74] The death toll was gigantic, and it is a terrible irony that the principal victims of socialist progress in China were workers and peasants.

72 Tanner, H. M., *China: A History*, v. 2: *From the Great Qing Empire through the People's Republic of China*, 1644–2009, Hackett Publishing Company, Indianapolis / Cambridge, 2010, pp. 124–125.

73 Pines, Y., *The Everlasting Empire: The Political Culture of Ancient China and Its Imperial Legacy*, Princeton University Press, Princeton and Oxford, 2012, p. 164.

74 Gray, J., *Rebellions and Revolutions: China from the 1800s to 2000*, second edition, Oxford University Press, Oxford, 2002, pp. 324–380.

In Iran, the oscillation between constitutional and absolute monarchy and the late Shah's modernist reforms terminated in 1979 with the most radical break with the past that Iran has ever endured. It was much less murderous than the Chinese example, but only slightly less destructive. The Shiite theocracy and the dictatorship of legal scholars which now govern Iran were invented by the Ayatollah Khomeini, inspired more by contemporary radicalism in Latin America than by any traditional Shiite practice.[75] It was a utopian and naïve attempt to free Iran from the dead hand of the past as represented by the Shah, and it remains illegitimate in the eyes of orthodox Shiite clerics who had always been politically quiescent.[76] The Islamic Republic still takes a dim view of ancient Iranian, especially pre-Islamic, history; but luckily the attempt to outlaw traditional music and visual art has failed.

As in China, so in Iran, it was not relativism that motivated those sad developments, but simply the belief that the past must be destroyed to make way for a new and better world. Some of the worst revolutionary excesses in both countries have, it is true, been curtailed or reversed—notably in the reforms of Deng Xiaoping and Mohammad Khatami. But the Islamic Republic of Iran is still going strong, with no viable alternative to replace it. And despite China's market reforms and change of attitude to religion, the project of deracination and re-education continues in Xinjiang and Tibet.

75 Abrahamian, E., *Khomeinism: Essays on the Islamic Republic*, University of California Press, Berkley, 1993.

76 Saffari, S., 'The Legitimation of the Clergy's Right to Rule in the Iranian Constitution of 1979', *British Journal of Middle Eastern Studies*, 20 (1), 1993, pp. 64–82; Momen, M., *An Introduction to Shi'i Islam: The History and Doctrines of Twelver Shi'ism*, Yale University Press, 1985, pp. 295–296.

No Revaluation of Values

In the West, there is one notable inheritance from the past that has not yet been wholly effaced. This is the Christian moral system. Its survival is something of a paradox. If, after the Reformation, no one could agree on religion anymore, how could there be any consensus on morality or on how to live a good life? The old Aristotelian ethics of virtue were accordingly abandoned over the course of the Reformation and the Enlightenment. When nature itself came to be seen as a universal mechanism of efficient causes, no room was left for a distinctly *human* nature. This is what Condorcet and his ilk implied by their doctrine of the perfectibility of man. If there was no human nature, neither was there any specifically human good, nor any activities or practices to bring about that good. The collapse of virtue ethics explains why there seems to be no way to settle contemporary questions as to how human beings ought to live, what is good or evil, and the relationship between morality and politics.

This problem is consummately analysed by Alisdair MacIntyre in his famous book *After Virtue.*[77] The best that most people can manage is what MacIntyre calls 'emotivism': the idea that originally Christian moral judgements are nothing more than statements about our own feelings. In other words, something is good simply because we approve of it. The metaphysics that once supported Christian moral claims have been disavowed, the church has fragmented, and its power has diminished. And yet, no viable or remotely appealing alternative to Christian morality has been proposed. David Hume and Immanuel Kant assumed that Christian morality was true, but tried—and failed—to give it a purely rational basis. Nietzsche and

77 MacIntyre, A., *After Virtue: A Study in Moral Theory*, third edition, Notre Dame, University of Notre Dame, 2007.

the Nazis were the last to try to get rid of it altogether, and they too failed. The American *Declaration of Independence* insists that certain Christian assumptions about human nature are 'self-evident' truths, and the French *Rights of Man and the Citizen* assumes much the same. Jeremy Bentham, the utilitarian philosopher, called such assertions 'nonsense upon stilts', since they admitted of no justification.[78] It may have escaped Bentham, but the influence of Christian morality upon the moral philosophy of the Age of Reason is enormous but wholly unacknowledged—a fact which attracted the wrath of Nietzsche and which inspired Carl Becker's series of essays called *The Heavenly City of the Eighteenth-Century Philosophers*. More recently, Tom Holland's book *Dominion* has shown that the modern language of human rights simply asserts Christian claims about equality and dignity and so forth, without any attempt at justification.[79]

The paradoxical result of all this is that the hottest of contemporary hot-button issues are both attacked and defended with reference to the same moral principles. Both advocates and critics of abortion,[80] pornography,[81] and assisted suicide[82] confront

78 Bentham, J., 'An Examination of the Declaration of the Rights of Man and the Citizen decreed by the Constituent Assembly in France' in *The Works of Jeremy Bentham*, edited by John Bowring, 11 vols., Edinburgh, 1843, vol. II, pp. 491–529.

79 Holland, T., *Dominion: How the Christian Revolution Remade the World*, Basic Books, New York, 2019.

80 Green, E., 'A Pastor's Case for the Morality of Abortion', *The Atlantic*, May 26, 2019 (retrieved from https://www.theatlantic.com/politics/archive/2019/05/progressive-christians-abortion-jes-kast/590293/).

81 Gryboski, M., 'Lutheran Pastor Defends 'Ethically Sourced Porn,' Wants to Remove 'Shame' From Industry', *Christian Post Reporter*, November 7, 2018 (retrieved from https://www.christianpost.com/news/lutheran-pastor-defends-ethically-sourced-porn-wants-to-remove-shame-from-industry.html).

82 Cartwright, J., 'Assisted Dying: A Christian Argument', *The Guardian*, July 9, 2009 (retrieved from https://www.theguardian.com/commentisfree/belief/2009/jul/09/assisted-dying-christianity-religion).

one another with similar appeals to the Christian concepts of dignity, mercy, compassion, and autonomy. The revaluation of values, which Nietzsche looked forward to, has not happened. But it is as though we are wandering in the ruins of an ancient morality which we still reflexively accept but no longer fully understand.

Postmodernism

Otherwise, all universalizing ideas were dead. Or so Jean-François Lyotard argued in his 1979 book *The Postmodern Condition*. The term 'postmodern' had been used before in reference to art, but Lyotard was first to apply it to Western culture in general. The basic argument was that the big ideas of the past, particularly the recent past, had led only to disappointment. Progressive movements of every kind—science, religion, the old ideologies, and especially Marxism—had failed to usher in the utopias that they had promised. No one believed in them, and no one could even agree on reality anymore because no one understood it. Here Lyotard's limited understanding of chaos theory appeared to justify his claims. We could not look to universal theories or narratives to tell us who we are, or what our purpose is, because they had led only to failure.

Instead of grand narratives (or 'metanarratives', as Lyotard called them), all we had left were 'language games' and a fragmentary jumble of local or personal 'small narratives', which were mutually contradictory.[83] This goes a long way to explain why the gradual divergence of science from the humanities was accelerated and completed in the postmodern age. Every body of knowledge and human pursuit has been separated and partitioned into distinct

83 Lyotard, J.-F., *The Postmodern Condition: A Report on Knowledge*, University of Minnesota Press, Minneapolis, 1984.

fields, with no apparent relationship among them. The idea of the full exercise of all human faculties by a single person seems strange now. We can hardly imagine Bill Gates distinguishing himself as a theologian like Leibniz or Newton, or Arnold Schwarzenegger writing architectural treatises like Alberti. But we smile at the fact that Brian May, the guitarist from the band *Queen*, is also an astrophysicist, and note it as a quaint eccentricity. An Avicenna or an Alberti would have flourished in any civilizing epoch, but not in our own age of narrow, atomized specialization and pointillist focus on minutiae.

But Lyotard's postmodernism was, in a sense, rather unoriginal. In 1562, Henri Estienne published *The Outlines of Pyrrhonist Philosophy*. It was an exposition of the ideas attributed to a certain Pyrrho, as recorded by the second-century Graeco-Roman philosopher Sextus Empiricus.[84] Pyrrho, incidentally, was supposedly a younger contemporary of Aristotle. One of the main arguments of Pyrrho and Sextus amounted to a denial that sensory experience could lead to certain knowledge about the world, and it proved extraordinarily influential on Michel de Montaigne.[85] In his own writings, Montaigne added the idea that all men's senses were defective in different ways and could not be reconciled. A radical scepticism took root—reflected notably in Pierre Charron's *On Wisdom* (published in 1601) and most famously in Descartes' *First Meditation*—and it has remained an obsession in French thought ever since. To me at least, postmodernism looks like the latest iteration of this obsession. And I suppose that it is

84 For more detail, see the introduction to Sextus Empiricus, *Outlines of Scepticism*, edited by Julia Annas and Jonathan Barnes, Cambridge University Press, Cambridge, 2000, pp. xi–xxxi, and the ensuing translated text also.

85 Greengrass, M., *Christendom Destroyed: Europe 1517–1648,* Penguin Books, London, 2014, pp. 209–210.

not surprising that a trend which took hold amidst the calamities of the Reformation, the Wars of Religion, and the Thirty Years' War reasserted itself after the disasters of the twentieth century.

In another sense, postmodernism was late to the game, since it merely reflected and described changes that had already begun in the 1960s. The American civil rights movement, feminism, the sexual revolution, environmentalism, alternative lifestyles, and the beginning of globalization all undermined prevailing modes of thought and called attention to marginalized people and unfamiliar places and ideas.[86] Much good came of these developments, before they hardened into political correctness in the 1990s. But what was good came at a high cost. Like his hippie forerunner, the new Postmodern Man was cut off from his ancestors' ideas and customs; and he revelled in eclecticism, in contradictions, in absurdities, and in disruption of norms. He had no idea where he came from, where he was, or where he was going, and that was how he liked it. The 1960s were fittingly concluded with the moon landing, the 'giant leap for mankind' which took our species further than we have ever been from where we belong; and, intellectually, it seems that we have not yet returned.[87]

When I was at school and in undergrad in the late 1990s and early 2000s, it was still possible to hear young people claim to be existentialists and hippies. Some would start sentences with 'when the revolution comes . . .' without any obvious irony. Their parents, ex-hippies perhaps from the Baby Boom, may have told them, or more probably they got it all from parodies on *The Simpsons*. In any

86 Marwick, A., *The Sixties: Cultural Revolution in Britain, France, Italy, and the United States, c. 1958–1974,* Oxford University Press, Oxford, 1998.

87 Conrad, P., *Modern Times, Modern Places: How Life and Art Were Transformed in a Century of Revolution, Innovation and Radical Change*, New York, Alfred A. Knopf, 1999, pp. 693–694.

case, the sixties cast a long shadow over the rest of the twentieth century and beyond; and even Millennials, who claim to hate the Boomers, seem strangely fond of the Boomers' most formative moments right down to re-enacting 1968-style street rioting in 2020.[88] But no one reads Sartre anymore. Postmodernism has taken over where existentialism left off.

Some say that postmodernism was only a transitional phase or an interregnum between modernism and some new era whose character has yet to be defined. Postmodernism, they say, died at the end of the nineties. Others say that the curtain came down with attacks of 9/11 or the death of the postmodernist luminary Jacques Derrida in 2004.[89] But I do not believe that the postmodernist era has ended, for the scepticism of grand narratives is alive and well and still justifies some of the most important of contemporary beliefs. The globalized world requires a person to hold multiple, contradictory perspectives at once, since antithetical 'grand narratives' might cause conflict. Practitioners of Social Justice and Critical Race Theory follow the postmodernists in rejecting all hierarchies of value, certainty, conviction, and other 'hegemonic' modes of thought. Whether they know it or not, conspiracy theorists such as Alex Jones share the postmodernist belief that knowledge is socially constructed. And popular emphasis on the 'small narratives' of personal truth and lived experience is a powerful stimulus to libertarianism across the political spectrum.

88 Andrews, H., *Boomers: The Men and Women Who Promised Freedom and Delivered Disaster*, New York, Sentinel, 2021, pp. 191–197.

89 Bauman, Z. / Bordoni, C., *State of Crisis*, Polity Press, Cambridge, 2014, pp. 76–97; Pluckrose, H. / Lindsay, J., *Cynical Theories: How Activist Scholarship Made Everything about Race, Gender, and Identity — and Why This Harms Everybody*, Pitchstone Publishing, Durham, North Carolina, 2020, pp. 45–66.

The Decline of Institutions

On that sad note, we can return to Kenneth Clark's judgement with which I began this chapter. Helen Andrews does exactly this at the end of her book *Boomers*, and we should follow her analysis. Clark's judgement was pronounced as he was wandering about the University of East Anglia, observing the Baby Boomer undergraduates conversing or reading books in the library. He seemed to take comfort in the idea that so many young people, such as those he had observed, were so 'bright-minded', 'curious', and 'critical'. They may have wanted to abolish existing institutions, but they would soon realize, as Clark thought, that 'it was institutions that made society work'. Andrews rightly calls Clark's optimism 'misplaced',[90] and I would add that his judgement about the future of institutions was rather naïve.

After the Bronze Age collapse, only the merchants of Phoenicia emerged from the wreckage stronger; after the fall of western Rome, it was the church. In contrast, only banks, credit card companies, and certain other corporations seem to have grown stronger since the Second World War, despite having very little to offer. Every other Western institution has been badly weakened or destroyed altogether. So many examples can be chosen to show this, that the problem is not where to begin the list, but where to end it. It was already too late when President Carter addressed Americans in 1979 about the energy crisis and also decried 'a growing disrespect for government and for churches and schools, the news media and other institutions'.[91] Nowadays, a recent Gallup poll has shown that only

90 Andrews, H., *Boomers: The Men and Women Who Promised Freedom and Delivered Disaster*, New York, Sentinel, 2021, p. 197.

91 Lipset, S. M. / Schneider, W., 'The Decline of Confidence in American Institutions', *Political Science Quarterly*, 8 (3), 1983, pp. 379–402.

33 percent of Americans have confidence in major institutions such as government, the medical system, and law enforcement—a symbol of a long process of neglect and atrophy paralleled everywhere.[92]

But it is not just large institutions that have deteriorated. Smaller, local, civic clubs and little volunteer societies are arguably in worse shape. The decline of such associations was famously pointed out in 1953 by Robert Nisbet in his book *The Quest for Community*.[93] The arguments of that text were revisited and reinforced in *Bowling Alone*, Robert Putnam's famous study of the collapse of American social intercourse, published in 2000.[94] Since then exhortations to reconnect with institutions and to strengthen social bonds have appeared periodically—most recently in Timothy P. Carney's *Alienated America* and Yuval Levin's *A Time to Build*, published respectively in 2019 and 2020.[95] So, there is good reason to think that the problem was getting worse even before the COVID-19 lockdowns.

The Culture of Narcissism, Atomization, and Identity Politics

The relativism and subjectivity of the early twentieth century has given way to extreme self-regard in our own time: the 'culture of

92 Brenan, M., 'Americans' Confidence in Major U.S. Institutions Dips', *Gallup*, July 14, 2021 (retrieved from https://news.gallup.com/poll/352316/americans-confidence-major-institutions-dips.aspx).

93 Nisbet, R., *The Quest for Community: A Study in the Ethics of Order and Freedom*, with an introduction by Ross Douthat, Wilmington, Delaware, ISI Books, 2019 (originally published 1953).

94 Putnam, R., *Bowling Alone: The Collapse and Revival of American Community*, 2000.

95 Carney, T. P., *Alienated America: Why Some Places Thrive While Others Collapse*, Harper Collins, New York, 2019; Levin, Y., *A Time to Build: From Family and Community to Congress and the Campus, How Recommitting to Our Institutions Can Revive the American Dream*, Basic Books, New York, 2020.

narcissism' identified first by Christopher Lasch in the late 1970s. This is not to say that everyone can now be diagnosed clinically as a narcissist. Narcissism, Lasch thought, was rather the spirit of the late twentieth century, typified by repressed anger and self-hatred, by the sham insight of self-help, by escapism into grandiose self-conception, by fear of ageing and death, by mid-life crises, and by the manipulation of other persons as instruments of gratification.[96] Some observers would go further. Bruce Cannon Gibney describes the still-dominant Baby Boomers as 'a generation of sociopaths', whose selfishness, improvidence, licentiousness, sexual promiscuity, wastefulness, drug use, and so on have lasted well beyond the 1960s when most of them came of age.[97] No generation has more bafflingly aimed both at 'living in the moment', as though there were no future, and at a sort of ageless, deathless process of never-ending self-cultivation in which the past counts for nothing. Gibney notices another seeming paradox: contrary to what one might have supposed, the Boomer fixation on the present and the future did not usher in an era of constant improvement. Scientific and technological development began to stall in the 1970s, and public infrastructure has been deteriorating since the 1950s. Nor (says Gibney) has there been much social progress lately. Narcissists and sociopaths are especially bad at cooperating with others and sustaining harmonious social interaction. Such people are incapable of seeing any point to volunteer groups, because of their failure to identify with posterity and their inability to feel themselves part of history.

96 Lasch, C., *The Culture of Narcissism: American Life in an Age of Diminishing Expectations*, originally published in 1979, W. W. Norton & Company, New York, 2018.

97 Gibney, B. C., *A Generation of Sociopaths: How the Baby Boomers Betrayed America*, Hachette Books, New York, 2018 (originally published 2017).

Atomization is accordingly worse now. Isolation from the communities, institutions, and sense of history that once gave life meaning, the practice of virtue, civic participation, family formation, and so forth, count for nothing in and of themselves. What matters most, as far as I can tell, is that everything be open to free, autonomous choice. There is no worse sin than curtailing seemingly endless possibilities. This, of course, is a paradox: to choose one thing means that you have rejected something else, hence, the contemporary aversion from commitment to persons, places, and causes—an aversion well symbolized in Joachim Trier's 2021 film *The Worst Person in the World.* This film is a portrait of Julie, an ageing millennial woman who cannot commit herself to anything of lasting significance, lest she abridge the array of free choices before her, as she drifts from one failed relationship to another. Julie is a fictional character, of course, but she typifies the loneliness and isolation of the present moment, just as Brett Easton Ellis' character Patrick Bateman in *American Psycho* represented the darkest aspects of the 1980s culture of narcissism.

But the problem cannot simply be boiled down to loneliness. The idea of free, autonomous choice presupposes that the exercise of the will is necessary in order to actualize a private 'inner self'.[98] This idea takes shape within the thought of American philosopher John Rawls, whose book *A Theory of Justice* established free choice as the dominant theory of contemporary liberalism.[99] One can see it as the latest phase of the individualism inaugurated by Petrarch. One can hear in it distant echoes of Descartes, Rousseau, Kant, and Bergson, as well as harmonies with the postmodern notion of small narratives

98 I am following the analysis in Fukuyama, F., *Liberalism and Its Discontents*, Farrar, Straus and Giroux, New York, 2022, pp. 47–63.

99 Rawls, J., *A Theory of Justice*, revised edition, Harvard University Press, Cambridge, 1991.

and the supremacy of lived experience. Anyway, the ultimate exercise of the will without guidance, without authority, without judgement, and without purpose is, I daresay, bad for us, since the autonomous chooser inevitably becomes a person bereft of character and moral depth.[100] Worse, sooner or later we realize that our inner selves are not really autonomous. Others must acknowledge and respect us. Autonomy, rightly understood, is better exercised by groups and communities with a common wisdom and shared capacity greater than those of any single person. But such groups, as I said before, have been weakened or destroyed altogether. Accordingly, disaggregated and unhappy individuals have little recourse but to turn to the state for recognition and acknowledgement amidst the loneliness and flatness of contemporary life. As Francis Fukuyama has lately demonstrated, this is the origin of identity politics: a problem which now places enormous strain on common, civic life and political institutions alike.[101]

Here I will stop. The story of decline that I have just rehearsed is only a brief summary of recent trends that have produced what Kenneth Clark called a civilization without a centre. It is just enough, I hope, to get a clear sense of the overall problem. But I do not wish simply to diagnose or describe a disease. I want to suggest some remedies also. So, next, we will revisit the three main outcomes of civilized life that I mentioned earlier—clarity, beauty, and order—and discuss the present state of each one, and what may be done to restore them.

100 Sandel, M. J., *Liberalism and the Limits of Justice*, second edition, Cambridge University Press, Cambridge, 1998, pp. 179–183.

101 Fukuyama, F., *Identity: The Demand for Dignity and the Politics of Resentment*, Farrar, Straus and Giroux, New York, 2018.

CHAPTER IV

Clarity

If names are not rectified, speech will not accord with reality.
Confucius, *Analects*, 13.3

OUR SPECIES HAS BEEN CAPABLE of attentive observation for at least forty thousand years. Such, at least, is suggested by the lifelike and energetic depictions of animals within the Lascaux and Altamira caves. Yet it seems that we realized only comparatively recently that the world could not only be observed, but also understood. At the root of this discovery is confidence in our powers of perception and reason. But what is more important is the belief that our understanding of the world can be explained—that our thoughts, feelings, and ideas can be made intelligible to others who have not necessarily shared our experiences. This sense of clarity is vitally important to civilization; for, without it, people could not be certain of understanding one another, no knowledge could be communicated between people, nor could what we know be enlarged by the great variety of human experience.

Clarity requires close correspondence between perception and expression. This principle takes visible shape in the earliest writing systems. Instead of a series of arbitrary signs representing the *sound* of a word, as in alphabetic writing, our ancestors began with the *image*. Drawing what you see and using the pictures to express your thoughts implies a belief in the proximity of perception, thought, and language. Accordingly, pictographic writing, such as Egyptian hieroglyphs, conveys and encourages solidity and realism; and even intellectual and emotional states are represented by images of the physical expressions or gestures accompanying them. The old view was that this method was an impediment to abstract thought, but I cannot agree.[1] The elegant appearance and realistic imagery of Egyptian hieroglyphs means that abstract ideas can be made not only vivid, but also pleasing to look at.[2] Much the same can be said of Sumerian cuneiform and Chinese characters, which also involve pictographic realism and visualization of abstract concepts, albeit in a more stylized manner.[3] The longevity of pictographic writing proves how well suited it is to human thought and communication. It lasted about three thousand years in Egypt and Mesopotamia, and it is still used in China where the most abstract principles of Confucian and Daoist philosophy have always been represented by pictures.

Pictographic writing systems remind us that clear thinking and expression began with a clear image of the world. The same principle

1 Gardner, A., *Egyptian Grammar: Being an Introduction to the Study of Hieroglyphs*, third edition, Oxford University Press, London, 1973, p. 4.

2 Ritner, R. K., 'Egyptian Writing' in Daniels, P. T. / Bright, W., *The World's Writing Systems*, Oxford University Press, Oxford, 1996, pp. 73–81.

3 Michalowski, P., 'Mesopotamian Cuneiform' in Daniels, P. T. / Bright, W., *The World's Writing Systems*, Oxford University Press, Oxford, 1996, pp. 34–43; Boltz, W. G., 'Early Chinese Writing' in Daniels, P. T. / Bright, W., *The World's Writing Systems*, Oxford University Press, Oxford, 1996, pp. 191–199.

is at work in the most vivid and arresting poetry of the ancient world, such as we find in the epics of Assyria and the Hebrew Bible. In the *Descent of Ishtar* (a Neo-Assyrian poem), the underworld is 'the house of darkness', 'a road whose course does not turn back', where the inhabitants 'eat dust and clay'.[4] The *Song of Solomon*, from the sixth century BC, employs every conceivable metaphor to describe love, jealousy, and the pleasures of the body to startling effect. The vividness of the Homeric poems comes from the so-called epic simile, which, as a rule, compares a strange and unfamiliar thing to some aspect of common experience. Accordingly, Hector leaping into battle is like a wave crashing upon a ship, and his rout of the Achaeans is like a lion attacking a herd of cattle;[5] Trojan watchfires are as numerous as the stars in the night sky;[6] the gleam of Achilles' spear is as the appearance of the evening star,[7] and so forth. Such similes became conventional in poetry because you must be able to imagine clearly what you hear or read in order to understand it.

Plato applied this idea to thought in general, and he was first to advance a model of the visual and verbal operation of the mind. In the dialogue called the *Philebus*, Socrates describes thinking as the work of an inner 'scribe writing words in our souls' whose work is accompanied by 'a painter who paints images in our souls to illustrate what the writer has written'.[8] This is a concise expression of the fact that clear thinking involves word and image together.

4 Reiner, E., *Your Thwarts in Pieces, You Mooring Rope Cut: Poetry from Babylonia and Assyria*, Horace H. Rackham School of Graduate Studies at the University of Michigan, Ann Arbor, 1985, pp. 29–49.

5 *Iliad*, XV.624–636.

6 *Iliad*, VIII.555–560.

7 *Iliad*, XXII.317–320.

8 Plato, *Philebus*, 38e9–39c6.

Unsurprisingly, the works of Plato are models of clear thought illustrated with vivid, accessible images. They address some of the most abstract subjects (the nature of love, of justice, of piety, and so on) in an idiom combining the best features of formal prose and ordinary conversation. Plato's contemporary Xenophon adheres to the same standard of clarity in his writing, and it is perhaps not merely a coincidence that he was also a student of Socrates.

Socrates was the great opponent of the sophists: tutors for hire who purported to teach virtue to the sons of Greek aristocrats, along with the usual subjects of rhetoric, music, mathematics, and so on. But for Socrates they were pedants and quibblers, preoccupied more with verbal artistry than with reality and truth—what we call *sophistry*. Socrates, Plato, and Xenophon were not their only detractors. The playwright Aristophanes and the philosophers Aristotle and Isocrates also took up the fight against the casuistry and relativism of the sophists. When it came to relativism, no sophist was worse than Protagoras, whose dictum 'man is the measure of all things' meant that individual persons constructed their own truth. And in his dialogue *The Sophist*, Plato outright accuses sophists of fabricating a bogus alternative reality, which was all the worse for being superficially plausible. The only antidote was to understand the world as it really is through clear communication free of distortion and artifice.

Plato was right on this point, but another aspect of his influence misled the Western mediaeval world somewhat. The Platonic emphasis on the unchanging, eternal world of forms was exaggerated in the doctrines of the so-called Neoplatonists who flourished in Late Antiquity and whose work was rediscovered amidst the Carolingian Renaissance. The Neoplatonists tended to view the world of forms as the only true reality and believed that what the senses perceived merely represented or symbolized the higher, truer world. This suited the passionate faith of the Middle Ages only too well, and its need to 'worship the ineffable under visible signs'.[9] The love of symbolism might have produced an incoherent mass of allegories or a 'wild phantasmagoria', as Jan Huizenga says, were it not for the fact that every image and picture had been carefully analysed and assigned its place within a vast thought-system—a world that is alive to us in the poetry of Chrétien de Troyes and the *Romance of the Rose*, and which is trapped in amber in the later allegorical tapestries known as *The Lady and the Unicorn.*

The same love of symbolism also entailed the personification of abstract ideas, such as the cardinal virtues or the seven deadly sins, which are represented as actual characters in art and literature. Perhaps the only such personification that remains with us is the figure of death who once appeared as a jolly skeleton in the mediaeval *danse macabre* and who is now represented by the grim reaper. Obviously, symbols, allegories, and personifications can communicate truth. But they cannot be taken to an extreme without damaging consequences. It is not possible to live a healthy and full life if you view the world as *just* an agglomeration of symbols. That mode of thought prevents us from seeing things as they really are, and can easily produce contempt for the world. Moreover, if you see everything as an allegory, you are dangerously close to living in a Don Quixote-style fantasy world. And so, one of the most important transformations in European intellectual history was the sudden burst of clarity that made Western Christendom perceive the hard reality beneath the symbol.[10]

9 See the discussion of this tendency in Huizenga, J., *Autumntide of the Middle Ages: A Study of Forms of Life and Thought of the Fourteenth and Fifteenth Centuries in France and the Low Countries*, translated by Diane Webb, edited by Graeme Small and Anton van der Lem, Leiden University Press, Leiden, 2020 (originally published 1919), pp. 301–315.

10 Pieper, J., *Guide to Thomas Aquinas*, Ignatius Press, San Francisco, 1991, pp. 44–47.

It was the renewed interest in the works of Aristotle which inspired this transformation. It happened in the thirteenth century, and it began with Albertus Magnus (c. AD 1200–1280), although his illustrious student Thomas Aquinas usually gets all the credit. The superiority of Aristotle (and associated commentaries by Avicenna and Averroes) struck these two men profoundly. Aristotle was for them the personification of intellectual energy, and no subject, it seemed, had eluded his intelligence. Discussion of the soul, sensory perception, memory, imagination, cognition, cosmology, motion, meteorology, ethics, quantity, time and space, and studies of biology informed by careful observation—these qualities made the study of Aristotle irresistible, and any attempt to ban him (and there had been some) was bound to fail.[11] What Aristotle seemed to show was that all that was apparent to the senses was real and intelligible in itself. And so, Aquinas and his ilk hit upon the philosophical justification for studying the here-and-now. Obviously, this mode of thought could be antagonistic to prevailing religious ideas, and in a later age it would lead to a kind of worldliness and materialism among lesser men than Aquinas. Contemporary critics charged that it was enough to know about God without bothering with his creation; Aquinas replied that an error about nature would lead to muddled thinking about God.[12]

There was, however, a problem with Aristotle, or so some later intellectuals began to think. Aristotle knew the importance

11 Lindberg, D. C., *The Beginnings of Western Science: The European Scientific Tradition in Philosophical, Religious, and Institutional Context, Prehistory to A.D. 1450*, second edition, University of Chicago Press, Chicago and London, 2007, pp. 227–253. On the struggles to ban Aristotle's works, see Grant, E., *The Foundations of Modern Science in the Middle Ages: Their Religious Institutional, and Intellectual Contexts*, Cambridge University Press, Cambridge,1996, pp. 54–83.

12 Pieper, J., *Guide to Thomas Aquinas*, Ignatius Press, San Francisco, 1991, p. 48.

of careful observation and the experience of the senses. Memory follows sense experience; and through memory, an observer uses his intuition or insight to determine the universal features of things. But, in the Aristotelian writings, knowledge gained from experience is always presented as the product of a deductive demonstration, like a Euclidean mathematical proof.[13] This meant beginning from 'first principles': universal definitions or assumptions from which nothing further could be deduced. The actual phenomena of nature came second. Aristotle began his *Metaphysics* with the famous generality that 'all men by nature desire to know' and then gradually gets into a discussion of what wisdom is.[14] This approach worked well for biological growth or other seemingly organic developments. For example, we have the very Aristotelian idea that living beings move toward end-states or goals: the goal of a seed is to become a plant, the goal of a child is to become an adult, and so forth, because it is in their nature to do so. Similarly, the goal of practising virtue was the Good Life, which human beings are naturally inclined to pursue. Such deductions from the 'nature of things' made less sense, though, when it was asserted, for instance, that rocks fall to the ground simply because it is in their nature to do so.[15] So, it would be easy to accuse Aristotle and his followers of the capital crime of failing to test their assumptions under controlled conditions.

13 Lindberg, D. C., *The Beginnings of Western Science: The European Scientific Tradition in Philosophical, Religious, and Institutional Context, Prehistory to A.D. 1450*, second edition, University of Chicago Press, Chicago and London, 2007, p. 48.

14 Aristotle, *Metaphysics*, I.180a.

15 Robertson, R., *The Enlightenment: The Pursuit of Happiness 1680–1790*, Penguin Books, 2020, p. 42; Lindberg, D. C., *The Beginnings of Western Science: The European Scientific Tradition in Philosophical, Religious, and Institutional Context, Prehistory to A.D. 1450*, second edition, University of Chicago Press, Chicago and London, 2007, pp. 50–51.

Aristotle, though, would have replied that what he wanted to observe and understand was *nature as it really was* without artificial constraints.[16]

There is much to be said for this point of view. And approaching the world with a set of ideas about how it works can certainly help us to see the world more clearly. But in the age of exploration and discovery, many of the old assumptions would not do. The flood of new information called too many of them into doubt, and demanded instead a heavy emphasis on experience and facts alone.[17] The word 'fact' itself came into use at this time. Galileo Galilei (1564–1642) seems to have been the first to use it for something that had occurred or which had been observed to be true. For Francis Bacon, a 'fact' meant whatever could be proved by experiment—an idea for which he gets far too much credit because he did not actually originate it. The much earlier Roger Bacon (1220–1292) and his mentor Robert Grosseteste (1175–1253) were the first European scholars to speak of the *scientia experimentalis*, meaning knowledge through trial and experience. Yet even they had borrowed the concept from the work of Ibn al-Haytham who had emphasized confirming knowledge through a process of rigorous testing, which he called *i'tibar* in Arabic.[18] And, of course, it was the Byzantine grammarian and theologian John Philoponus (d. c. 570) who had first put to the test and corrected Aristotle's erroneous theory of falling bodies, and about a thousand years later Galileo imitated him.[19] Anyway, Francis Bacon tends to get

16 Lindberg, D. C., *The Beginnings of Western Science: The European Scientific Tradition in Philosophical, Religious, and Institutional Context, Prehistory to A.D. 1450*, second edition, University of Chicago Press, Chicago and London, 2007, p. 51.

17 Greengrass, M., *Christendom Destroyed: Europe 1517–1648,* Penguin Books, London, 2014, p. 210.

18 Falk, S., *The Light Ages: The Surprising Story of Mediaeval Science*, W. W. Norton and Company, New York, 2020, pp. 115–116.

19 Lindberg, D. C., *The Beginnings of Western Science: The European Scientific Tradition*

all the credit for the so-called *inductive* method and experimentation, whereby one begins with observable facts, infers general principles from them, and then tests them—the reverse of reasoning from Aristotelian first principles.

The late sixteenth and early seventeenth centuries were accordingly something of a heyday for factual representation, lifelike paintings, true histories, and so forth. There was also considerable fascination with very unusual or surprising things, monsters, and freaks; and these were put on display in Cabinets of Curiosities where they could be pondered or marvelled at. Induction suited this age perfectly. But without a framework of assumptions (like those of Aristotle) to hold all this information together, the new world of facts seemed to crumble before the scepticism of Montaigne and the doubts of Descartes. And it is a paradox of European intellectual history that, as facts proliferated, so did uncertainty and relativism.[20]

But the truth is that we do not need Plato, Aristotle, or Bacon to see the world clearly and to communicate about it. What we need is confidence—confidence in our senses and intellect to understand the world and confidence that the truth is the same for everyone. Matta ibn Yunus (AD 870–940), who was one of the luminaries of the Abbasid translation movement, succinctly expressed these two ideas in the context of a tenth-century dialogue about the merits of logic and grammar recorded by Abu Hayyan al-Tawhidi (AD 930–1023).[21] 'In matters apprehended by the intellect', Matta

in Philosophical, Religious, and Institutional Context, Prehistory to A.D. 1450, second edition, University of Chicago Press, Chicago and London, 2007, pp. 310–311.

20 Greengrass, M., *Christendom Destroyed: Europe 1517–1648*, Penguin Books, London, 2014, p. 210.

21 The Arabic text and English translation of this debate can be found in Margoliouth, D. S., 'The Discussion between Abu Bishr Matta and Abu Sa'id al-Sirafi on the Merits of Logic and Grammar', *The Journal of the Royal Asiatic Society of Great Britain and Ireland*, January, 1905, pp. 79–129.

said, 'all men are alike, as for example four and four are eight with all nations'. His opponent, Abu Sa'id al-Sirafi, considered that a gross oversimplification, and rejected philosophy because what had been invented by Greeks could not, in his opinion, be of value to Turks, Indians, Persians, or Arabs. Al-Tawhidi favoured that sort of parochial relativism also, and he included Greek philosophy among the 'invasive sciences' which in his opinion had no place in Arabic thought and language. Similarly, the achievements of al-Farabi, Avicenna, and Averroes, founded as they were on Aristotelian logic, provoked hostility from conservative Muslim jurists—most famously from al-Ghazali (AD 1058–1111) and Ibn Taymiyyah (AD 1263–1328).[22] Modern scholars have been tempted to accuse those two of snuffing out Islamic science and philosophy in favour of anti-intellectual dogmatism. This is not entirely true, since science pressed on for some time despite them, but their refusal to trust both human reason and the evidence of their senses was a blow to intellectual confidence.[23]

The Islamic Golden Age was distinguished by confidence in all branches of knowledge. While scientists and philosophers assimilated the Greek heritage, historians and raconteurs rummaged through Byzantine, Iranian, Indian, and Chinese literature and historiography. This huge array of material might have amounted to an inchoate mass of anecdotes or disjointed aphorisms encumbered by long chains of witnesses and authorities, or *isnad*s are they are called in Arabic. Earlier Arabic historiography was like this before writers developed confidence in their powers of narrative unity and

22 Ezzaher, L. E., *Three Arabic Treatises on Aristotle's* Rhetoric: *The Commentaries of al-Farabi, Avicenna, and Averroes*, Southern Illinois University Press, Carbondale, 2015.

23 Adamson, P., *Philosophy in the Islamic World: History of Philosophy Without Any Gaps*, volume 3, Oxford University Press, 2016, pp. 140–146; 358–364.

synthesis.[24] But the writers of the ninth and tenth centuries had that confidence, and were models of clarity. Al-Jahiz, the greatest stylist of that age, described good prose as brief, clear, and free of mannerism and affectation. The works of Baladhuri, Dinawari, Ya'qubi, Ibn Mu'tazz, Ibn 'Abd Rabbih, Mas'udi, and so on adhere to the same principles.[25] Their vivid and elegant histories may still be read for pleasure. The great jurist and historian al-Tabari (AD 839–923) notably broke the mould, employing long chains of references and multiple conflicting narratives about the same event. He has won respect from modern academics in search of historical anecdotes, but he is not especially accessible or clear. After the fall of the Western Roman Empire, it took more than a millennium for the writers of the Scottish and French Enlightenment to cast aside the florid and verbose Latin of the Renaissance in favour of brevity and clarity in their native languages. This same sense of clarity appeared in the east after the fall of the Sasanian Empire after a much shorter interval.

Al-Ghazali's doubts about reason and his own senses are presented in two books. The first is the famous *Incoherence of the Philosophers* and the second is *The Deliverance from Error*, a work that is little known in the West.[26] Taken together, the force of those works bears a superficial resemblance to the central assumption of postmodernist philosophy. In the late twentieth and early twenty-first centuries, doubt in our powers of perception and reason have been rooted in

24 Robinson, C., *Islamic Historiography*, Cambridge University Press, Cambridge, 2003, pp. 18–30.

25 Khalidi, T., *Islamic Historiography: The Histories of Mas'udi*, State University of New York Press, Albany, 1975, pp. 19–26.

26 Al-Ghazali, *Deliverance from Error and the Beginning of Guidance*, translated by W. Montgomery Watt, Islamic Book Trust, Selangor, Malaysia, 2005 (originally published in 1953 by George Allen & Unwin Ltd under the title *The Faith and Practice of Al-Ghazali*).

the experience of two horrific world wars and the failure of ideology. Likewise, al-Ghazali's doubts (and those of Ibn Taymiyyah) arose amidst the slow dismemberment of the Abbasid Caliphate from the late ninth century onward and its violent destruction by the Mongols in AD 1258. Perhaps we can say that the horrors of the thirteenth and twentieth centuries had comparable outcomes in that both were severe psychological blows, and both gave way in the end to doubt and cynicism. Yet before this happened in the East, there was a great flowering of Islamic mysticism, or Sufism, which sadly has no Western parallel in our own time. Al-Ghazali, who was himself a Sufi, came at the beginning of this flowering; and Ibn Taymiyah, who hated all forms of mysticism, came at the end. A brief digression on this subject has some bearing on our discussion of clarity.

Sufism developed out of a sense of personal piety and the purification of inner worship and awareness. Its aim was personal union with God, and it was inspired in part by Christian mysticism, which it eventually surpassed. Exploring the hidden meanings behind the literal word of the Qur'an and the formalities of the shariah had no place within the conventional piety of jurists and scholars, but Sufism encouraged it. The mystical life of a Sufi was characterized by states of ecstasy, comparable to transports of rage, hallucinations, or euphoria. Such experiences, brought on by meditation, fasting, dancing, or intoxication, would obviously be to some extent subjective, but not so subjective as to defy mutual understanding and communication. The proof of this is that the Persian mystical poetry of Sana'i, Attar, Rumi, and Jami are a unitary genre of universal human interest, as shown by the widespread appeal of Rumi, the greatest of those poets, even in translation.[27]

27 Ciabbatari, J. 'Why Is Rumi the Best-Selling Poet in the US', *Between the Lines*, BBC Culture, October 21, 2014 (https://www.bbc.com/culture/article/20140414-americas-best-selling-poet).

So, it is not hard to see why Sufism would have flourished amidst the calamities of political collapse and the Mongol irruption. It may even have done so *because* of those problems, for Sufism's emphasis on personal piety was for many the only consolation amidst the butchery and devastation of the thirteenth century.[28] Sufism could easily be misunderstood as a turning away from a troubled world, in favour of private fantasy, credulity, superstition, passivity, pessimism, and contempt of intelligence and knowledge.[29] And so it may have been for some people who knew no better. But it is wrong to think of Sufism as prefiguring the escapist distortions of reality of the hippie movement or rave culture. For its purpose was to see and to understand reality *with greater clarity*, such as when the solution to a problem suddenly appears, when a fit of anger has passed, or when a person can at last look at his own shortcomings and pettiness with objectivity.[30] Mysticism was the counterpart, not the enemy, of reason and philosophy.

Accordingly, the Sufis looked beyond the outward appearance of formal public worship and Islamic law. The forms of religion were still binding on all believers, but the rules were only really valid if their inward spirit could be grasped—a principle familiar from Christianity also. Sufis would accordingly belittle the apparent

28 The arguments of various scholars to this effect are summarized in Lane, G., *Early Mongol Rule in Thirteenth-Century Iran: A Persian Renaissance*, Routledge, London, 2003, pp. 226–232; See also Arberry, A. J., *Aspects of Islamic Civilization: The Moslem World Depicted Through Its Literature*, second edition, Ann Arbor, The University of Michigan Press, 1971, pp. 16–17.

29 Rypka, J., *History of Iranian Literature*, first published in 1956, translated from the German by P. van Hopte-Pope, D. Reidel Publishing Company, Dordrecht, 1968, pp. 232–233.

30 Hodgson, M. G. S., *The Venture of Islam: Conscience and History in a World Civilization, Volume 1: The Classical Age of Islam*, University of Chicago Press, Chicago, first edition, 1977, pp. 392–409.

differences among religions. Modern interpreters and translators of the poetry of Rumi, for instance, tend to construe this tendency as a kind of relativism, but this is wrong.[31] The Sufis overlooked religious allegiance in favour of a person's spiritual and moral qualities in order to emphasize what is common, what is *universal*, in all religions. Even idolaters who venerated stones were held by the Sufis to worship the one God, since it was the best approximation of the truth that they knew.

That sense of goodwill, as well as detachment from the turmoil of the day, meant that popular loathing of the Mongol conquerors never comes across in the works of the Sufi mystics. This was true even when they themselves, like Rumi, Sa'di, and Attar, endured many horrors of war. Not so for Ibn Taymiyyah, who hated and condemned the conquerors. He thought of himself as the defender of the wreckage of Islam against the barbarians even after the Mongols themselves converted to it—a conversion which he considered illegitimate anyway.[32] Ibn Taymiyyah accordingly dispensed with philosophy and mysticism alike and called the faithful to a puritanical, originalist vision of Islam. This was not exactly the end of Sufism, but Ibn Taymiyyah, not Rumi, had the last word. The doubt and confusion following the destruction of the Caliphate never entirely abated, and the apparent certainty of literalism has lately triumphed over inner, spiritual clarity.

In our own time, the doubt and uncertainty that followed the two World Wars has not yet abated either, and still finds justification in the doctrines of postmodernism. To put it as charitably as

31 Ali, R., 'The Erasure of Islam from the Poetry of Rumi', *The New Yorker*, January 5, 2017 (https://www.newyorker.com/books/page-turner/the-erasure-of-islam-from-the-poetry-of-rumi).

32 Adamson, P., *Philosophy in the Islamic World: History of Philosophy Without Any Gaps*, volume 3, Oxford University Press, 2016, pp. 358–364.

possible, this mode of thought is a pessimistic rejection of certainty, especially that of the exploded ideologies. Michel Foucault, for instance, seems not to have denied the existence of the real world; but he argued that human bias got in the way of perception, and that socio-political power, not reality, was the standard of truth. Jacques Derrida and Jean François Lyotard emphasized language instead of power. For them, objectivity, science, technology, and so on were a mere language game; and, contrary to all common sense, words did not refer to the real world and could not represent it or communicate it to others. Similarly, the postmodern irrationalist philosophers preached the relativity of truth and falsity, refusing any epistemological distinction between science, religion, and mythology.[33] All these doctrines—like those of al-Ghazali and Ibn Taymiyyah—have a common suspicion of reason, empiricism, and logic; and this suspicion is inspired by a belief that we cannot grasp the whole truth. There is, however, a key difference. Al-Ghazali and Ibn Taymiyyah never gave way to relativism. Their point was that God, through his revelation, is the guarantor of truth, objectivity, and falsehood; but postmodernism is in practice a denial of the existence of these principles altogether, and an assertion of relativism.

Apart from the banal observations that knowledge and perception can be shaped by power, that culture and belief can influence one another, and that language can sometimes be tricky, postmodernism is otherwise fallacious. The mere fact that something *can* be doubted does not mean that we cannot know the truth; indeed, doubt may really be the first step toward the truth. Long before Descartes, Peter Abelard (AD 1079–1142), the near contemporary of al-Ghazali, put

33 Sidky, H., 'The War on Science, Anti-Intellectualism, and Alternative Ways of Knowing in 21st Century America', *Skeptical Inquirer*, 2 (2), 2018, pp. 38–43.

this well when he said 'by doubting we come to inquiry, and by inquiry we perceive the truth'.[34] But the worst feature of postmodern thought is that it is bereft of clarity; and in place of clarity there is a huge mass of pompous literary allusions, pastiche, baroque rhetorical figures, faux-scientific jargon, and abstruse nonsense. Here is a famous example:

> Indeed dialectical critical realism may be seen under the aspect of Foucauldian strategic reversal of the unholy trinity of Parmenidean / Platonic /Aristotelean provenance; of the Cartesian-Lockean-Humean-Kantian paradigm, of foundationalisms (in practice, fideistic foundationalisms) and irrationalisms (in practice, capricious exercises of the will-to-power or some other ideologically and/or psycho-somatically buried source) new and old alike; of the primordial failing of western philosophy, ontological monovalence, and its close ally, the epistemic fallacy with its ontic dual; of the analytic problematic laid down by Plato, which Hegel served only to replicate in his actualist monovalent analytic reinstatement in transfigurative reconciling dialectical connection, while in his hubristic claims for absolute idealism he inaugurated the Comtean, Kierkegaardian and Nietzschean eclipses of reason, replicating the fundaments of positivism through its transmutation route to the superidealism of a Baudrillard.

That quotation is from Roy Bhaskar's book *Plato Etc.,* originally published in 1994.[35] In the year of its publication, that single

34 Abelard P., *Sic et Non* (eds. Boyer, B. B. / McKeon, R.), University of Chicago Press, Chicago, 1976, p. 103.

35 Bhaskar, R., *Plato etc: The Problems of Philosophy and Their Resolution*, Routledge, London, 2010 (second edition).

sentence—and it is a *single* sentence—won first place in the *Philosophy and Literature* Bad Writing Contest. Its obscurity and abstractness, its lack of any clear mental image, now characterize typical 'academic' prose. That this sort of writing is indeed nonsense was first established by the famous Sokal hoax in 1996, when physicist Alan Sokal published a parody article full of postmodern jargon and deliberate non sequiturs in the journal *Social Text*. The leading lights of postmodernism, including the journal's editors Frederic Jameson and Andrew Ross, were unable to distinguish their own field from bullshit.[36] But this was not the end of postmodernism. For it has become the main intellectual impetus behind all Social Justice movements, Critical Theory, identity politics, and everything else that may be considered characteristic of the 'post-truth' age. The fuzzy, diffuse, and often meaningless ideas associated them have recently been documented, quoted, and dissected by Helen Pluckrose and James Lindsay in their book *Cynical Theories*.[37]

Nevertheless, the appeal of postmodernism is very hard to overcome. Since the 1960s, and long after the Sokal hoax, postmodernist doctrine has flourished in Western universities, where students of every political persuasion imbibed it. Well-meaning, albeit naïve, professors seem to have believed that relativity of truth and falsehood would usher in a more open, tolerant, and virtuous society—a state of affairs famously lamented in *The Closing of the American Mind* by Allan Bloom.[38] In this respect, the proponents

36 For more on this depressing subject, see Sokal, A. / Bricmont, J., *Fashionable Nonsense: Postmodern Intellectuals' Abuse of Science*, Picador, New York, 1998.

37 Pluckrose, H. / Lindsay, J., *Cynical Theories: How Activist Scholarship Made Everything about Race, Gender, and Identity — and Why This Harms Everybody*, Pitchstone Publishing, Durham, North Carolina, 2020.

38 Bloom, A., *The Closing of the American Mind: How Higher Education Has Failed Democracy and Impoverished the Souls of Today's Students*, the 25th Anniversary Edition, Simon and Schuster Paperbacks, New York, 2012 (originally published 1987).

of postmodernism are very much like the sophists, for both claim to know and to impart *virtue*. Anyone peddling a quick route to virtue should immediately put us on our guard, and relativity of truth and falsehood has not produced a better society, only the most debilitating confusion. The new sophists' disconnection from reality and their avoidance of clarity mean that no communication is possible with them. They do not understand that words describe reality and that we speak or write in order to name and identify things that are real, and to identify them for *others*.[39] In place of dialogue, postmodern expression is a *soliloquy*, aiming at ideological purity and the superficialities of academic complexity, but not at the truth. It is not an attempt to describe the world as it really is and to discuss it. It is rather like a pre-recorded message of propaganda, repeated incessantly, exhausting and degrading everyone who hears it—a phenomenon that can be especially loathsome when it takes the form of repetitive sloganeering on Twitter. And yet, I say again, it obviously appeals to certain people.

In contrast to Pluckrose and Lindsay, Thomas de Zengotita presents a more sympathetic critique of postmodernism.[40] He too finds that postmodernism is the main ideological force behind identity politics, along with every other aspect of the 'Age of Trump' that we now live in. 'Crazy confusion' is the main feature of this age. But the postmodernist Left have long ceased to be disruptive—especially in comparison with the Trumpian Right. For no modern movement, nor any single person, has done more to upend norms, disrupt conventions, transgress boundaries, or question metanarratives than Donald Trump. And nothing represents the relativity of truth

39 Pieper, J., *Abuse of Language, Abuse of Power* (translated from German by Lothar Krauth), Ignatius Press, San Francisco, 1992 (second edition).

40 De Zengotita, T., *Postmodern Theory and Progressive Politics: Toward a New Humanism*, 2018.

better than right-wing conspiracy theories. Accordingly, progressive postmodernism has failed; and it was a necessary failure. De Zengotita argues that, confronted with this ironic reversal, serious intellectuals steeped in postmodernism must admit defeat. They have no choice, as he says, but to step away from the confusion, and create 'new master narratives, stories that can tell us who we are today, in this context, but also, and at the same time, who we are in general'.[41] In other words, de Zengotita means a recovery of a kind of universal humanism as the inevitable consequence of the postmodern failure.

That would be an appealing outcome, as attractive perhaps as Sufi religious universalism. But I cannot agree that it is inevitable. And it certainly would not happen without a return to clarity of perception, thought, and expression. Meaningful and dignified human existence depends on perceiving the world as it really is and living in accordance with that truth—an idea very close in spirit to the Confucian concept of the 'rectification of names' mentioned in this chapter's epigraph. Josef Pieper, the great Catholic Platonist, says that 'the natural habitat of truth' is in language, and therefore in clear interpersonal communication.[42] We could also say that clarity is a necessary property of mathematics, visual art, architecture, and music. And so it is. But it is in interpersonal communication that we now have the greatest need for clarity.

41 De Zengotita, T., *Postmodern Theory and Progressive Politics: Toward a New Humanism*, 2018, p. 357.

42 Pieper, J., *Abuse of Language, Abuse of Power* (translated from German by Lothar Krauth), Ignatius Press, San Francisco, 1992 (second edition), pp. 35–36.

CHAPTER V

Beauty

> The carpenter stretcheth out his rule; he marketh it out with a line; he fitteth it with planes, and he marketh it out with the compass, and maketh it after the figure of a man, according to the beauty of a man . . .
>
> Isaiah 44:13

WHAT IS THE RELATIONSHIP between beauty as a principle or a value and civilization? This is as hard a question to answer, since it is likely that our most ancient ancestors had a sense of aesthetics long before settled life appeared. The regular and balanced design of ancient hand axes was imposed deliberately—a sign of an early and universal human satisfaction with symmetry.[1] This innate satisfaction with symmetry

1 Wynn, T., 'Handaxe Enigmas', *World Archaeology*, 27 (1), 1995, pp. 10–24; Mithen, S., *The Prehistory of the Mind: A Search for the Origins of Art, Religion and Science*, Thames and Hudson, London, 1996, pp. 132–136.

and the ability to impose form upon raw material are surely the genesis of what we now call art. The artistic impulse seems to have been with us from the very beginning. So, we should be very careful about distinguishing between civilized art and any other kind.

Nevertheless, it seems obvious to me that civilization allowed our innate aesthetic sense to develop fully. Cave paintings of the Upper Palaeolithic clearly indicate an ability to hold an image of something in the mind and then to represent it accurately, often beautifully, but without an overall structure or narrative. The art of early settled life, as at Çatalhöyük for instance, lacks a strong aesthetic sense but is easier for us to interpret because of its narrative force. And the full development of civilized art unites a sense of aesthetics with narrative power.

An excellent early example of this appears on a large alabaster vase from the temple of Uruk in Mesopotamia, dating to the fourth millennium BC.[2] The vase commemorates the Sumerian festival of the new year in four parallel registers carved in relief. The lowest register shows a pair of undulating lines from which grows an alternating series of plants, probably barley and reeds. Directly above this we see sheep walking to the right. Above that a procession of identical nude men marches leftward, each carrying different agricultural offerings to the goddess. The highest register has suffered some damage, but may still be understood as depicting the ritual marriage of the goddess Innana and her consort Dumuzi, patron deities of the city of Uruk. The narrative force of the

2 Suter, C. E., 'Kings and Queens: Representations and Reality' in Crawford, H. (ed.), *The Sumerian World*, London, Routledge, 2013, pp. 201–226, pp. 206–207; Bahrani, Z. 'Performativity and the Image: Narrative, Representation, and the Uruk Vase' in Ehrenberg, E. (ed.), *Leaving No Stones Unturned: Essays on the Ancient Near East and Egypt in Honor of Donald P. Hansen*, Winona Lake (Indiana), Eisenbrauns, 2002, pp. 15–22.

vase is emphasized by the flat bands which divide and frame the registers: the effect is like that of a storyboard or comic strip. No less significantly, this is the first example in art history of people, plants, and animals standing firmly on the ground within an area representing space.[3] The Uruk vase also reminds us of the unity of beauty and utility, since the vessel itself would have been used in the religious festival depicted on it. And this sense of beauty and utility clearly goes well beyond our ancient ancestors' satisfaction with symmetrical hand axes.

We are no longer used to thinking of the union of utility and beauty. A signal proof is that our modern distinctions among art, craft, and technology were unheard of in ancient times. The Latin *ars*, which is the origin of our word 'art', was used for any kind of practical skill, technical or scientific knowledge, as well as what we would call a work of art. But in the sixteenth century, painters and sculptors began to be held in higher esteem than decorative artists, woodworkers, potters, smiths, and so on; and thereafter we have always maintained a distinction between the work of artists, which is purely aesthetic, and that of craftsmen, which emphasizes practical utility. The effect of this separation on visual art is unfortunate. It has led many people (especially adherents of modern 'trad' movements) to assume that an artist's only aim should be beauty. Even aesthetic philosopher Roger Scruton seemed to think that all would be well in the art world if there were a renewed emphasis on beauty.

The problem is that beauty can be deceptive.[4] Nothing is more likely to persuade us that all is well, when really it is not, than beautiful images, and fine words will convince us to do evil things

3 Honour, H. / Fleming, J., *The Visual Arts: A History*, fifth edition, New York, Harry N. Abrams, 1999, pp. 52–53.

4 I am following the arguments in Eco, U., *On Beauty*, London, MacLehose Press, 2010.

more readily than naked force. The twentieth-century experience with Fascist and Communist propaganda is enough to prove the point. Yet even the tendency toward idealism in art can be considered pernicious. The practice of portraying Christ and his Apostles as muscular athletes, or the invented speeches in Thucydides' *History*, for instance, take us far from the truth, since it is easier to believe what is improbable or imaginary if it has a pleasing appearance. Plato grasped this point and belaboured it. According to Plato, beauty had an existence independent of any physical form, and it did not correspond with what we see. Plato therefore dismissed practically everything that we would call art as a base copy of true beauty. For that reason, Plato considered art to be morally harmful, and he advocated banning it from schools in favour of teaching geometry instead.[5]

Plato's view is too extreme for most people to take seriously. But there is a kernel of truth in what he says. The Baroque, Rococo, and Neo-Classical emphasis on beauty went too far, and it provoked a reaction in favour of the fear, awe, and horror of the Romantics and their successors. These feelings exhausted themselves in about a century, and contemporary art tends to avoid both beauty and sublimity. Much modern art avoids physical forms altogether, as in Barnett Newman's abstract stripes of colour. Some art now even seems to aim deliberately at ugliness, such as the grim and pornographic mannequins of Cindy Sherman, or Lucian Freud's emphasis on his models' least appealing features. And Maurizio Cattelan's banana taped to a wall seems more like a spoof than anything else.

An artwork does not need to avoid ugliness in order for it to be good. Roman portrait busts make no attempt to hide people's

5 Timaeus, V, 55e–56c; Phaedrus, 244a–250d; Republic, 603a–603e.

physical imperfections. Many fine statues depict the most violent and disgusting scenes from classical mythology, such as the Laocoön group or Perseus with the head of Medusa. Images of the crucifixion of Jesus, such as that by Matthias Grünewald, are often grim and disturbing. Musical settings of the passion story, like those of Schütz or Bach, produce similar feelings, as do the requiem masses of Morales and Victoria. The tragedies of Aeschylus, Sophocles, Marlowe, and Shakespeare can be frightening or revolting. Those are all superb works of art. So, it would be wrong to say that the problem with the works of Newman, Sherman, Freud, and Cattelan boils down to their lack of beauty. They are certainly ugly, but their ugliness is secondary to their banality and lack of imagination; and in the case of Cindy Sherman and Maurizio Cattelan, I detect a will to shock us. Modern critics justify this shock value as 'pushing boundaries', or alerting people to their historical predicament and reminding them of perpetual change and so forth.[6] But such justifications are disingenuous.

Plato may have understood, and exaggerated, the beguiling nature of beauty, but he did not anticipate the danger of deliberately provoking anger, disgust, or fear which we find in contemporary art. Both extremes of beauty and ugliness can be equally manipulative. And self-conscious ugliness is just as mendacious as superficial beauty, since neither reflects the world as it really is. This is a good lesson for the age of round-the-clock news coverage and social media, which thrive on shocking images. The air-brushed model of the 1990s has given way to plastic surgery and deceptive Instagram filters. The overall affect may be superficially attractive to some but at the root of it is a lie. Further contemplation of this lie will end in disgust and cynicism. Plato was surely right to look beyond pleasing appearances, but we

6 Scruton, R., *Beauty: A Short Introduction*, Oxford, Oxford University Press, 2011, p. 141.

must avoid transforming beauty into an invisible abstraction and detaching it entirely from utility.

Both common sense and the evidence of ancient hand axes show that our aesthetic sense has always been based on harmonious proportion. We do not call ungainly, disproportionate things beautiful, and we distinguish between harmonious music, and that which is out of tune. This idea of beauty as proportion found almost literal expression in Egyptian art, which was executed according to a specific standard of measurement, commonly called the Egyptian canon. This meant dividing up a blank surface into little squares, and ensuring that each part of the eventual picture always filled about the same number of squares relative to the other parts. Some of these grid lines are still clearly visible on unfinished tomb paintings, and in other cases paint has chipped off finished works and revealed the lines beneath. To judge by the Biblical quotation at the beginning of this chapter, Assyrian and Babylonian artists seem to have followed a similar procedure, but the Near Eastern canon has been little studied.[7] Much more work has been done on the Egyptian canon, usually with too much rigidity, since scholars once thought that Egyptian artists always followed one and the same canon throughout Egyptian history. We now know that this is not true, and artists were more flexible than formerly believed.[8] Nevertheless, Egyptian artists always adhered to the idea that beautiful images could be made according to mathematical rules.

This concept is surely what inspired Pythagoras, a Greek philosopher of the late sixth and early fifth centuries BC. Pythagoras believed that the world was an orderly and intelligible form, not

7 Azarpay, G., 'Proportional Guidelines in Ancient Near Eastern Art', *Journal of Near Eastern Studies*, 46 (3), 1987, pp. 183–213.

8 Gay, R., *Proportion and Style in Egyptian Art*, Austin, University of Texas Press, 1994, pp. 64–123.

a chaotic mess. A natural progression of thought suggested to Pythagoras a correspondence between form and beauty, and that both could be understood according to mathematical rules. This theory seemed justified by the ratios governing musical sounds, the intervals between notes, and the relationship between the length of a string and the pitch that it produces when struck. Music and beauty were therefore governed by the same laws. A highly influential expression of this was the theory of the Music of the Spheres: a beautiful harmony produced by the perfect, circular motion of the planets which human ears were too feeble to hear. This idea reached the mediaeval world, where it inspired John Scotus Eriugena to conceive of the beauty of creation as a harmony of diverse voices, and Honorius of Autun to describe the universe as a cithara, a guitar-like instrument, whose different strings vibrate in harmony together.[9] St Hildegard of Bingen explained the proportions of the human body as expressing the harmonious plan of God's creation. Copernicus placed the sun at the centre of his universe, not simply because it made sense of the Persian mathematical models which he had copied, but also because it was in keeping with Pythagorean ideas of heavenly geometry. This is why Kepler jokingly called Pythagoras 'the grandfather of all Copernicans'.[10] And Kepler, for his part, claimed to have discovered a correspondence between the velocity of the planets and musical intervals.[11]

The precise ratios of Pythagoras and the Egyptians gave way to a more flexible sense of general proportions in classical Greek

9 Honorius, *Liber XII Quaestionum*, 2.

10 Africa, T. W., 'Copernicus' Relation to Aristarchus and Pythagoras', *Isis*, 52 (3), 1961, pp. 403–409.

11 Godwin, J., *Harmonies of Heaven and Earth: Mysticism in Music from Antiquity to the Avant-Garde*, Rochester, Vermont, Inner Traditions International, 1994, pp. 219–225.

statuary.[12] This is best exemplified in the work of the Greek sculptor Polycleitus for whom beauty was not to be found in the separate parts of a work, but in the proportions of each part in relation to the others and to the work as a whole. Polycleitus himself is supposed to have said that 'the beautiful comes about little by little through many numbers'.[13] Yet his approach to the proportions of a statue was subordinated to movements of the body represented, to changes in perspective, and to the position of the eventual viewer.[14] The Egyptian canon could be applied before executing the artwork, but Polycleitus and his followers had to take into account the whole experience of beholding the final product in different circumstances, and adjust its proportions accordingly. This more flexible approach would eventually change, though. In Byzantine art, there is a return to more rigid ideas of proportion, similar in principle to the Egyptian canon. Much the same can be said for the late Mediaeval paintings of Cennino Cennini, whose treatise on art owes much to Byzantine models. But the sense of measurement, whether absolute or relative, is far more evident in Romanesque and Gothic architecture than in painting, from which it nearly vanished altogether. Mediaeval man emphasized theories of harmonious proportion but expressed them more through architecture, music, and mystical theology than through art.

This changed in the Italian Renaissance. A canon of human proportions once again came to be seen as a rational basis for beauty, as well as an expression of mystical harmony.[15] The urge to achieve

12 I am following Panofsky, E., *Meaning in the Visual Arts*, Chicago, University of Chicago Press, 1955, pp. 55–88.

13 Philo Mechanicus, *Syntaxis*, 4.1.49.20.

14 Pliny, *Natural History*, XXXV.5; Vitruvius, *de Architectura*, III.1; Galen, *Placita Hippocratis et Platonis*, V.3.

15 Panofsky, E., *Meaning in the Visual Arts*, Chicago, University of Chicago Press, 1955, pp. 88–93.

the same mathematical perfection in the visual arts as in music was revived. It reached its peak in the rediscovery of linear perspective: a technique held to be both beautiful and an accurate representation of the world. Pomponius Gauricus revived the Pythagorean idea that the proportions of the human body were visual realizations of musical harmony. Giovanni Paolo Lomazzo connected those proportions with the pagan gods, with astrology, and with many other antiquarian and mythological themes. Leon Battista Alberti began to identify human proportions with those of buildings in order to show the architectural symmetry of the body and the humane qualities of architecture—an idea derived ultimately from the Roman architect Vitruvius.[16] This was all quite extravagant, even by the standards of the day, and reverence for a mathematical theory of proportion was not always matched by rigorous methods.

But no one was more rigorous than Alberti, Leonardo, and Dürer. Both Alberti and Leonardo accepted the classical tradition, but sought to verify it by observing and measuring nature. Instead of imposing mathematical rules on the world, they sought to derive them from observation. In the words of Erwin Panofsky, they intended 'to discover the ideal in an attempt to define the normal'.[17] Alberti claimed to have verified his few observations and measurements in consultation with many other experts. Leonardo preferred to multiply his studies of nature, as reflected in his copious notebooks. Dürer surpassed both in precision and variety of measurement, and his *Four Books on Human Proportion* is the apogee of the theory of beauty as mathematical proportion.[18]

16 Alberti, *De Re Aedificatoria*, VII.13.

17 Panofsky, E., *Meaning in the Visual Arts*, Chicago, University of Chicago Press, 1955, p. 94.

18 Panofsky, E., *Meaning in the Visual Arts*, Chicago, University of Chicago Press, 1955, pp. 99–104.

But Dürer went too far. His precision and complexity seemed to construe the study of proportion as an end in itself. It went well beyond the limits of utility and artistic practice. In this respect, Dürer's study of proportion was more like the illustrations in medical textbooks, such as *Gray's Anatomy*, than a theory of beauty. The triumph of the Renaissance was to balance principles of mathematical proportion, organic movement, and the subjective experience of the viewer. From the time of Dürer onward, that balance began to be disrupted and those principles began slowly to diverge, as the distinctions between artists, craftsmen, and architects grew.

Panofsky argues that the emphasis on the subjectivity of art undermined the theory of harmonious proportion more than anything else.[19] Seventeenth-century Dutch painters and the Impressionists of the nineteenth century had no need of a theory of proportion, he says, since solid objects and the human form meant nothing in comparison with the light and air of unlimited space in which they delighted. The distortions of people and objects preferred by the Mannerists and Expressionists suggest a similar conclusion, and contemporary artists seem to have abandoned measurement altogether. The result has not been good. To paraphrase Umberto Eco: who has not had the experience of leaving a modern gallery and hearing the patrons ask 'what was it meant to represent?' or 'is that what they call art?'[20] Panofsky's observations are surely right, but he missed the cause of the problem. The cause is not that subjectivity has been exalted over harmonious proportion, because this state of affairs is the *result* of a deeper disturbance. We have not

19 Panofsky, E., *Meaning in the Visual Arts*, Chicago, University of Chicago Press, 1955, p. 106.

20 Eco, U., *On Beauty*, London, MacLehose Press, 2010, p. 417.

lost our sense of beauty, because (though tastes may change) it is innate. But there is, as we have seen, a link between art and cosmology. Artists depict the world as they see and understand it, and what early twentieth-century science taught, or what people thought it taught, was new and startling.[21] Kenneth Clark touched on this fact for only an instant, observing that 'the incomprehensibility of our new cosmos seems to me, ultimately, to be the reason for the chaos of modern art'.[22] We can pursue this matter further.

It began with a series of misunderstandings of what was then cutting-edge physics. Picasso and Braque, the originators of Cubism, drew inspiration from atomic theory and quantum mechanics, and gave us a vision of a disorderly and fragmented world in parallel with the unpredictable movements of particles.[23] When Wassily Kandinsky read Rutherford's description of the atom in 1911, somehow all things become transparent to him 'without strength or certainty', as he himself said, and he founded a new style of abstract art which came to dominate the entire twentieth century.[24] Marcel Duchamp claimed to know little of science, but his masterpiece, now commonly called *Large Glass*, made between 1915 and 1923, was apparently inspired by Einstein's theories of special and general relativity, and his idea of spacetime as four dimensional. The original title of this work is *The Bride Stripped Bare by Her Bachelors, Even*, and it was intended as a scientific and

21 Fernández-Armesto, F., *Out of Our Minds: What We Think and How We Came to Think It*, London, One World Books, 2019, pp. 348–349.

22 Clark, K., *Civilisation*, 1969, p. 245.

23 Parkinson, G., 'Revolutions in Art and Science: Cubism, Quantum Mechanics, and Art History' in Malloy, V. V., *Modern Art in the Age of Einstein*, Cambridge, Mass., The MIT Press, 2018, pp. 99–113.

24 Conrad, P., *Modern Times, Modern Places: How Life and Art Were Transformed in a Century of Revolution, Innovation and Radical Change*, New York, Alfred A. Knopf, 1999, p. 83.

mathematical allegory of frustrated desires illustrated by a 'bride' suspended above a group of 'bachelors' below. The bride, who is not subject to the force of gravity, floats in what is supposed to be the fourth dimension, beyond the reach of the three-dimensional bachelors who are subject to the force of gravity—but anyone who did not read Duchamp's pompous and semi-coherent notes, published in 1967, would never have discerned any of this.[25] And the abstract painter Robert Delaunay and Futurist Enrico Prampolini had also been experimenting with a fourth dimension respectively in painting and set design at about the same moment.[26]

But then, in 1936, came the *Dimensionist Manifesto.* It organized and articulated the principles which had originally inspired Kandinsky and his successors. Its author, the Hungarian poet Charles Sirató, urged his readers to accept that 'Space and Time are no longer separate categories . . . and thus all the old limits and boundaries of the arts disappear'.[27] Sirató's ideas had been influenced by Cubism and Futurism; but pride of place went to Einstein's theories, which he called 'the European spirit's new conceptions of space-time'. Painting, as Sirató declared, would go from two to three dimensions, and sculpture from three to four. Many artists,

25 Henderson, L. D., 'The Dimensionist Manifesto and the Multivalent Fourth Dimension in 1936: Sirató, Delaunay, Duchamp, Kandinsky, and Prampolini' in Malloy, V. V., *Modern Art in the Age of Einstein*, Cambridge, Mass., The MIT Press, 2018, pp. 58–60; Conrad, P., *Modern Times, Modern Places: How Life and Art Were Transformed in a Century of Revolution, Innovation and Radical Change*, New York, Alfred A. Knopf, 1999, pp. 80–82.

26 Henderson, L. D., 'The Dimensionist Manifesto and the Multivalent Fourth Dimension in 1936: Sirató, Delaunay, Duchamp, Kandinsky, and Prampolini' in Malloy, V. V., *Modern Art in the Age of Einstein*, Cambridge, Mass., The MIT Press, 2018, pp. 57–58, 64–68.

27 Sirató, C. T., 'The History of the Dimensionist Manifesto and Related Texts' in Malloy, V. V., *Modern Art in the Age of Einstein*, Cambridge, Mass., The MIT Press, 2018, pp. 170–175.

including Kandinsky, signed this manifesto, but precisely how it would or could be fulfilled never became clear. Dimensionism itself attracted little attention amidst the rise of Nazism, the Second World War, and the Soviet occupation of Hungary; but, just as Marinetti had done, Sirató identified and described trends that remain influential.

The artists who had endorsed Dimensionism, and those who followed them, had abandoned accurate depictions of the world. In the struggle to represent a universe which they could not see and did not understand, they lost all sense of narrative force, as well as the principal unity of beauty and utility. But they were not always interested in the accurate representation of science, either. The little they knew of physics inspired them to question everything they had previously understood about reality, and to make art reflecting the doubt and confusion that remained. Behind all this was a misinterpretation, since no one seemed to grasp that Einstein's universe was a determinist one, which obeyed physical laws, and which we could understand and describe. Einstein firmly believed this and objected to the quantum mechanics of Niels Bohr which seemed to suggest the opposite. It would be hard to blame people for noticing that contradiction and feeling utterly bewildered. But the new irrational and chaotic universe had been shaped to fit the reality of mechanized warfare, mass murder, totalitarianism, atom smashers, and nuclear bombs.

But it is one thing to say that we do not yet understand the universe and another to say that the universe is permanently unintelligible. If we cannot persuade ourselves that the universe is orderly and coherent, whether we now grasp it or not, no exhortation to harmonious proportion or beauty will have any effect. This is where the search for a grand Theory of Everything would be especially helpful. So far, the most promising candidate for a theory to explain all physical aspects of the universe is superstring theory (string theory for short). In contrast to a universe of point-like ingredients with mostly empty internal structures, string theory posits that the most basic building blocks of everything are ultra-microscopic vibrating strings, and certain patterns of vibration give rise to different masses and force charges. When these vibrating strings and their behaviour are properly understood (a feat well beyond my own small mathematical capacity), the old incompatibility between general relativity and quantum mechanics vanishes. And so, if string theory is right, it brings us back to the idea of an orderly cosmos, intelligible according to mathematical laws. Its emphasis on resonant patterns of vibration and different tensions on tiny strings invites Pythagorean analogies. Brian Greene, the great popularizer of string theory, accordingly speaks of the 'cosmic symphony', the 'music of string theory', and 'an aeolian universe'—the comparison being to an aeolian harp, a sort of box zither from which sounds are made when the wind passes over the strings.[28] This metaphor is incidentally almost identical to the one employed by Honorius of Autun nearly a thousand years earlier, though Greene seems not have known about it. Anyway, as good as it may sound, there is still a long way to go. What string theory lacks in mathematical and experimental proof it makes up for in elegance and imagination. But we may yet live to see it tested and proved,[29] and we may yet see a see new generation of artists inspired by a vision of an orderly and rational universe.

However this may be, aesthetic concerns will be taken most seriously when they bear directly on people's lives. So, I will end this chapter with a short discussion of architecture, which, more

28 Greene, B., *The Elegant Universe: Superstrings, Hidden Dimensions, and the Quest for the Ultimate Theory*, New York, W. W. Norton, 2003, p. 135.

29 On the efforts to test string theory, see Gubser, S. S., *The Little Book of String Theory*, Princeton, Princeton University Press, 2010, pp. 1–6, 117–158.

than any other art, is capable of making our lives better and fuller. Buildings not only protect us from the elements, but also facilitate and shape social interaction because we live or work, or conduct other business in them, and are surrounded by them in every human settlement. Architecture is the best means that we have for defining space and marking it out for some meaningful purpose. No less importantly, permanent structures represent continuity over time and mankind's rootedness in a place and in a community.

The ancients believed in what might be called an anthropology of architecture. The Roman architect and theoretician Vitruvius believed that 'no building can be satisfactorily ordered in the absence of analogy with the correct proportions of the human body'.[30] I suspect that Vitruvius did not invent this concept, but he seems to have been first to write it down. Alberti, who effectively revived Vitruvian principles in the fifteenth century, did not know about Palaeolithic hand axes, but he suspected that our attraction to buildings designed with symmetry across a vertical axis was innate, and had the same source as our preference to symmetry in the human body. He even argued that the vertical structure and openings of an architectural façade had the same visual properties as the human face and body.[31] Andrea Palladio accepted this implicitly, but like Leonardo he sought out the ideal in a meticulous study of an enormous number of ancient structures; and, like Dürer, he attempted to work out the precise ratios of architectural parts that would produce a beautiful building. Many Palladian buildings, such as the Georgian houses of the eastern United States, are very beautiful, indeed; but whether their beauty arises from following

30 Vitruvius, III.i.1.

31 *De Re Aedificatoria*, IX.5; Onians, J., *Neuroarthistory: From Aristotle and Pliny to Baxandall and Zeki*, New Haven, Yale University Press, 2007, p. 45.

Palladio's exact mathematical ratios, and not a more general sense of symmetry, is an open question.

Two important ideas follow from Vitruvius' anthropology of architecture. The first is that architecture is in a sense an extension of our own bodies, making up for our natural defenselessness against the elements. A further progression of thought might suggest that an imperishable stone building could be a metaphorical extension of our own mortal bodies into spacetime, but this does not seem to have occurred to the Dimensionists. The second idea is simply that good architecture must be on a human scale. It should not challenge our standards and perceptions, but rather meet and satisfy them. We should no more expect people to accommodate themselves to ugly and uncomfortable architecture than we would expect them to adjust to foul-tasting and un-nutritious food. And so, it seems to me that neglecting to make our buildings beautiful is a serious failure.[32] It is, at least, a notable aberration, since beauty had always been considered an important element of architecture until the twentieth century.

What changed? The same trends that inspired Cubism and Dimensionism also influenced architecture. Austrian architect and professor Otto Wagner (1841–1918) preached a doctrine of architectural realism in which a building's form was to be determined by its purpose, and he rejected rehashing older, ornate styles in favour of functional simplicity. It would have been easy to feel this way, being surrounded by unimaginative Viennese baroque architecture. It fell to Wagner's disciple Adolf Loos (1870–1933) to declare war on every form of decoration and ornament and inaugurate the

32 I am following Rennix, A. / Robinson, N. J., 'Why You Hate Contemporary Architecture', *Current Affairs*, October 31, 2017 (https://www.currentaffairs.org/2017/10/why-you-hate-contemporary-architecture).

Modernist school.[33] He compared ornament to primitive tattooing, which probably says more about the derivative and superficial baroque classicism of Loos' time than anything else. 'Freedom from ornament is a sign of spiritual strength', wrote Loos in his manifesto *Ornament and Crime*, originally delivered as a lecture in 1910 and published later in 1913.[34] Emperor Franz Joseph may have hated it, but the so-called Looshaus at Michaelerplatz in Vienna is an elegant attempt to simplify architecture to its essential elements.[35] Loos's approach caught on and twentieth-century architecture has tried to adhere to the maxim that form follows function. I say 'tried' because the maxim was not always understood or observed.

Contempt for ornament eventually led in unpleasant directions. Futurist architects like Antonio Sant'Elia thought that we had surpassed the use of all traditional building materials, and favoured only concrete, iron, and glass. Mies van der Rohe followed him, inaugurating the unimaginative trend toward huge towers of steel and glass that disfigure modern cities.[36] But, when it comes to downright ugly architecture, Brutalism (so called from the French expression for raw concrete or *béton brut*) probably comes first to most people's minds. Soulless masses of concrete, steel, and glass in angular geometric shapes have arisen everywhere in the world, often in the form of depressing modular housing developments. No

33 Johnston, W. M., *The Austrian Mind: An Intellectual and Social History 1848–1938*, University of Chicago Press, Chicago, 1983, pp. 150–151.

34 A translation of *Ornament and Crime* can be found in Conrads, U., *Programs and Manifestoes on 20th-Century Architecture*, the MIT Press, Cambridge, 1970, pp. 19–24.

35 Masheck, J., *Adolf Loos: The Art of Architecture*, I.B. Tauris, London and New York, 2013, pp. 1–32.

36 Conrad, P., *Modern Times, Modern Places: How Life and Art Were Transformed in a Century of Revolution, Innovation and Radical Change*, New York, Alfred A. Knopf, 1999, pp. 290–291.

name is better associated with Brutalism than that of Swiss-French architect Le Corbusier. It was he who outdid Wagner and Loos, saying: 'this taste for decorating everything around one is a false taste, an abominable little perversion'.[37] His utopian plans to demolish the Marais quarter in Paris, and to bulldoze most of Moscow, and erect gigantic concrete towers were mercifully never realized. Brutalism ought to have been discredited by such ideas, and Le Corbusier with it. But Modernist architecture in general and Brutalism in particular were simple and cheap, and developers embraced them.

Brutalist buildings may have been soulless and ugly, but at least you could live and work in them, as many people still do. This was not always true of other Modernist styles. The Modernist house that Le Corbusier designed and built for the Savoye family outside Paris in 1929 appeared to be a triumph of functional simplicity: it is all empty, unadorned spaces and right angles. The only problem was that it was a failure. The perfectly flat roof allowed rainwater to accumulate; and within a week the house was flooded. 'The house which you built in 1929', wrote Madame Savoye to Le Corbusier, 'is uninhabitable'. She wrote that to him in 1937, and only the outbreak of the Second World War and the Savoyes' flight out of France saved Le Corbusier from legal action.[38] This is all quite ironic. Le Corbusier followed the Futurists in emphasizing the beauty of machinery such as low-pressure ventilating fans, huge electrical turbines, and airplanes. He loved aeronautics and claimed that his favourite chair was the seat of a cockpit. But the difference between the Villa Savoye and all that machinery was that the machinery could at least be expected to work properly.

37 Le Corbusier, *The Decorative Art of Today*, translated by James Dunnett, the MIT Press, Cambridge, Mass., 1987, p. 90.

38 De Botton, A., *The Architecture of Happiness*, Penguin Books, London, 2014 (originally published in 2006), pp. 57–66.

Postmodernist architecture, best exemplified by the work of Peter Eisenman, is even worse. A master bedroom divided in two by a wall so that a couple could not sleep together; a large hole in the floor and a stairway that ran directly into a wall; a house completely devoid of bathrooms—these were some of the characteristics of Eisenman's houses, and the owners of one of them even published a book lamenting the difficulties of living amidst such 'features'.[39] The idea of designing a building without human beings in mind seems comically absurd, but that was Eisenman's approach. He defended himself in a public debate with fellow architect Christopher Alexander at Harvard University in 1982.[40] Eisenman claimed to be influenced by the postmodernist, deconstructionist trinity of Barthes, Foucault, and Derrida, and stressed the importance of incongruity, disharmony, and even anxiety in his architecture. 'A world of total harmony is no harmony at all', he said, as though there were some virtue in asserting that 'the role of art or architecture might be just to remind people that everything wasn't all right'. In contrast, Alexander invoked the ideal of harmony and the architecture of the cathedral at Chartres in the hope of finding common ground. Eisenman sniffed:

> I think it is a boring building. Chartres, for me, is one of the least interesting cathedrals. In fact, I have gone to Chartres a number of times to eat in the restaurant across the street—had a 1934 red Mersault wine, which was exquisite—I never went into the cathedral. The cathedral was done *en passant*. Once you've seen one Gothic cathedral, you have seen them all.

39 Frank, S., *Peter Eisenman's House VI: The Client's Response*, Watson-Guptil Publications, New York, 1994.

40 Originally published in the magazine *Lotus International* 40, 1983, pp. 60–68. It has been transcribed here: http://www.katarxis3.com/Alexander_Eisenman_Debate.htm.

Alexander broke down in the face of such philistinism, claiming 'I feel sorry for the man. I also feel incredibly angry because he is fucking up the world'. He predicted that people would soon see through Eisenman's postmodernist claptrap, but this did not prove true as far as elite opinion was concerned. Alexander and his species of small-scale, hand-made architecture were soon forgotten, and Eisenman went on to win awards, to design ever larger structures, and to teach at several prestigious universities. One feels, though, that awards would have little value if ordinary people do not like your buildings.

Therein lies the main problem. Eisenman and his followers are less interested in satisfying the public than in pleasing other architects. The work of Frank Gehry, the celebrity architect par excellence, typifies this trend, since his buildings are strongly detested outside a narrow circle of critics and award committees. Consider, for instance, the mostly negative reactions to Gehry's Guggenheim Museum in Bilbao, completed in 1997,[41] or the 2006 open letter to Gehry by Jonathan Lethem in response to the gigantic development proposed for Atlantic Yards in Brooklyn.[42] Polls, such as one conducted in 2020 by the National Civic Art Society in America, consistently show an overwhelming preference for traditional architecture when it comes to public buildings.[43] But architects of Modernist and postmodernist

41 Goodman, D., *A History of the Future*, The Monacelli Press, New York, 2008, pp. 214–215.

42 The letter can be found here: https://slate.com/culture/2006/06/an-open-letter-to-frank-gehry.html. Three years later Gehry was stripped of his leading role in the project.

43 *Americans' Preferred Architecture for Federal Buildings: A National Civic Arts Survey Conducted by The Harris Poll* (https://static1.squarespace.com/static/59bfe5dbf14aa1b6bbb12cd0/t/5f845dfda65e566a0e0a8d32/1602510358640/Americans%27-Preferred-Architecture-for-Federal-Buildings-National-Civic-Art-Society-Harris-Poll-Survey.pdf).

schools prefer to give people what they think they should want rather than what they ask for—a notable departure from the traditional idea of an artist in service to a patron or a public. A good example of this is the housing development commissioned in 1923 near Bordeaux by French industrialist Henri Frugès. He had asked Le Corbusier to build modern-style housing for his factory workers and Le Corbusier obliged, deliberately avoiding any allusions to local architectural features or generally rustic qualities. The result was a series of plain, unadorned boxes, rectangular windows, bare walls, and flat roofs. The houses, as far as I know, were more structurally sound than the later Villa Savoye. But they too failed in the sense that the inhabitants immediately began to embellish their houses with shutters, window casements, wallpaper, picket fences, and the most un-Modernist of all features: pitched roofs.[44] The drive toward ornament is evidently hard to suppress, and elite notions of what people *should* want is usually wrong.

The postmodernists, alas, have never been deterred by this. In his debate with Christopher Alexander, Eisenman said that deference to public taste in music, for example, would produce Mantovani-style schlock instead of Beethoven, and so the architect should *impose* taste upon the public. Eisenman was simply convinced that he and his fellow architects knew best and everyone else would just have to get used to it. But the comparison with music is fallacious, as Rennix and Robinson have astutely pointed out in their excellent 2017 article called 'Why You Hate Contemporary Architecture'.[45] I am not especially fond of Beethoven (neither are Rennix and

44 De Botton, A., *The Architecture of Happiness*, Penguin Books, London, 2014 (originally published in 2006), pp. 163–166.

45 Rennix, A. / Robinson, N. J., 'Why You Hate Contemporary Architecture', *Current Affairs*, October 31, 2017 (https://www.currentaffairs.org/2017/10/why-you-hate-contemporary-architecture).

Robinson), and luckily I am not forced to listen to him at all times; but the buildings in which we all live and work are essential to civilized life, and it is impossible to avoid objectionable architecture when it surrounds us everywhere and when we have to live in it.

A revival of beautiful buildings does not mean a return to any particular style. It must rather begin with the anthropology of architecture that I described before. Nothing could have been more bizarre to the Roman architect Vitruvius and his imitators than the postmodernist idea that people must learn to accommodate themselves to jarring and uncomfortable buildings. We must understand instead that buildings are put up to meet our needs, and that no process of adjustment or accommodation should ever be necessary. The human needs satisfied by architecture are neatly summed up in the so-called Vitruvian triad: 'beauty, stability, usefulness'. This is founding principle of all good architecture. No element of the triad can be satisfied without the others. The proof of this is furnished by Modernist and postmodernist architecture: beauty is obviously not a by-product of a purely functional building, the strongest structure will not long be tolerated if it is not beautiful, and stability and utility by themselves do not guarantee permanence.[46] We can contrast the long-term use and value of traditional architecture with more recently built objects of immediate consumption and short lifespan.[47]

Léon Krier is perhaps the greatest disciple of Vitruvius now living. Krier is the guiding intelligence behind a number of traditional architectural projects throughout the world, but he is most famously associated with Poundbury in Dorset, England. Poundbury is an experiment in traditional and neo-classical architecture and the philosophy of New Urbanism patronized by Prince Charles. Critics

46 Krier, L., *The Architecture of Community*, Island Press, Washington, 2009, p. 259.
47 Krier, L., *The Architecture of Community*, Island Press, Washington, 2009, p. 250.

call Poundbury a 'feudal Disneyland',[48] a slur almost as unfair as describing the work of Le Corbusier as a totalitarian EPCOT Center. Poundbury is small, elegant, and walkable, but not hostile to the automobile. Traffic is notably controlled not through signs or lights, but by the width of streets and strategic placement of obstacles. Thirty-five percent of all housing is affordable and interspersed throughout the town, but without distinction of architectural style, so as to facilitate interaction among people of different social backgrounds. The idea is to keep the population to about 4,500 and to keep the town small. If Poundbury needs to grow, growth must be an organic reproduction of the town around another nearby centre, not endless outward sprawl. In spite of its critics, Poundbury has proved popular since its beginnings in the 1980s. The inhabitants are happy. Property values are 29 percent higher there than in the surrounding area, and this is as good an indication as any that people want to live there.[49] Yet, it must be said that the architectural styles of Poundbury are not in keeping with those of the surrounding area, and its building materials are not sourced locally.

Will the principles of New Urbanism embodied by Poundbury catch on? We shall see. Krier warns that we may find ourselves becoming New Urbanists and reviving beautiful architecture whether we wish to or not. Nothing, he says, has enabled the excesses of Modernist and postmodernist architecture more than the abuse of fossil fuels, since the most unpleasant features of those styles are

48 Wainwright, O., 'A Royal Revolution: Is Prince Charles's Model Village Having the Last Laugh?', *The Guardian*, October 27, 2016 (retrieved from https://www.theguardian.com/artanddesign/2016/oct/27/poundbury-prince-charles-village-dorset-disneyland-growing-community).

49 Shields, B., 'Fit for a King: Prince Charles' Experimental City Is Proving Critics Wrong', *The Sydney Morning Herald*, June 25, 2021 (retrieved from https://www.smh.com.au/world/europe/fit-for-a-king-prince-charles-experimental-city-is-proving-critics-wrong-20210722-p58bz9.html).

made possible only by concrete, glue, plastic, and other artificial products which require or are actually derived from petroleum. And this is to say nothing of the enormous environmental and human cost of heating and air conditioning required by architecture that takes no account of climate and meteorology. As we wean ourselves off fossil fuels, or as they run out, the gigantism and ungainly distortions of Modernist and postmodernist architecture will cease to be possible. The result will be a forcible return to traditional building techniques with natural materials and traditional styles. Structures built accordingly cannot fail to appear humane and beautiful, and nothing beyond a human scale will be possible. This is a comforting thought in a way. But it is sad to think that the revival of architectural beauty might only come about because of immense environmental degradation and self-destructive waste.

CHAPTER VI

Order

It is not good that the man should be alone.

Genesis 1:18

There is nothing so good or so convenient for people as order.

Xenophon, *Oeconomicus*, VIII.iii

AN IDEAL OF HUMAN ORDER can be derived from much of what we see around us. Observation suggests that at least some things are not random. They are intelligible and predictable. The behaviours of ants or bees, the regular migration of birds, the change of the seasons, the cycle of day and night, the phases of the moon, and the movements of the stars can all be interpreted as signs of an orderly universe. Our ancient ancestors saw these things and used them to make predictions, and these surely helped them to gather food, to reproduce, and to avoid danger. A natural progression of thought suggests that there must also be some organizing principles for mankind just as there are for other animals and natural phenomena. But for a long time, the nature of this ancient order was subject to considerable debate. Aristotle was right to declare that man naturally lives in a society, but he was wrong to assume that it had always been the city-state or *polis*. Both Hobbes and Rousseau were wrong to assume that men and women were originally solitary. And contemporary liberal thought wrongly construes the solitary individual as the basic unit of society.

Human beings have never been solitary.[1] We have always lived in groups. Studies of other primates can tell us a little about what ancient human groups were like. Frans de Waal's studies of the turbulent world of chimpanzees, for instance, reveals many features that we would recognize instantly as political: efforts at conflict resolution, compromise, reciprocal exchange, and even what de Waal calls Chimpanzee Machiavellianism.[2] There are even leadership contests when one alpha male and his supporters challenge and try to replace the reigning ape and his cronies. A chimp called Mike notably overthrew and replaced his group's dominant male, cowing him into submission by banging some empty kerosene cans which he had stolen from primatologist Jane Goodall.[3] Mike had been a physically unimpressive figure, but his coup succeeded in outsmarting and overthrowing the reigning party—the first primate putsch that we know of, though there have surely been others over the past three million years. So, politics in one form or another has probably always been with us.

1 Fukuyama, F., *The Origins of Political Order: From Prehuman Times to the French Revolution*, Farrar, Straus and Giroux, New York, 2011, pp. 26–31.

2 de Waal, F., *Chimpanzee Politics: Power and Sex among Apes*, Hopkins University Press, Baltimore, 1998 (1982).

3 Goodall, J., *In the Shadow of Man*, revised edition, Houghton Mifflin, New York, 1988 (1971), pp. 112–119; Goodall, J., *The Chimpanzees of Gombe: Patterns of Behavior*, Harvard University Press, Cambridge, 1986, pp. 424–429.

So has inequality. The various goods found in Neanderthal burials must indicate differences in social and political position. The famous example of Shanidar cave in Iraq holds the remains of a very old Neanderthal man who had lost an eye and the use of one arm and whose legs had been disabled.[4] His community had plainly held him in some esteem, as they had carefully buried him in the foetal position with flowers and medicinal herbs. It follows that he may have been a political leader or perhaps an elder whose wisdom had been especially valued by his community. The most ancient burials of *homo sapiens* point to greater inequalities. At Sunghir near Moscow, a cemetery was established twenty-eight thousand years ago.[5] The body of an elderly man was buried there along with a cap sewn with fox teeth, thousands of ivory beads on his clothes, and twenty ivory bracelets. There are also a boy and a girl, about eight or twelve years old. They were buried with huge spears, bracelets, and necklaces all carved in mammoth ivory, as well as buttons made of fox teeth; and three thousand five hundred ivory beads had been poured over the bodies by mourners. The older man may well have been a leader of some kind, but the children cannot have been honoured because of any personal achievement.

Politics, competition, inequality—they have always been with us. There is no reason to think otherwise. Graeber and Wengrow's recent book *The Dawn of Everything* infers this from the same evidence that I just described. They argue, though, that our ancestors were probably not confined to one and the same political and social system at all times and in all places. In other words, apart from always living in groups, ancient men and women may have experimented with different forms of social order and government

4 Trinkaus, E., *The Shanidar Neanderthals*, Academic Press, New York, 1983.

5 Trinkaus, E. *et al.*, *The People of Sunghir: Burials, Bodies, and Behavior in the Earlier Upper Paleolithic*, Oxford University Press, Oxford, 2014.

in the remote past: they may even have been rigidly hierarchical for half the year and more independent for the other half in the manner of some contemporary Inuit, Nambikwara, or Crow peoples.[6] We can never know for certain. But the point is that the theory of an ancient age of equality and innocence without politics and without social order is wholly imaginary. The question for us is what constitutes a *civilized* political and social order.

The answer goes something like this. Beyond biology and the observable world, our ancestors' sense of order was also influenced by what they did not see. At some point in the very remote past, the idea arose that there was more to the cosmos than our senses could grasp.[7] Our senses, after all, can deceive us and contradict one another, and hallucinations and dreams, which have always been important in mystical experiences, appear to give access to another realm which cannot normally be perceived.[8] But the same notion of a world beyond the senses is also suggested by two other modes of thought which we now consider to be entirely rational. First, we can cite any sort of imaginative planning. When one of our ancestors designed a tool or other object in his mind before attempting to make it, he would have thought that the imperfect result of his labour was only a copy of his perfect mental image, and something that was not real could not have been copied. This is the distant origin of Platonic thought. Second, the use of numbers would have led to the idea that oneness, two-ness, three-ness, and so on were real even though they could not be seen or felt and even though they

6 Graeber, D. / Wengrow, D., *The Dawn of Everything: A New History of Humanity*, Signal, McClelland and Stuart, 2021, pp. 102–111.

7 Fukuyama, F., *The Origins of Political Order: From Prehuman Times to the French Revolution*, Farrar, Straus and Giroux, New York, 2011, p. 36.

8 Fernández-Armesto, F., *Out of Our Minds: What We Think and How We Came to Think It*, London, One World Books, 2019, pp. 49–56.

were unattached to physical objects. This may seem strange until we remind ourselves that the abstract mathematics of our own time is wholly inaccessible to the senses but nevertheless real.

The theory of an invisible order that could influence human society probably gave rise to a new form of leadership. The religion suggested by Palaeolithic cave paintings seems to have been one of shamanic visions, trances, and spiritual journeys to the other world. Privileged access to the forces that make the world as it is, and the possibility of discerning their will or influencing them, would have conferred on Palaeolithic visionaries a charismatic authority to rival the brute strength of any alpha male and his cronies. The visionary or shaman would accordingly have commanded enormous social and political power in his little community, and may conceivably have been its main leader. But the forces with which he communicated are entirely mysterious to us. To judge by Palaeolithic art, the nature of those forces seems to have been unclear to the shamans also. There are no obvious depictions of gods or goddesses, nor any symbols of abstract ideas like fertility, peace, or love. The curious blend of human and animal imagery, which we do find in Palaeolithic art, must represent ideas about the powers governing the cosmos which were not yet clearly defined—a fluid state of affairs befitting the world of wandering hunter-gatherers.

This changed in the Neolithic period, when religious ideas crystallized and public rituals took definite forms. The evidence for these developments is strange and macabre by contemporary standards, but quite persuasive nonetheless. Throughout the Neolithic Near East, we find that skulls were removed from bodies long after death, cleaned, and covered with a layer of plaster.[9] In

9 The evidence is summarized and discussed in Hayden, B., *Shamans, Sorcerers, and Saints: A Prehistory of Religion*, Smithsonian Books, Washington, 2003, pp. 185–188

order to create a more lifelike appearance, the eye-sockets were covered with shells, and paint was applied representing facial features and hair. All over the Near East, but most famously at the site of Jericho, we find that skulls were kept within houses, perhaps on display, or stored within special receptacles. Similar in principle was the practice of burying the dead under the floors of houses at Çatalhöyük. Some form of public liturgy associated with the skull cult seems to have taken place in specially appointed communal sites at the centre of Neolithic settlements. A striking example of such places has been found at Göbekli Tepe in southwestern Anatolia. Eleven thousand years ago, gigantic limestone pillars were erected there; and amidst the stones archaeologists have found numerous fragments of human skulls, which had probably been hung up or otherwise put on display there.[10] Perhaps the stone masks and mysterious human figurines found at various Neolithic sites featured in public ritual also, but we can only guess how.

Such practices, sustained over the course of thousands of years, point to a cult of ancestors.[11] Such a cult would have had enormous benefits for those who believed in it. Dead ancestors could be portrayed as providing guidance for important decisions, as dealing out rewards and punishments for various behaviours, and as granting legitimacy to a king or a shaman, or to any other figure of authority. It would be easy to see the ancestor cult as a method of social control, imposed by elites to establish order within the world's

and Cauvin, J., *Naissance des divinités; naissance de l'agriculture*, CNRS editions, Paris, 1994, pp. 185–211 (pp. 105–120 in the English version, *The Birth of the Gods and the Origins of Agriculture*, Cambridge University Press, Cambridge, 2000).

10 Gresky, J. *et al.*, 'Modified Human Crania from Göbekli Tepe Provide Evidence for a New Form of Neolithic Skull Cult', *Science advances*, 3 (6), 2017 (https://www.science.org/doi/10.1126/sciadv.1700564).

11 Hayden, B., *Shamans, Sorcerers, and Saints: A Prehistory of Religion*, Smithsonian Books, Washington, 2003, pp. 183–185.

first cities. But this would be a misunderstanding, since the cult of ancestors appeared long before the development of agriculture and cities. To judge by the public shrine at Göbekli Tepe, for instance, there is a gap of at least five thousand years between them.

The implications of that last fact must be emphasized. Every ritual behaviour expresses deeper ideas or beliefs. The cult of ancestors implies a new belief in stability over time and in the permanence of the human population in a given place. It implies belief in the importance of a shared past; and it also suggests a particular view of the future. Those now living can look forward to veneration as ancestors after death, and their present offspring and future descendants may be imagined doing likewise. These are the beliefs that persuaded people to settle down for the first time in history, and to develop all the other amenities of civilization. And people began to do so while the old hunting and gathering economy was still going strong, long before the agricultural economy and the first states.

It is sometimes supposed that the appearance of agriculture and the state did away with ties of kinship and ancestors. In place of those ties, so the thinking goes, came allegiance to the state and the bureaucracy through which it projected power. But this development took a very long time, occurring first in China in the third century BC.[12] Far from limiting ties of kinship, the earliest civilizations actually enlarged them through the metaphorical extension of the smallest social group: the household. We see this first at Çatalhöyük.

The settlement at Çatalhöyük was dense and populous, supporting as many as ten thousand souls. Houses were so close

12 Fukuyama, F., *The Origins of Political Order from Prehuman Times to the French Revolution*, Farrar, Straus and Giroux, New York, 2012, p. 101.

together that there were no streets, and people must have walked on their roofs to get from one house to another. The town flourished for about a millennium between 7500 BC and 6400 BC. And yet there is no evidence of a central authority or bureaucracy, nor any sign that the inhabitants held ranks in a government or other hierarchy.[13] But neither did the inhabitants aim at any egalitarian ideal, as would be reflected in, say, uniformity of material culture or neighbourhoods distinguished by size of house.[14] Households, nevertheless, built up various collections of hunting trophies, burial platforms, and volcanic glass, and they accumulated their own histories. Each household was a centre of private religious rites and other domestic routines which remained stable for a long time. Houses were inhabited for between fifty and one hundred years, and then dismantled and reconstructed. Walls, hearths, ovens, and so on all went back exactly where they had been before according to the same design. Ancestors were consistently buried under houses and honoured by the inhabitants for generations. Obviously, much remains mysterious about the society of Çatalhöyük, but here we have a vision of political order without a central government, without either egalitarianism or hierarchy, and without agriculture. There were only interconnected households.

This model persisted and was enlarged. The earliest and most successful states were structured as a network of households scaled upward from families, to institutional households, and beyond to the entire polity. The king (if there was a king) was held to be the

13 Hodder, I., *The Leopard's Tale: Revealing the Mysteries of Çatalhöyük*, Thames and Hudson, London, 2006.

14 Graeber, D. / Wengrow, D., *The Dawn of Everything: A New History of Humanity*, Signal, McClelland and Stuart, 2021, p. 222. See also Mithen, S., *After the Ice: A Global Human History 20,000–5000 BC*, Harvard University Press, Cambridge, 2003, pp. 88–96.

father or master, and heads of sub-households were sons or servants. Society was 'a hierarchy of households nested within households with the royal household at its apex'.[15]

The evidence for the ancient concept of the state-as-household is presented exhaustively by J. David Schloen in his very long book *The House of the Father as Fact and Symbol.* We can note some of its key points here. In the languages of Mesopotamia, there is no word for the state itself. There is not even a distinct Sumerian or Akkadian word for 'palace', for both languages used a periphrasis meaning 'great household'. Nor is there a concept of a bureaucratic 'office' as distinct from the person who occupies it, since the legitimacy of officials was assured by personal ties with the ruler. Our friend Shulgi's Third Dynasty of Ur is a good illustration of what this meant in practice. Temples and irrigation works were managed by independent families. Cylinder seals used by officials were re-issued whenever a new king came to the throne in order to emphasize personal ties. And kings projected power abroad through marriage alliances which achieved almost literal expansion of the royal household. This model, allowing for regional variation, took hold everywhere, and was dominant throughout the entire Bronze Age.

The model of society as a network of households outlasted the Bronze Age collapse. After that calamity, Hesiod's advice for any self-respecting man was 'first find a house, a wife, an ox and a plough'.[16] Aristotle interpreted this to mean that the smallest unit of society was the household, and therefore the foundation of his ideal city-state. For Aristotle, the idea of a society of autonomous individuals was impossible, since 'a person incapable of being part

15 Schloen, J., *The House of the Father as Fact and Symbol: Patrimonialism in Ugarit and the Ancient Near East*, Studies in the Archaeology and History of the Levant 2, Eisenbrauns, Winona Lake, 2001, p. 208.

16 Hesiod, WD, 405.

of a community, or so self-sufficient as to have no need to do so' must be 'either a beast or a god'.[17] In other words, an individual man was but an imperfect part of a greater community, and ancient society as a whole was a sort of community of communities. 'The part is ordered to the whole as the imperfect to the perfect', wrote Thomas Aquinas, and so an individual man is merely 'part of the perfect community'.[18] Aquinas was a man of the high Middle Ages, but he was expressing a very ancient train of thought.

Ancient households and the communities that they formed were at a considerable distance from the power of a central government (if one even existed), and possibly beyond its reach entirely—a fact which troubled ancient advocates of powerful states. The confusion and divided loyalties following the Peloponnesian War, for instance, presented seemingly insoluble social and political problems because the Athenian government could not rein in mutually hostile factions: so why not simply abolish every social and spiritual allegiance and replace them with loyalty to the state alone? This is what Plato recommended in his *Republic*. He was notably a failure as a political adviser; and Platonic political ideas did not take hold anywhere. Roman military despotism, however, was another matter.

From the rise of Julius Caesar onward, the Roman state was increasingly suspicious of civil societies, independent families, private industry, and religions which it could not control. The persecution of Christianity, the confiscation of private wealth, the destruction of noble families, and state monopolies of certain industries are cases in point. Most telling, though, is the Roman attitude to social, religious, and commercial associations or *collegia*, as they were called. Their role in the Roman economy is doubtful,

17 Aristotle, *Politics*, I.20.
18 *Summa Theologiae*, I-II, q. 90.

but their main functions were to hold public ceremonies, to honour civic leaders and solicit their patronage, and to defend the interests of their members. They also integrated aliens and ordinary Romans into urban society, so as to make life 'more amenable and less chaotic'.[19] But the imperial government hated and feared the *collegia* because of the loyalty they commanded and their political influence. Julius Caesar outlawed all but the most ancient *collegia* in 64 BC: the younger ones had apparently been fomenting political violence. The Emperor Augustus relaxed the ban somewhat, but required all *collegia* to have the sanction of the emperor or the senate.[20] Trajan famously refused to allow Nicomedia to have a *collegium* of firemen, because he feared it would become little more than a secret society.[21] Every sort of *collegium* was banned in Pompeii after an outbreak of unrest.[22] In the early second century AD, the emperor Hadrian allowed them more freedom until they were all entirely subsumed under state control by the emperor Aurelian a hundred years later.[23]

The fall of the Western Roman Empire gradually gave way to a long period of decentralization in which power was contested between princes and popes, and in which personal allegiance resided not with the state but rather with the family, the town, the guild, the parish, the local corporation, the university, or the monastery. The classic study of such mediaeval associations is Susan

19 Verboven, K., 'Introduction: Professional Collegia: Guilds or Social Clubs?', *Ancient Society*, 41, 2011, pp. 187–195.
20 Boatright, M. *et al.*, *The Romans, from Village to Empire: A History of Rome from Earliest Times to the End of the Western Empire*, Oxford University Press, Oxford, 2011, p. 237.
21 Pliny, *Epistles*, X.34.
22 Tacitus, *Annals*, XIV.17.4.
23 Boatright, M. *et al.*, *The Romans, from Village to Empire: A History of Rome from Earliest Times to the End of the Western Empire*, Oxford University Press, Oxford, 2011, p. 438.

Reynold's *Kingdoms and Communities in Western Europe*.[24] Reynolds shows that both peasants and town-dwellers established voluntary associations as expressions of their interests and values. The resultant institutions (commonly called guilds) were modelled on the ideal of sibling relationships within a household, united by mutual affection, and reinforced with oaths. They were founded for various purposes, but they all demonstrated the 'essence of brotherhood' in the same ways: eating and drinking together, pledging themselves to do good works, and even performing what we might call social-welfare functions like pooling expenses for weddings and funerals. Incidentally, much the same functions were performed in the East by Abbasid-era civic and fraternal associations, known as *futuwwa*, which covered everything from youth gangs to mutual aid societies, commercial guilds, sports clubs, and Sufi orders.[25]

Such groups could certainly be threatening to higher powers. In AD 884, for instance, king Carloman of the West Franks cracked down on villages forming guilds for the purpose of vigilante justice. Simon de Montfort (who was the earl of Leicester in the early thirteenth century) forbade the formation of any fraternal organizations without consent of the local feudal lord. And associations devoted to helping the poor were usually held in suspicion everywhere, since their economic interests were opposed to those of a given town's rulers. Nevertheless, guilds proliferated because of the warmth and sociability that they offered. The plague had given them a new lease of life, but they were not a response to any particular difficulty, and

24 Reynolds, S., *Kingdoms and Communities in Western Europe 900–1300*, second edition, Oxford University Press, Oxford, 1997.

25 Hodgson, M. G. S., *The Venture of Islam: Conscience and History in a World Civilization, Volume 2, The Expansion of Islam in the Middle Periods*, The University of Chicago Press, Chicago, 1974, pp. 125–131.

tended to satisfy a need for association beyond economic need.[26] One of their important goals was to reconcile feuding parties and to restore friendship. There were, of course, revolts against tyrannical lords, as in the Saxon Rebellion between 1073 and 1075, or the Peasants' Revolt in late fourteenth-century England, but such uprisings were reactions to particular injustices and not attempts to overthrow and replace a largely stable and harmonious social order.

The ideal of order for which the guilds and other mediaeval institutions stood was reinforced by a flexible approach to law also. Far from the arbitrary dictates of an emperor, or inscrutable bureaucratic regulations, law was indistinguishable from local custom, and was largely unwritten. This is the state of affairs that many people still mistake for chaos, tyranny, or anarchy. Now, there must have been nonconformists, and as Reynolds says 'underdogs', who struggled with authority; but it was hardly a time of oppression, much less dull uniformity. On the contrary, the enormous interest in Arabic scholarship, which we discussed earlier, suggests an age of curiosity and imagination.[27] Clarity of thought in such scholars as Abelard and Aquinas can be contrasted with contemporary academic obscurantism and nonsense. We can also notice a love of light and decoration in Cluniac ornament and Romanesque and Gothic architecture. The great cathedral churches, which Peter Eisenman sniffed at, were projects lasting well beyond the lifespan of a normal mediaeval person. This is a sign of the solidity of groups, their long-term powers of imagination and cooperation, and the stability of values over many generations. We are certainly not dealing with

26 Bossy, J., *Christianity in the West: 1400–1700,* Oxford University Press, Oxford, 1989, pp. 57–63.

27 For more detail, see the most recent treatment of Western mediaeval science: Falk, S., *The Light Ages: The Surprising Story of Mediaeval Science*, W. W. Norton and Company, New York, 2020.

faceless, non-personalities ground down by superstition and feudal service. It is true that the earlier, fantastical epic tradition of *Beowulf* and the Finnsburg Fragment harks back to a time of barbarism, portrayed in all its grim ferocity in the 2022 film *The Northman*; but in such later mediaeval works as the Icelandic Sagas, the *Divine Comedy*, the *Decameron*, and the *Canterbury Tales*, we are a long way from that age of brutality and violence.

Unfortunately, such an age was to return. The upheavals of the Protestant Reformation put enormous strain upon the mediaeval social order, and it broke down.[28] Catholic and Protestant forces clashed in Switzerland in the late 1520s and early 1530s. Meanwhile in the 1520s, the so-called Peasants' War in Germany brought the 'pressure-cooker atmosphere' of the early Reformation to a climax.[29] Apocalyptic, millennial movements followed, such as the Melchiorites at Amsterdam and the Anabaptist theocracy at Münster in the early 1530s. Violence escalated. Monasteries and churches were pillaged. Images were destroyed, and there began a new era of burning in effigy, organized destruction of books, verbal aggression, judicial repression, and huge massacres.[30] The Peace of Augsburg in 1555 was supposed to calm everything down; but it was basically a stalemate after Holy Roman Emperor Charles V's defeat of the Schmalkadic League. In any case, Lutheran ideas had already spread

28 For the Reformation in general, see Gregory, B. S., *The Unintended Reformation: How a Religious Revolution Secularized Society*, The Belknap Press of Harvard University Press, Cambridge, 2012. For the collapse of Christendom, see Greengrass, M., *Christendom Destroyed: Europe 1517–1648,* Penguin Books, London, 2014.

29 Greengrass, M., *Christendom Destroyed: Europe 1517–1648,* Penguin Books, London, 2014, p. 341. For this violent conflict, see Baylor, M. G., *The German Reformation and the Peasants' War: A Brief History with Documents,* Bedford / St. Martin's, Boston and New York, 2012.

30 Greengrass, M., *Christendom Destroyed: Europe 1517–1648,* Penguin Books, London, 2014, pp. 394–396.

everywhere and could not be eradicated by warfare. Exhausted by the struggle, Charles V abdicated in the following year. French Protestants and Catholics fought eight civil wars between 1562 and 1598, and skirmishes continued until 1629. Philip II's crackdown on heresy in the Netherlands in 1566 provoked a revolt which lasted until 1648. The Thirty Years' War, between 1618 and 1648, drew nearly the entire European continent into multiple rounds of bloodshed, with the ensuing plague and famine killing perhaps as many as twelve million people. Incidentally, the tension and anxiety of this time can still be felt in the music of Heinrich Schütz, who lived through the war. Meanwhile, in England, Puritan opposition to king Charles I erupted into two civil wars in the 1640s.

On the eve of the Reformation, guilds were active and growing everywhere, albeit more so in urban areas. At Rouen, for instance, there were some 40,000 inhabitants, but 131 sodalities, including both social groups and those representing artisanal trades.[31] In many places, even beggars had their own confraternities; and, of course, people might belong to more than one guild. But in the sixteenth century, such associations came to be viewed as misguided. Martin Luther himself argued that they were little more than a waste of money that could be put to better use. Amidst increasing upheaval, the old guilds and associations carried on as best they could. But the division within the church spread throughout society and promoted conflict among them. This suggested the need for a stronger central authority to assure order between antagonists who could not see eye to eye. Royal absolutism was the response, and the French jurist and political aide Jean Bodin (1530–1596) was its great exponent. His theory of monarchy, articulated in his *Six Books of the Commonwealth*,

31 Greengrass, M., *Christendom Destroyed: Europe 1517–1648*, Penguin Books, London, 2014, pp. 317–318.

owes much to the Roman legal tradition and the Justinianic notion that the sovereign was the source of law without being bound by law. Bodin accordingly sought to bring all the heterogeneous codes and legal systems of France under the absolute authority of the king, much as the emperor Justinian had done, and much as contemporary states insist upon uniform legal systems. The primary role of the monarch for Bodin was to exert 'force and violence' in order to restrain the antithetical factions recently set loose by the Reformation.

But Bodin was not *just* an apologist for absolute monarchy. He argued that the family and all other civil associations were the basis of society and antecedent to the state. Such societies were held together not by the fear of violence but by friendship, and they were natural products of man's social instinct. Bodin's great insight was to distinguish the sovereign's supreme authority from both government and from the state itself. In practice, this would mean an individual's obedience to the crown while most functions of what we would call government were exercised by smaller, local institutions. Royal power would be limited not by laws, but by custom and tradition. There would be a great variety of local cultures, as well as multiple personal allegiances. The best and most prosperous kingdoms, says Bodin, were those in which diverse groups and associations flourished; and it is the mark of a tyrant to suppress or extinguish them.

Bodin's ideas about the family were perhaps the last great assertion of the old theory of the household. He knew nothing about Çatalhöyük, of course, but Bodin was right to observe that 'a community of a number of heads of households, or of a village, a town, or a province, can subsist without there being any commonwealth', by which he meant a higher, central authority.[32]

32 Bodin, *Six Books of the Commonwealth*, III.vii.

But even where there is a central government, its authority stops at the family's threshold, beyond which public law does not apply. Within the household, the rule of the father is supreme: child, wife, servants, and so on are all in his custodianship. Bodin even reasserted the old Roman idea of the *patria potestas*: the father's absolute authority over the life and death of his children. This will strike us now as extremely unpalatable, but it should be understood in the spirit of checking the potentially despotic power of the state. Similarly, Bodin was an adamant defender of family property. If the state could interfere in customs of inheritance and thereby alienate private property, there would be no limit to its tyranny. The family must remain a single economic unit if it is to be socially and morally virtuous.

But it was not Bodin's views on institutions and family that caught on, but those on absolutism. Amidst the upheavals of the Reformation, in the eyes of political theorists all human relationships and associations became suspect. Only the individual man was a fact, and only a powerful central state could maintain order. This was the intellectual trend that shaped the thought of Hobbes and Rousseau and nearly everyone who followed them.

No two political philosophers are more often contrasted or considered to be so implacably opposed as Hobbes and Rousseau. Rousseau himself explicitly rebutted Hobbes in his writings, of course. But no two philosophical antagonists were in greater agreement on essentials. They both assumed an originally solitary humanity, and they arrived at visions of politics in which all subsidiary associations are dissolved, leaving only the individual man and the all-powerful state. Hobbes, who incidentally had worked as Francis Bacon's secretary, wished the state to assist the individual man in his escape from the strictures of class, tradition, and religion, and to create a new morality founded on individual virtue. Rousseau similarly saw the state as the highest and *only* moral community. There was no morality, no freedom, no community outside the state. Needless to say, this conception of political and social order has no grounding in history or anthropology; and yet it has been highly influential.

It has also been extraordinarily destructive. In Rousseau's ideal state, the individual man would be 'compelled to be free'. Exactly what this would mean was unclear until the Terror of 1793, in which insufficient revolutionary zeal was grounds for execution.[33] But the state which demands the total subordination and allegiance of the individual, foreshadowed originally by Plato, did not emerge until later. How did it emerge? The historical process that I described in the third chapter of this book led to the release of the individual person from all or nearly all ancient bonds of kinship, family, homeland, social class, guild, village, and so forth. The result was a mass of atomized individuals with few if any ties to ancestral tradition, place, society, or one another, ground down by industrial capitalism into nothing but economic units. Nineteenth-century liberals saw the breakdown of institutions as a work of progressive liberation, and their successors share this view. But those who cherished stability, rootedness, coherent moral beliefs, continuity of culture and religion, and human interdependence saw it differently. They saw only disruption, confusion, a sense of purposelessness, loneliness, and a frustrated need for belonging. What was left was what Robert Nisbet called the 'quest for community'.[34]

The need for belonging could be easily channelled toward political ends, as all demagogues and aspiring tyrants of the early

33 Andress, D., *The Terror: The Merciless War for Freedom in Revolutionary France*, Farrar, Straus and Giroux, New York, 2005, pp. 244–276.

34 Nisbet, R., *The Quest for Community: A Study in the Ethics of Order and Freedom*, with an introduction by Ross Douthat, Wilmington, Delaware, ISI Books, 2019 (originally published 1953).

twentieth century understood. When all subsidiary associations had been dissolved, the individual would encounter fellowship for the first time only in conformity with the masses, under the command of a great leader:

> The man who is exposed to great tribulations, as the first advocate of a new doctrine in his factory or workshop, absolutely needs that strengthening which lies in the conviction of being a member and fighter in a great comprehensive body. And he obtains an impression of this body for the first time in the mass demonstration. When, from his little workshop or big factory, in which he feels very small, he steps for the first time into a mass meeting and has thousands and thousands of people of the same opinions around him, when, as a seeker, he is swept away by three or four thousand others into the mighty effect of suggestive intoxication and enthusiasm, when the visible success and the agreement of thousands confirm to him the rightness of the new doctrine and for the first time arouse doubt in the truth of his previous conviction—then he himself has succumbed to the magic influence of what we designate as 'mass suggestion'. The will, the longing, and also the power of thousands are accumulated in the individual.[35]

Those are the words of Adolf Hitler. But the sentiment is the same as Rousseau's doctrine of the General Will which, as Rousseau believed, was the only source of political legitimacy and the foundation of political order.[36] Everyone would have to conform

35 Hitler, A., *Mein Kampf*, translated by Ralph Mannheim, Houghton Mifflin Company, The Riverside Press, Cambridge, Mass., 1943, pp. 478–479.

36 Rousseau, J. J., *Le Contrat Social*, II.3; Drucker, P. F., *The Future of Industrial Man: A Conservative Approach*, William Heinemann, Ltd., London, 1943, pp. 138–139.

to it. The French revolutionaries, Robespierre and Saint-Just, did not entirely succeed in enforcing that conformity. But the Nazis accomplished it by accelerating the process of atomization, which was already far advanced, and by bringing every aspect of society into line with Nazi ideology.

The Nazis talked a good deal of claptrap about the family as 'the germ cell of the nation' and so on, but all this meant in practice was reducing the family to the single task of reproduction—breeding more people in service to the state.[37] The family was no safe haven from the reach of the Nazi Party which sought to invade and to dominate it. Marriages were rigorously policed in order to ensure racial homogeneity. All pro-natal organizations were controlled and funded by the state, and welfare policies directed at young mothers came with mandatory indoctrination in Nazi ideology. The state strictly forbade any and all formal associations between families. All political associations, apart from the Nazi Party, were illegal. Local governments were abolished and reconstituted in utter subordination to the central government, thereby abolishing federalism. Trades unions were all dissolved and replaced by the German Labour Front, which was an organ of the state. Agrarian associations were subsumed within the Reich Food Estate. All clubs, groups, fraternal organizations, and so forth were outlawed. Even recreation and leisure became the responsibility of the state alone in the Strength Through Joy programme, through which the Nazi government funded concerts, plays, libraries, gymnastics, hiking, and even vacations. It is astounding to think that, in the 1930s, Strength Through Joy became the largest tourism operator in the world.[38]

37 Pine, L., *Hitler's 'National Community': Society and Culture in Nazi Germany*, second edition, Bloomsbury, London, 2017, pp. 118–125.

38 Pine, L., *Hitler's 'National Community': Society and Culture in Nazi Germany*, second edition, Bloomsbury, London, 2017, pp. 31–41.

I want to emphasize the atomization of society on which the Third Reich was built. There are two important symbols of this. The first is that absurd Nazi greeting: the 'Heil Hitler' salute.[39] It is not a handshake, an embrace, or some other gesture performed in intimate proximity: you have to stand well back from others in order to do it right, and two or more persons cannot even perform it together without striking one another unless they are far apart. It is especially ill-suited to rallies in which people stand very close together. No more antisocial gesture has ever been made compulsory, as far as I know. The second fact is that the Third Reich, which was supposed to last a thousand years, lasted a mere twelve, and the mutual collapse of the state and society was total. This is the best possible proof of the complete identification of society with the Nazi state. No institution, custom, or other aspect of Hitler's 'national community' survived, no one attempted any sort of revival, and the German people did not resist the Allied occupation. In the absence of the Nazi state, the only thing that had lately given life any meaning, a wave of suicides overcame Germany beginning with Hitler himself, and high-ranking party members, generals, SS officers, and ordinary people followed him.[40]

In contrast to the Third Reich, the Soviet Union lasted longer, and could be considered more successful. But it too operated on the same atomizing logic, albeit with different justification, and it too collapsed. Marxist hostility to civil society, as well as the traditional affiliations of family, community, religion, and all other 'bourgeois' institutions, became Soviet policy, and reached its peak

39 Evans, R. J., *The Third Reich in History and Memory*, Oxford University Press, Oxford, 2015, pp. 119–123.

40 Huber, F., *Promise Me You'll Shoot Yourself: The Downfall of Ordinary Germans in 1945*, Penguin, London, 2019.

under Stalin.[41] Local and regional governments were brought under direct Bolshevik control. Enormous numbers of peasant farmers were killed off, and those who remained alive were forced into collective farms run by the state. Ever-increasing production goals divided the proletariat by mutual resentment, thereby preventing workers from uniting against the government. Constant ideological cleansing of the civil service, guilt by association, enforced denunciation of relatives and friends, internal passports, outlawing differing factions within the Communist party—such measures left nothing but the disaggregated individual and state. In the 1920s, the Soviet Union had even gone as far as to outlaw marriage, and to make divorce a matter of minutes, in order to dissolve the family altogether. But these policies went too far and were reversed.

Both Nazism and Soviet Communism are gone now. Their promotion of disaggregation and their hostility to household and family have vanished. But all is not well with liberalism: the vision of human order which seemed indestructible at the end of the twentieth century. Lately, the rise of populist leaders such as Orbán and Trump, or autocratic ones like Putin, have caused advanced thinkers to suspect that something is amiss. Something is indeed wrong within all liberal democracies, but most observers do not understand what the problem is.

To put it simply, liberalism also promotes disaggregation and atomization. Like Francis Bacon, the Futurists, and tyrants of all sorts, liberalism promises a break with the past by freeing the individual from all ancestral and institutional ties. The inner logic to this process was, as John Stuart Mill put it, derived from a view of

41 Arendt, H., *The Origins of Totalitarianism*, new edition with added prefaces, Harcourt Brace Jovanovich Publishers, San Diego-New York-London, 1973, pp. 320–323.

history as a perpetual 'struggle between liberty and authority'.[42] Mill and his fellow liberals were convinced that progress, both moral and technological, was a law of history. The solitary individual was the fundamental building block of society, and ever-expanding personal freedoms and autonomy were not only desirable but also inevitable. And so, it has always been easy for liberals to sweep away the injustices, superstitions, and prejudices of the past. But it is enough to say that something is 'old' to invite a liberal to abolish it—hence the project of abolition did not stop at the repudiation of aristocratic privileges, slavery, the autonomy of the church, local self-government, seemingly irrational mediaeval legal practices, and so on. Some evil things were surely obliterated. But innumerable beneficial things, such as small, local institutions and family bonds, have also been eroded or destroyed in the quest for individual freedom. Worse, liberalism does not replace the institutions and customs that it effaces. The rubbish of the past is cleared away, and man is left free—free, but disaggregated, atomized, alone. This may go a long way to explain why every modern tyranny has grown out of a liberal political order.[43] The French constitutional monarchy of 1791 was organized according to liberal principles, but gave way to the Reign of Terror in about two years. Kerenski's liberal government collapsed into Bolshevism after half a year. And the Nazis were elected from within the ultra-progressivist Weimar Republic.

Those who have now begun to fear that something is wrong with liberal democracy are late to the game. Orbán and Putin announced, perhaps prematurely, the end of liberalism in 2014 and

42 Mill, J. S., *On Liberty*, In Focus, edited by John Gray and G. W. Smith, Routledge, London, 2003, p. 23.

43 Drucker, P. F., *The Future of Industrial Man: A Conservative Approach*, William Heinemann, Ltd., London, 1943, pp. 134–135.

2019, respectively.[44] But the problem did not begin with them, and liberalism has had its critics from the beginning. In our own time, no sooner had the Soviet Union fallen than the spread of liberalism in Eastern Europe began to arouse fear and suspicion. This is brought home in the late Pope John Paul II's book *Memory and Identity*. Many of his fellow Poles, said the pope, feared that their nation, its identity, and traditions would soon be dissolved within an increasingly homogeneous world. In other words, what Soviet Communism had failed to achieve by force might be accomplished with popular consent by liberal democracy.[45] Moreover, elections might be free and fair, but policies would stay the same. Political discourse would be circumscribed within the ever-narrowing limits of acceptable liberal opinion. There would be no tolerance of dissent, since liberalism was presented as rational and obviously good. Anyone who thought otherwise was not only wrong but also stupid.

The late pope's analysis was prescient. And in his observations, it is easy to see the reason for the rise of right-wing populism, since it was the only force promising to challenge the liberal consensus—a mode of thought recently taken up by Polish professor and former politician Ryszard Legutko.[46] The same pattern has been repeated throughout the former Eastern Bloc, and it is also taking shape in the West. Liberal elites grow increasingly suspicious of mass

44 Csaba Tóth, 'Full Text of Viktor Orbán's Speech at Băile Tuşnad (Tusnádfürdő) of 26 July 2014', *The Budapest Beacon*, July 29, 2014 (https://budapestbeacon.com/full-text-of-viktor-orbans-speech-at-baile-tusnad-tusnadfurdo-of-26-july-2014/); Barber, L. *et al.*, 'Vladimir Putin Says Liberalism Has "Become Obsolete"', *Financial Times*, June 27, 2019 (https://www.ft.com/content/670039ec-98f3-11e9-9573-ee5cbb98ed36).

45 Pope John Paul II, *Memory and Identity: Conversations at the Dawn of a Millennium*, Rizzoli, New York, 2005, p. 48.

46 See, for instance, Legutko, R., *The Demon in Democracy: Totalitarian Temptations in Free Societies*, translated by Teresa Adelson, Encounter Books, New York, 2018.

politics and seek ever tighter control on political processes, while populists inveigh against an unaccountable and corrupt elite. This is why elections are more and more portrayed as mass indictments of incompetence or corruption than anything else.[47]

So, in contrast with Francis Fukuyama's famous announcement in 1992, the future of liberalism does not look so good now. Of course, there was something of a misunderstanding, since Fukuyama predicted that future problems would come from within liberal democracy, and not from outside.[48] He did not suggest that liberalism was invincible, or that it had no weaknesses, but this is not what many of Fukuyama's readers took from his arguments. His readers had clearly been unaware of the steady stream of criticism directed at liberalism, beginning with Joseph de Maistre and Louis Veuillot who inveighed against its original eighteenth- and nineteenth-century forms.[49] Pope Pius IX published a concise takedown of liberalism in the form of his *Syllabus of Errors*, an appendix to his *Quanta Cura* encyclical issued in 1864.[50] Many thoughtful critiques of liberalism have appeared since then. Not all are in an ultra-Catholic mode. Consider, for instance, former Marxist James Burnham's 1964 book *The Suicide of the West*, whose

47 Kratsev, I., 'Is East-Central Europe Backsliding? The Strange Death of the Liberal Consensus', *Journal of Democracy*,18 (4), October, 2007, pp. 56–63.

48 Fukuyama, F., *The End of History*, with a new afterword, Free Press, New York, 2006 (originally published 1992), pp. 300–339; Roussinos, A., 'Why Fukuyama Was Right All Along', *Unherd*, September, 2020 (retrieved from https://unherd.com/2020/09/why-fukuyama-was-right-all-along/).

49 See, for instance, de Maistre, J., *l'Essai sur le principe générateur des consitutions politiques et d'autres institutions humaines*, la Société typographique, Paris, 1814; de Maistre, J., *du Pape*, Charpentier, Paris, 1841; and Veuillot, L., *L'Illusion libérale*, Palmé, éditeur des Bollandistes, Paris, 1866.

50 The encyclical in question can be found here: https://www.vatican.va/content/pius-ix/la/documents/encyclica-quanta-cura-8-decembris-1864.html.

title suggests a very dim view of the subject indeed.[51] Latterly, the problems of liberalism have been analysed by Patrick Deneen in his book *Why Liberalism Failed*; as de Tocqueville did, he also predicts a slide into a kind of tyrannical statism.[52] In contrast, Joel Kotkin claims to foresee the imminent collapse of liberalism into an age of stagnancy and hierarchy which he mistakenly calls 'neo-feudalism'.[53] Catherine Liu's 2021 book *Virtue Hoarders* offers something close to a traditional Marxist critique of liberalism, the superiority complex of its self-appointed 'professional managerial class', and their contempt for ordinary working people.[54] All the virtue-signalling, policing of language, Critical Race Theory, and other oddities associated with contemporary liberalism can be understood, says Liu, as tactics to befuddle the working classes, to atomize them, and to prevent solidarity among them. One does not have to be a Marxist to see much truth in this analysis. But Liu does not proceed beyond denouncing capitalism and its odious class of professional managers.

Liberalism certainly has its defenders also. As I was editing this book for publication, Francis Fukuyama's *Liberalism and Its Discontents* appeared.[55] It is a rather anaemic defense of liberalism; but, since it is the work of a true believer, we should take it seriously. Fukuyama rightly denounces the absurdities and excesses of left- and

51 Burnham, J., *Suicide of the West: An Essay on the Meaning and Destiny of Liberalism*, with a new forward by John O'Sullivan and introduction by Roger Kimball, Encounter Books, New York, 2014 (originally published in 1964).

52 Deneen, P. J., *Why Liberalism Failed*, 2018.

53 Kotkin, J., *The Coming of Neo-Feudalism: A Warning to the Global Middle Class*, Encounter Books, New York, 2020.

54 Liu, C., *Virtue Hoarders: The Case Against the Professional Managerial Class*, University of Minnesota Press, Minneapolis, 2021.

55 Fukuyama, F., *Liberalism and Its Discontents*, Farrar, Straus and Giroux, New York, 2022.

right-wing liberalism: what many now call identity politics and neo-liberalism, respectively. So far so good. But how do we get back to a more moderate form of liberalism? Fukuyama urges a return to objectivity, shared truths, and the scientific method—all of which, he says, are (or should be) robust pillars of liberalism. The more elaborate forms of postmodernism must be condemned. It is also refreshing to read Fukuyama's invective against the pernicious simulacrum of reality on the Internet, in Hollywood, and in video games. These bogus fantasy worlds have encouraged, as he says, an epidemic of utopianism, outrage, and virtue-signalling which allow people to feel complacent about real problems without taking real action against them. And the radical free-market economics that have hollowed out the middle class, destroyed institutions, shipped jobs overseas, and weakened governments are accused and denounced also.

Who can disagree with this analysis? But the question is: how does Fukuyama's favourite ideology[56] point the way out of this mess? Everything that makes liberalism bland, uninspiring, frustrating, and lonely, Fukuyama salutes as the antidote to present problems. The virtue of liberalism, he says, is that it 'lowers the aspirations of politics' away from any particular vision of human flourishing, upon which there will never be unanimity.[57] As I say, this is not especially inspiring, and it is somewhat misleading. We do not need a unanimous prescription for the Good Life so much as unanimity that the Good Life is, as Aristotle would say, *naturally* worth aiming at, and a constant discussion of how to do so.

56 That liberalism is indeed an ideology is proved in Burnham, J., *Suicide of the West: An Essay on the Meaning and Destiny of Liberalism*, with a new forward by John O'Sullivan and introduction by Roger Kimball, Encounter Books, New York, 2014 (originally published in 1964), pp. 103–131.

57 Fukuyama, F., *Liberalism and Its Discontents*, Farrar, Straus and Giroux, New York, 2022, p. 6.

What is worse, though, is that Fukuyama has misunderstood the nature of the problem. The extremes of neo-liberalism and identity politics are *not* two mutually hostile beasts fighting over the body of liberalism. They are better understood, as Catherine Liu would remind us, as allies, since the progressivist Left and neo-liberal capitalists now walk together hand-in-hand, laying traps for the working man, their mutual foe. An obvious proof of this alliance is the tendency of large corporations to co-opt progressivist liberal causes and slogans—a phenomenon which Vivek Ramaswamy has analysed in his book *Woke, Inc.*[58] So, Fukuyama's readers may well wonder how *more* liberalism could be the solution to the problems which liberalism created in the first place.

Equally odd is Fukuyama's suggestion that the only alternative to liberalism is tyranny. If we take the apostles of open borders and Antifa at their word, then outright anarchy will be the probable outcome if such people prevail. Various right-wing proposals for what may replace liberalism are presented in Matthew Rose's book *A World After Liberalism*, many of which are grim, and yet not all could be considered tyrannical.[59] But we should remind ourselves that tolerance, the rule of law, and the sanctity of contracts, which Fukuyama makes so much of, long predate liberalism. And the idea that there is no alternative to liberalism but tyranny arises from a failure of historical memory. Let me add, incidentally, that precisely none of the ancient amenities of civilization arose under a liberal political order.

Unlike Fukuyama, I am not so sure that any remedy is possible. It is tempting to think that liberalism could be informed by external

58 Ramaswamy, V., *Woke, Inc.: Inside Corporate America's Social Justice Scam*, Center Street, New York, 2021.

59 Rose, M., *A World After Liberalism: Philosophers of the Radical Right*, Yale University Press, New Haven, 2021.

discussions of freedom and autonomy. The fact that liberalism bills itself as the only workable vision of human freedom seems rather myopic to me. I can hardly conceive of a serious discussion of freedom without classical philosophy, without Judaism, without Christianity, without Islam, without the mediaeval scholastics, without ancient and modern republicanism, without anthropology, without the ethics of virtue and duty.[60] Nor should we accept the idea that free choice *by itself* is the only way to assure personal autonomy. As my friend the philosopher Ljiljiana Radenovic would remind us, it matters not only *what* you choose but also *why* you choose it.[61] If your highest good is something that you have little or no control over, such as money or fame, choosing those things will actually diminish your autonomy. Yet if we value things that depend only upon ourselves, such as kindness, generosity, or love, we shall become more autonomous. And likewise, if we choose those things for their own sake, we are more autonomous than if we subordinate those choices to other ends, such as ingratiating ourselves with others. But here is the problem: if liberalism were informed by such discussions, would it still be liberalism?

Anyway, there are many people who want to tell others what to do, but few who want to be told. This is why I suspect that ideas of freedom and autonomy will be with us for some time. Nevertheless, liberalism's internal problems are going to make for very hard going unless they can be resolved. I can point out three of them here.

First, we have the constellation of phenomena that we call the culture war: pulling down statues, cancel culture, pronouns, Twitter

60 *Cf.* Legutko, R., *The Demon in Democracy: Totalitarian Temptations in Free Societies*, translated by Teresa Adelson, Encounter Books, New York, 2018, p. 45.

61 Radenovic, L., 'From Deficient Liberalism Toward a Deeper Sense of Freedom', *Social Epistemology Review and Reply Collective*, 10 (6), 2021, pp. 20–25.

mobs, campus social justice crusades, and so forth. They all arise not from the spirit of Marxism, as some critics assert, but from within liberalism itself. Everyone who demands a 'safe space', a trigger warning, the deplatforming of an objectionable speaker, or the cancellation of an antagonist does so in the name of individual freedom and autonomy—not ideological purity or conformity with a party line. On the other hand, their opponents oppose those things not because they reject individual freedom. Far from it. Their opposition amounts to asserting other liberal values, most especially free speech and academic freedom. And so, the resultant conflict is best analysed as a liberal civil war: a contest between antithetical personal freedoms.

Second, whereas the liberal tendency toward atomization appears as a natural outcome of freeing individuals from social bonds, there is another liberal tendency that is equally natural but more paradoxical. This is the drive toward homogeneity of culture. Homogeneity? Surely nothing could be farther from a liberal's mind, since no one talks of diversity more than liberals do. This is true. And yet the loudest demands for diversity always appear alongside the most stultifying uniformity. The culture warriors, campus activists, identitarians, intersectionalists, deplatformers, and so on are all basically the same: they sound the same, they borrow jargon and slogans from one another, and very often they even look the same. In principle, they seem to stand for an endless variety of group identities, but in practice the only outcome is individual autonomy.[62] In this respect, the liberal Left is in full agreement with their most rabid right-wing libertarian opponents.

Third and last comes identity politics. Identity politics arises when all the disaggregated, autonomous individuals produced by

62 Deneen, P. J., *Why Liberalism Failed*, 2018, p. 124.

liberalism have nowhere to turn but to the state. It is the latest iteration in Nisbet's 'quest for community' that I mentioned before. It is a quest, as Francis Fukuyama would remind us, for protection and recognition either because there are no subsidiary institutions left or because those that remain are too weak to help. The result is that more powers are ceded to the state, the process of atomization is accelerated, atomization promotes a stronger urge for meaning and belonging, and the cycle starts over again. This makes identity politics one of the most self-destructive responses to the problems of liberalism. Fukuyama's book *Identity* has lately predicted that the corrosive effect of identitarianism will be outcomes observed in the failed states of Afghanistan, Iraq, Syria, and Libya, where one's opinions, job, neighbourhood, income, and marriage prospects are all circumscribed by identity alone.[63] There is something to what he says. But I believe that the problem in the West would be far worse, since we are not dealing with ancient, deeply rooted communities united by faith and language, but rather with an individualism and subjectivity more radical than ever before.

We shall see how these internal problems play themselves out. Whatever happens, the task before us is not to invite or coerce people into ever greater autonomy, but to *reconnect* them. We can begin by acknowledging two important truths. The first is that we are all naturally embedded within relationships of kinship and descent, and the second is that we all inherit cultural and social patrimonies.[64]

63 Fukuyama, F., *Identity*, 2018. Incidentally, Fukuyama predicted the rise of identitarianism in his more famous book *The End of History* (Roussinos, A., 'Why Fukuyama Was Right All Along', *Unherd*, September, 2020 (retrieved from https://unherd.com/2020/09/why-fukuyama-was-right-all-along/); Fukuyama, F., *The End of History*, with a new afterword, Free Press, New York, 2006 ((originally published 1992)), pp. 300–339.

64 Rose, M., *A World After Liberalism: Philosophers of the Radical Right*, Yale University Press, New Haven, 2021, p. 154.

Our ancient ancestors were well served by understanding these facts; and stable, durable societies were the result. Kinship and patrimony notably subsist within households and other institutions modelled on them. It is those bodies which maintain and transmit culture; without them, none of the heroes of civilization like Shulgi of Ur would have appeared. And so, it is the household that should be the first focus of renewal—a renewal made all the more urgent because of the COVID-19 pandemic and its aftermath.

Lockdowns, closures of houses of worship, businesses, schools, and so on meant that the family was practically the only society left in which human contact was still possible. Parents with small children closed ranks and hunkered down. Young workers who lost jobs returned to their parents' houses. Seniors who lived with family were lucky to escape the disaster of long-term care homes. Nearly every household was forced to become office, workshop, restaurant, school, nursery, club house, infirmary, and gymnasium. The transformation was by no means easy, and mental health came under considerable strain. Some families may even have been broken apart by the tension between remote work, or no work, and online school. However, the challenge called to mind not the need for more state intervention, but rather the sort of mutual assistance which one family can give another, as well as the kind of small-scale social interaction that can only occur in a neighbourhood, a public park, or a common area. The whole experience urges us to imagine how much worse the isolation would have been without the institution of the family.

It should not have taken a pandemic to prove it, but families are unquestionably conducive to the common good, and I know of no greater force for strengthening an individual person also. Much must obviously be sacrificed to live in common with others, but forming one's own family frees one from the isolation of contemporary life. I found that, after I was married, life's missing pieces suddenly fell into place: a household, stable employment, and a sense of rootedness and permanence.[65] This is how I came to understand what Peter Hitchens meant by calling the family 'a fortress of human liberty'.[66] Contemporary Western states may be more intrusive than ever before, but Bodin would surely rejoice that their authority does not yet reach beyond the family's threshold. Neither does the authority of any external person. No one can tell you, in your own house, how to raise your children, what to teach them, what to eat, when to go sleep, and so on. Moreover, parents may be persons of no importance outside, but in their own house, they are, to quote D. H. Lawrence, joint sovereigns of a 'little kingdom'.[67]

As the pandemic abates, I suspect that it will only be a matter of time before framers of public policy look for ways to help families and civil associations. I do not know what they may propose. Adapting tax systems to favour families and volunteer societies happens already, and will no doubt carry on. We might add better recognition in tax codes and pension law for stay-at-home parents also. Following Bodin, we might try to improve inheritance laws in order to preserve family property over generations. As my friend Sam Duncan suggests, governments could create a 'family lens' requiring the government to examine the impact of all future public policy on the family.[68] In theory, such analysis would at least weed out policies that are hostile or deleterious to family formation and stability. And

65 Harrington, M., 'Stop Hedging, Start Marrying', *New Social Covenant Unit*, March 26, 2021 (https://www.newsocialcovenant.co.uk/mary-harrington-blog-mhhbz/).

66 Hitchens, P., *The Abolition of Britain: From Winston Churchill to Theresa May*, Bloomsbury, London, 2018, pp. 208–224.

67 This is from Lawrence, D. H., *Apropos of Lady Chatterley's Lover*, Phoenix edition, Heineman, London, 1961.

68 Duncan, S., 'Families Should Be the Focus of Post-COVID Growth', *The Hub*, June 4, 2021 (https://thehub.ca/2021-06-04/samuel-duncan-families-should-be-the-focus-of-post-covid-growth/).

sooner or later, Western states will have to confront and try to reverse their declining fertility rates. But my reasoning above suggests that further intervention from the state *by itself* will only create new problems or exacerbate old ones. And so, I recommend turning away from the power of central government, and focusing on the politics of regions, cities, towns, neighbourhoods, and voluntary associations—in a word, localism.

Politics on a small scale will necessarily be closer to people's most important day-to-day concerns. Central governments, for instance, tend to have little or nothing to do with paving streets, collection of rubbish, school curriculums, local policing, zoning, and so forth. Dealing with such local matters may be frustrating, but it is at least a respite from the abstraction and depersonalization of national, or (worse) international, politics. Localism is also more robust than national politics, simply because there are fewer people involved. To quote Nassim Taleb, 'you build stronger bonds in meeting one person five times than in meeting five people once'.[69] Localism also gives you greater influence over your own community *as well as* greater influence over yourself, since a single voice is more readily heard by a few thousand or a few dozen others than by many millions. National politics also depends upon bureaucracy to enact policy accurately and consistently, but in practice this means uniformity and an abhorrence of local differences. With this in mind, we can see localism as the way to genuine diversity and variety.

Localism must also entail some economic changes. We must restore at least some of the household's old economic functions. Contemporary opinion holds that the purpose of the family

69 Taleb, N. N., *Scala Politica: Politics and Ethics Under Scaling and Uncertainty*, Stem Academic Press, 2021, p. 11.

is companionship, institutionalized affection, and the good psychological adjustment of children. These are nothing to sneeze at, but we must also recover the older idea that the family was an economy unto itself and fully self-sufficient, or nearly so. This concept is well articulated in Xenophon's dialogue called *The Oeconomicus*, in which the household, not the individual man, is presented as the smallest economic unit of society, and marriage is not merely a relationship for reproduction, but chiefly an equal partnership in the management of property and the education of children. Xenophon's idea of the total self-sufficiency of the household obviously makes most sense in rural areas, where food must be grown, harvested, and eaten locally. But, in the same spirit, city-dwellers might revive domestic skills and do-it-yourself know-how, as well as a sense of wealth based not so much on how much money one makes but on how much one does not need to spend. This is basically Susan Hayes' vision of reclaiming homemaking from the culture of consumerism.[70] At the very least, the fragility of distant supply chains and just-in-time delivery should invite a greater sense of preparedness from now on.

And what about the sort of civil associations that made the mediaeval world so dynamic? The aftermath of the pandemic will be an opportunity for revival. Restoring trust, however, may be difficult since many people may feel that their industry associations or trade unions did not fight hard enough to keep society open. There may be a lingering perception that the pandemic effectively transformed such groups into organs of the administrative state, relaying government orders rather than representing the concerns of their membership. However this may be, when the public-health

70 Hayes, S., *Radical Homemakers: Reclaiming Domesticity from a Consumer Culture*, Left to Write Press, New York, 2010.

side of things is under control once and for all, the heroes 'on the front line' will be those people who start or revive clubs, societies, volunteer groups, and other such institutions. Yuval Levin was already making a forceful case for institutional renewal on the eve of the pandemic.[71] The task may be harder now. One imagines, though, that the urge to return to the sort of groups where 'everybody knows your name', even if it is only the local pub, will be irresistible after such a long period of isolation and confusion. However, there are unfortunately many places in Europe and America where such institutions have disappeared altogether. In many cases, the pandemic will have been the final nail in the coffin. I am thinking of the post-industrial parts of Britain and Canada, or the American rust belt. What would the renewal of institutions look like in such places where it is most needed?

Timothy Carney, author of the book *Alienated America*, suggests a possible answer. In many parts of post-industrial America, the local church is often the *only* civic institution left standing after decades of deterioration. Accordingly, Carney suspects that, in the long run, the parish church may prove to be a source of renewal. [72] This possibility has ample historical precedent. After the fall of Western Rome, perhaps no local institution was more stable and durable than the parish. Warfare, plague, and other vicissitudes did not disrupt the form and function of parishes, and they were basically unchanged from at least the eighth century, through the upheavals of the Reformation and the Wars of Religion down to the nineteenth

71 Levin, Y., *A Time to Build: From Family and Community to Congress and the Campus, How Recommitting to Our Institutions Can Revive the American Dream*, Basic Books, New York, 2020, pp. 163–179.

72 Carney, T. P., *Alienated America: Why Some Places Thrive While Others Collapse*, Harper Collins, New York, 2019, pp. 281–299.

century when only their boundaries were adjusted.[73] Local parishes may well be just as stable and long-lived in our own time as they were in the remote past; but the sad truth is that religion itself is also in need of renewal.

John Lennon invited us to 'imagine no religion'. Well, we do not need to *imagine* it, because we have actually seen it many times already. A world without religion is not a world without mysticism or supernatural powers. It is not necessarily a world without public worship, either. A society without any religion at all might resemble that of the Azande people of South Sudan. The Azande, according to Edward Evans-Pritchard, had only the vaguest ideas about Mbori, the god who supposedly created the world, and showed no interest in theology.[74] Witchcraft, however, was a fixture of every aspect of public life, and was held to be responsible for every conceivable misfortune.[75]

In the West, the decline of religion has had similar consequences in the past. The epoch of the breakdown of Christendom produced Luther and Calvin, of course; but it was also the era of wild speculation in astrology, alchemy, and occultism, as attested by the careers of Girolamo Cardano, John Dee, Heinrich Agrippa, and Nostradamus (among many others).[76] The power and influence of the supernatural had always been taken for granted. Before the Reformation, intellectuals and theologians had explored the beneficent and malevolent uses of supernatural power in the

73 Reynolds, S., *Kingdoms and Communities in Western Europe 900–1300,* second edition, Oxford University Press, Oxford, 1997, p. 79.

74 Evans-Pritchard, E. E., 'Zande Theology', *Sudan Notes and Records*, vol. XIX, part 1, 1936, pp. 1–46.

75 Evans-Pritchard, E. E., *Witchcraft, Oracles and Magic Among the Azande*, Oxford University Press, Oxford, 1976.

76 Greengrass, M., *Christendom Destroyed: Europe 1517–1648,* Penguin Books, London, 2014, pp. 196–202.

context of medical treatments, incantatory prayers, holy water, relics, and so on. But it was the prerogative of the church, and the church alone, to wield that power. When that prerogative was called into doubt, strange things happened, and so the sixteenth and seventeenth centuries—not the Middle Ages—were the great era of monstrous births, celestial portents, witchcraft, demonic possession, werewolves, apparitions, ghosts, and so on. Stories of such things were widely circulated in pamphlets for the first time and became tropes in novellas, plays, and songs.[77] It was also the age of learned treatises on demonology and witchcraft, inquisitorial investigations, and parish visitations concerning magical and supernatural events. Both Catholics and Protestants engaged in such activities. But, ironically, the Protestants, who had set out to rid the world of superstition, achieved the exact opposite. By focusing on the immediacy of God in the world, they magnified the influence of the devil and his minions.[78] The worst consequence of this supernatural free-for-all was the European witch-craze.[79] Incidentally, there may be a parallel here with the fracture of Islam into myriad local and national groups, and the contemporary Saudi Arabian crackdown on magic and witchcraft.[80]

Speaking of Islam, the crisis of confidence and political turmoil following the collapse of the Ottoman empire and the abolition of the Caliphate in the 1920s provoked a good deal of supernatural

77 Greengrass, M., *Christendom Destroyed: Europe 1517–1648,* Penguin Books, London, 2014, pp. 492–493.

78 Greengrass, M., *Christendom Destroyed: Europe 1517–1648,* Penguin Books, London, 2014, p. 493.

79 Trevor-Roper, H., *The European Witch-Craze of the 16th and 17th Centuries*, Penguin, London, 1969.

80 Jacobs, R., 'Saudi Arabia's War on Witchcraft', *The Atlantic*, August 19, 2013 (https://www.theatlantic.com/international/archive/2013/08/saudi-arabias-war-on-witchcraft/278701/).

speculation.[81] Seances, communication with the souls of the dead, and belief in the influence of jinns flourished in Egypt with the encouragement of such figures as Ahmed Fahmy Abu al-Khair, Mohammed Farid Wagdy, Sheikh Tantawi Jawhari, and Hussein Hassan. They were scientists, scholars, and clerics, who might have ignored occultism in another age, but they embraced it in a moment of high tension and religious decline because they thought it vindicated their religion against the destabilizing claims of Western materialism and modernity. Even the early Muslim Brotherhood encouraged spiritualism; and from the 1950s onwards, the Syrian and Egyptian armies held regular seances until the practice declined in the 1970s. The idea was to help encourage a sense of pan-Arabism by summoning up the spirits of departed Caliphs, like Harun al-Rashid, and other Muslim luminaries. But this practice failed to foresee or avert Israel's victory in Six Day War in 1967, and this probably explains why it died out, only to be replaced by more puritanical forms of Islam.

Not even indifference to traditional religion, or even outright atheism, can deliver us from worship and mysticism. After the French Revolution came the short-lived Cult of the Supreme Being, then theosophy and spiritism.[82] In the late eighteenth century in China, the slow breakdown of Confucianism was attended by a hysterical fear of sorcerers who were believed to be stealing people's souls.[83] Later, the banning of religion in China

81 Cormack, R., 'Spiritualism Experienced Its Heyday in 20th-Century Egypt', *New Lines*, July 1, 2022 (https://newlinesmag.com/essays/spiritualism-experienced-its-heyday-in-20th-century-egypt/).

82 Strube, J., 'Socialist Religion and the Emergence of Occultism: A Genealogical Approach to Socialism and Secularization in 19th-century France', *Religion*, 26, 2016, pp. 359–388.

83 Kuhn, P. A., *The Soulstealers: The Chinese Sorcery Scare of 1768*, Harvard University Press, Cambridge, 1990.

and the destruction of temples and scripture amidst the Cultural Revolution produced the ersatz religion of Mao—not rational atheism. The Nazi hatred of Christianity gave way to the pan-Germanic mysticism of Heinrich Himmler. The churches and monasteries surrounding Moscow's Red Square had proved an embarrassment until the Soviets got their own place of worship: the tomb of Lenin.[84] His corpse, like that of an Orthodox saint, was preserved in a mausoleum, and annual processions of soldiers and nuclear missiles would pass before it in veneration.

The explanation for this tendency toward metaphysical speculation and worship should probably be sought within the structure of the human mind. Beliefs in unseen forces, ghosts, spiritual beings, witches, and so on are universal. They cannot be explained with reference to habit or a pre-scientific need to understand the world. Pascal Boyer, a cognitive anthropologist, has argued that the mind is predisposed by natural selection to infer the existence of non-physical beings or forces,[85] and I suspect that he is right. His argument means that the promise of the Enlightenment—that reason and science would triumph over metaphysics—will never come to pass. We will never escape the nagging feeling that there is something more to the world than what the senses can perceive. But without the structure of religion to contain and control it, belief in unseen beings and powers runs wild.

Here in the West, without the constraints once imposed by Christianity, metaphysical speculation has lately focused on mysterious forces, both personal and impersonal. On the one hand,

84 Conrad, P., *Modern Times, Modern Places: How Life and Art Were Transformed in a Century of Revolution, Innovation and Radical Change*, New York, Alfred A. Knopf, 1999, p. 238.

85 Boyer, P., *The Naturalness of Religious Ideas: A Cognitive Theory of Religion*, University of California Press, Berkeley, 1994.

we have the malevolent cabals pulling the strings above government or secretly undermining society. The classic conspiracy theories about Freemasons, the Illuminati, the Jews, Jesuits, or whoever fall into this category. On the other hand, we have such impersonal forces as blood, race, IQ, survival of the fittest, cultural Marxism, capitalism, the Patriarchy, feminism, unconscious bias, systemic racism, or whatever the latest bugbear may be. Such forces are believed to exert enormous influence everywhere and can only be resisted by special knowledge and rituals of expiation. I do not know how exactly to describe those beliefs succinctly. Following the late French pundit, Philippe Muray, we might call them 'occult', since they constitute beliefs in hidden supernatural influences outside the structure of religion.[86] A less inflammatory word might be 'gnostic' with its general dissatisfaction with the world, which is viewed as corrupt, and its emphasis on man's capacity to transform himself and the cosmos through secret knowledge. Or so the late Eric Voegelin defined it.[87]

That list of examples, which could certainly be enlarged, proves that occultism or gnosticism is found throughout the political spectrum. But two main forms of it are now rising out of the crumbling structure of Christianity. A right-wing gnosticism takes shape in a fascination with ancient paganism and the secrets of racial determinism—a mode of thought inaugurated by Nietzsche and latterly expanded by Julius Evola (1898–1974) who was himself an occultist in the more traditional sense of the term.[88] It could also be discerned in the QAnon conspiracy theory, whereby the quasi-divine power of

86 Muray, P., *Le XIXe Siècle à travers les âges*, Éditions Denoël, Paris, 1999.

87 Voegelin, E., *Science, Politics, and Gnosticism: Two Essays*, Gateway Editions, Washington, 1997.

88 Rose, M., *A World After Liberalism: Philosophers of the Radical Right*, Yale University Press, New Haven, 2021, pp. 39–63.

Donald Trump promised to root out the secret evil from within the 'deep state' and redeem America.[89] This idea is largely defunct now. The growing obsession with blood and belonging carries on, though, but tends to evoke amusement or disgust from most people so far.

Its left-wing counterpart is more popular and more influential. It promises esoteric knowledge whereby all-pervasive, 'systemic' racism can be discerned and exorcised. Its secret doctrine is Critical Race Theory, which had long been fermenting in the dark corners of academia.[90] But in the summer of 2020, amidst the tensions generated by lockdowns and the fear of pestilence, it exploded into a world-wide spiritual awakening, complete with its own sdoctrine of original sin, public confessions of wickedness and hereditary guilt, rituals of self-humiliation, baptism, and even foot-washing—all in reaction to the cruel murder of George Floyd. The later, unrelated death of the American Supreme Court Justice Ruth Bader Ginsburg added an apocalyptic element. Her admirers kept nocturnal vigils in which they held candles and sang John Lennon's *Imagine*, while young people took to Twitter and TikTok to announce the imminent end of the world.[91] The world did not end, of course, but now the gospel of Critical Race Theory, anti-racism, and unconscious bias is preached by elite corporations and universities throughout the English-speaking world.[92]

89 Muirhead, R. / Rosenblum, N. L., *A Lot of People Are Saying: The New Conspiracism and the Assault on Democracy*, Princeton University Press, Princeton, 2019, pp. 132–135.

90 Pluckrose, H. / Lindsay, J., *Cynical Theories: How Activist Scholarship Made Everything about Race, Gender, and Identity — and Why This Harms Everybody*, Pitchstone Publishing, Durham, North Carolina, 2020, pp. 111–134.

91 Hamid, S., 'America Without God', *The Atlantic*, April 2021 Issue (https://www.theatlantic.com/magazine/archive/2021/04/america-politics-religion/618072/).

92 Ramaswamy, V., *Woke, Inc.: Inside Corporate America's Social Justice Scam*, Center Street, New York, 2021, pp. 215–239.

Both forms of Gnosticism or occultism bear the mark of the religious system that once held them in check. This is most obvious on the gnostic Left. Social Justice, the Church of Diversity, 'wokeism'—whatever we want to call it—is *not* a form of neo-Marxism, as has recently been asserted by Mike Gonzalez, for instance.[93] It is better understood as a Christian heresy: a kind of post-Protestantism or perhaps the natural evolution of world-hating Puritanism. Some promising analysis in this connection appears in John McWhorter's book *Woke Racism.*[94] Most tellingly, the 'woke Elect' do not assert the destiny of the strong to rule over the weak: they demand justice, equity, and the total reversal of all power relations. Just as the last generation of pagan Romans heard Christians promising to turn subjects against rulers, and so on, we now hear promises to humble the mighty and to exalt the meek in everything from the call for safe spaces, to the MeToo movement, and the demand for transgender toilets.[95] Most wokeists would probably claim to reject Christianity, of course, albeit not with the same vehemence as the gnostic Right, who have followed Nietzsche and Evola into a pathological hatred of Christianity. And yet they too long for the social bonds and historical continuity that were once established and strengthened by that very religion.

Justice and belonging are understandable human needs. But without a religious framework to civilize them, they have become disordered and ugly, like a neglected and overgrown garden. Extreme progressives may claim to love justice; but they have no

93 Gonzalez, M., *BLM: The Making of a Marxist Revolution*, Encounter Books, New York and London, 2021.

94 McWhorter, J., *Woke Racism: How a New Religion Has Betrayed Black America*, Portfolio / Penguin, New York, 2021, pp. 23–60.

95 Holland, T., *Dominion: How the Christian Revolution Remade the World*, Basic Books, New York, 2019, pp. 523–533.

sense of forgiveness, nor of mercy. They demand confession, but offer no absolution. The maxim 'judge not, that ye be not judged'[96] has not reached them. This will lead only to a world of constant vendetta and merciless retribution. In contrast, the gnostic Right promises to vanquish Christianity once and for all and replace it with a new world of gods and heroes, united by ties of blood and soil. But without culture or patrimony, the new pagans will deliver only petty hatred and personal isolation.

That such diabolical forces can arise from the deteriorating edifice of religion tells me that we need to strengthen the foundation and repair the superstructure. We might start from the premise, well-advertised by the early church, that Christianity is a universal religion, open to everyone without distinction of race, country, language, social position, and so on. As St Paul remarked, 'there is neither Jew nor Greek, there is neither bond nor free, there is neither male nor female: for ye are all one in Christ Jesus'.[97] And similarly, he says 'there is neither Greek nor Jew, circumcision nor uncircumcision, Barbarian, Scythian, bond nor free: but Christ is all, and in all'.[98] Later in the second century AD, the author of the *Epistle to Diognetus* defended Christianity against its pagan accusers, invoking the paradoxical idea that a Christian was a foreigner in his own homeland and at home in every foreign country.[99] This sense of universalism was backed up by the original unity of the human family, since God 'hath made of one blood all nations of men'.[100] Properly understood, the unity spoken of by St Paul does not mean that all personal differences are effaced; but rather that

96 Matthew 7:1.
97 Galatians 3:28.
98 Colossians 3:11.
99 *Epistle to Diognetus*, V.
100 Acts 17:26.

no one has any special privileges because of them. Throw in the democratizing doctrine of original sin, and you have a vision of justice and equality which obliges everyone to acknowledge fault; but all are equally justified by grace and equally capable of union with Christ. In this respect, Christianity offers the exact opposite of popular contemporary alternatives, with all their immutable hierarchies of power and privilege.

Next comes the matter of Christian identity, community, and belonging. From the very beginning, Christianity has been unfairly accused of dissolving social bonds, corroding local customs, and severing ancestral ties. Tertullian (c. AD 155 to c. AD 220), who is often regarded as the founder of Western Christian theology, was aware of such complaints. If taken out of context, some of Tertullian's own arguments can be interpreted as demands for a radical break with the past and the complete reversal of ancestral custom.[101] But this is not really what Tertullian meant. On the contrary, he accuses his fellow Romans of neglecting their ancient customs and abandoning their ancestors' pious traditions. They had no right, therefore, to accuse Christians of doing likewise, Tertullian thought, since Christians had actually *restored* an older sense of piety and religious devotion.[102] Accordingly, Christianity would not sever ancestral ties or destroy ancient traditions, but rather renew, strengthen, and enlarge them. Likewise, Christians might be thought of as 'a new race of men', as we find in the *Epistle to Diognetus*,[103] but this implied a more expansive sense of community embracing the most various and most ancient of peoples, including the Jews and virtuous pagans. St Paul had insisted that Christians had

101 Tertullian, *Ad Nationes*, II.i.7, for example.

102 Tertullian, *Ad Nationes*, I.x.

103 *Epistle to Diognetus*, I.

Abraham as their ancestor through faith.[104] And just as Christ had announced the fulfilment, not the destruction, of the Jewish law, St Paul had explained Christianity as the confirmation of all former Hellenic philosophical speculation.[105] And so, far from the total reversal feared by the Roman elite, Christianity re-orientated believers backward to humanity's earliest past, and eventually became a repository of Graeco-Roman heritage.

Islam has many of the same qualities also. Islam also offers a spiritual patrimony and ancestry going back to Adam, the Hebrew prophets, learned pagans like Aristotle and Plato, and sometimes even the mythical kings and heroes of ancient Iran. Such an expansive sense of community comes across in the writings of Dinawari, Mas'udi, and Tabari, at least. The earliest Muslim political document, commonly called the *Constitution of Medina*, laid the groundwork for this universalism. That text describes the Muslim community, or *umma* as it is called in Arabic, as a single body embracing all Muslims, as well as Christians and Jews,[106] who all shared a similar commitment to Abrahamic monotheism and a common moral outlook. Wherever the worshipper turned, there was God: cult was the only difference.[107] With this in mind, there is reason to suspect that recent (largely political) hostility between Christians and Muslims will give way to solidarity—especially in the face of secular indifference and the corrosive effects of liberalism. What I hope for is something akin to what the late Archbishop Fulton Sheen described in a radio broadcast in 1947:

104 Galatians 3:5.

105 Acts 17:16–34.

106 Donner, F. M., *Muhammad and the Believers at the Origins of Islam,* The Belknap Press of Harvard University Press, Cambridge, 2010, pp. 228–232.

107 Qur'an 6:160–165; My analysis follows Hodgson, M. G. S., *The Venture of Islam: Conscience and History in a World Civilization, Volume 1: The Classical Age of Islam*, University of Chicago Press, Chicago, first edition, 1977, pp. 172–180.

'it is not a unity of religion we plead, for that is impossible when purchased at the cost of the unity of truth, but a unity of religious peoples, wherein each marches separately according to the light of his conscience, but strikes together for the moral betterment of the world through prayer, not hate'.[108]

A fond hope, perhaps; though the two greatest religions of Christianity and Islam have renewed people and nations in the past and may do so again. They have also renewed one another before, as in the Golden Age of the Abbasid Caliphate and the Western Middle Ages. But mutual renewal and respect will not happen again without self-respect and self-renewal. Pope John Paul II's *Memory and Identity* argues this exact point: respect for other cultures could only come from those who respected their own, and only a culture that had preserved itself could add to the variety of human experience. The defense of one's patrimony was, moreover, a moral duty implicit in the Mosaic commandment to honour one's father and mother. But, as the late pope pointed out, Christianity also directs the patrimony of human native lands to an eternal, heavenly homeland—a birth-right uniting and transcending every earthly heritage.[109] Of course, well-meaning people may shrug and say 'it is a fine ideal but I cannot believe it'. But I would say that most of us already act as though we do. Here in the West, we still accept the Christian vision of morality even without rational or metaphysical justification. Without metaphysics, that morality may last a little longer purely by force of habit, but I fear that sooner or later it will vanish unless we take greater interest in it.

108 The radio programme was called *Light Your Lamps* and the sermon was entitled 'Signs of Our Times'. There is a recording of it here: https://www.youtube.com/watch?v=s3e6mTMlM-s&t=1s.

109 Pope John Paul II, *Memory and Identity: Conversations at the Dawn of a Millennium*, Rizzoli, New York, 2005, pp. 59–99.

CHAPTER VII

The Future

Pécuchet takes a bleak view of mankind's future.

Modern man has been diminished and turned into a machine.

Final anarchy of the human race (Buchner, I.ii).

Impossibility of peace (id).

Barbarism through excess of individualism and delirium of science.

Three hypotheses: 1st, pantheistic radicalism will break all ties with the past—and an inhuman despotism will follow; 2nd, if theistic absolutism triumphs, the liberalism with which humanity has been saturated since the Reformation will fall, everything will be overturned; 3rd, if the convulsions since '89 vacillate endlessly between two outcomes, these oscillations will sweep us away with their own strength. There will be no more ideals, religion, or morality.

America will have conquered the world.

Future of Literature.

Universal vulgarity. Everything will be nothing but working-class debauchery.

End of the world because the heat will run out.

Bouvard has a rosy view of humanity's future. Modern man is making progress.

> Europe will be regenerated by Asia. The law of history being that civilisation goes from East to West,—the role of China,—the two humanities will be melded together.
>
> Future inventions: means of travel. Balloon.—Undersea boats with glass windows, always in calm waters, the sea turbulent only on the surface.—The fish and the countryside at the bottom of the ocean will be seen passing by.—Animals tamed—all sorts of cultivation.
>
> Future of literature (opposite of industrial literature). Future sciences.—Mastering the force of magnetism.
>
> Paris will become a winter-garden;—fruit orchards on the boulevard. The Seine filtered and warm,—abundance of precious and artificial stones,—lavish gilding,—house lighting—light will be stored, because some bodies have this property, like sugar, the flesh of certain molluscs at Bologna phosphorus. House façades will have to be whitewashed with a phosphorescent substance, and their radiance will light up the streets.
>
> Disappearance of evil because of the disappearance of want. Philosophy will be a religion.
>
> Communion of all peoples. Public festivals.
>
> We will travel to the stars,—and when the earth is used up, humanity will move to the stars . . .
>
> Gustave Flaubert, *Bouvard et Pécuchet*

THE PICTURE EMERGING FROM the last three chapters is not wholly bleak, but it is not exactly optimistic either. The prospect of renewal is not entirely remote; but, as far as I can tell, it is also not imminent. But all the historical examples which I have mentioned show that renewal is possible even at unlikely moments. The purpose of this chapter is to emphasize that point, and to show that there is at least one part of the world where a reorientation toward the past is now being attempted, however imperfectly.

The long epigraph above is an extract from the notes for the end of Flaubert's unfinished novel *Bouvard et Pécuchet*, published posthumously in 1881, but set in the late 1830s.[1] The book is a satire about two imbeciles, François Bouvard and Juste Pécuchet, who retire to the countryside and preoccupy themselves in absurd attempts to master various bodies of fashionable knowledge: farming, medicine, archaeology, spiritualism, and everything else that the typical nineteenth-century man would have had in his head. All their attempts miscarry dreadfully, and yet the two men never seem to give up. Despite this, *Bouvard et Pécuchet* lacks what we would recognize as a plot, and in this sense it prefigures *Seinfeld*, and similar postmodern comedies, as a novel 'about nothing'.[2]

1 The most recent English translation is *Bouvard and Pécuchet: the Last Novel of Gustave Flaubert, in a new translation from the French & with an introduction by Mark Polizzotti, followed by the Dictionary of Accepted Ideas and the Catalogue of Fashionable Ideas, and featuring a preface by Raymond Queneau*, Dalkey Archive Press, 2005. The passage I quoted is on pp. 276–277, but it is my own translation.

2 See Mark Polizzotti's introduction in *Bouvard and Pécuchet: the Last Novel of Gustave Flaubert, in a new translation from the French & with an introduction by Mark Polizzotti, followed by the Dictionary of Accepted Ideas and the Catalogue of Fashionable Ideas, and featuring a preface by Raymond Queneau*, Dalkey Archive Press, 2005, pp. vii–xvi.

To judge by Flaubert's notes, the novel was to conclude with the main characters' contrasting views of the future. Unbounded confidence in innovation, science, and technology, and so on is represented by the outlook of Bouvard. Scepticism about liberal individualism and fear of the breakdown of tradition and religion are expressed by Pécuchet. It would have required little foresight to sense that this dichotomy would last a long time. But, if anything, over the course of the twentieth century, the expectation of progress became more exaggerated than a Bouvard might have expected, and political and social upheavals at the same time were much more disruptive than the Pécuchets of the world imagined. Traditional religion has indeed declined, though it has not been replaced by philosophy, and probably never will be. American culture, through globalization, has indeed conquered the world. We have travelled to outer space, and conquered the moon, and there is now talk of colonizing other planets.

What is most surprising, though, is Bouvard's expectation that Western civilization would one day be regenerated by China. I do not know what could have inspired Bouvard's fictional expectation. It would have seemed strange in Flaubert's time. But now it appears almost prophetic, as I will demonstrate here.

By the late nineteenth century, the days when the Chinese emperor could address a European king 'with the patient manner appropriate in dealing with an importunate child'[3] had long been over. King George III's request for a permanent British diplomatic office in 1793, for instance, was met with the Qianlong emperor's respectful indifference. The British may have wanted to trade, but there was nothing that the Chinese needed from them. There was also a certain surprise that barbarians from so distant a country had

3 Russell, B. *The Problem of China*, George Allen and Unwin, London, 1922, p. 24.

shown any interest at all in Chinese civilization, since they would never be able to benefit from it:

> If you assert that your reverence for our Celestial Dynasty fills you with a desire to acquire our civilization, our ceremonies and code of laws differ so completely from your own that, even if your Envoy were able to acquire the rudiments of our civilization, you could not possibly transplant our manners and customs to your alien soil.[4]

That is what the Qianlong emperor said to George Macartney, the British envoy. Nevertheless, interest in Chinese civilization, whether real or feigned, would have made sense in the eighteenth century. An emperor would likewise have had every reason for confidence, not knowing what calamities were in store. But this changed amidst the chaos and bloodshed of the nineteenth and twentieth centuries. Few would have found a reason to speak favourably of Chinese civilization then, not least the Chinese themselves, many of whom blamed their humiliations on their ancestral culture.

There were some exceptions, though Flaubert and other Europeans had probably never heard of them. One was the intellectual Liang Qichao,[5] whom I mentioned earlier. He had admired the West, of course, and was one of the leaders of the translation movement that turned Darwin and Mill into Chinese. But his opinion of the West deteriorated with time. After a fact-finding expedition to America, and a personal interview with President Theodore Roosevelt, he

4 Backhouse, E. / Bland, J. O. P., *Annals and Memoirs of the Court of Peking (from the 16th to the 20th Century)*, Houghton Mifflin Company, Boston and New York, 1914, p. 324.

5 Xiao, Y., 'Liang Qichao's Political and Social Philosophy' in Cheng, C.-Y. / Bunnin, N. (eds.), *Contemporary Chinese Philosophy*, Blackwell, London, 2002, pp. 15–36.

judged American democracy as productive of 'mediocre politicians, corruption, disorder, racism, and imperialism'.[6] At the end of the First World War, he was downright disgusted with what he saw as the selfish individualism of the West and its materialistic hedonism. In his view, those forces had led only to brutal violence—not freedom and dignity as promised.[7] China should therefore reject Western culture and preserve its ancestral values. Liang Qichao's view of the future was expressed in a novel he wrote in 1902. It is about a descendant of Confucius visiting the 2062 World's Fair in Shanghai where he delivered a lecture on the coming of democracy to China—a vision of both continuity and development.[8] Another exception was the philosopher Liang Shuming (1893–1988).[9] Western science and technology, he thought, might raise everyone's standard of living, but otherwise the West was crippled by a great spiritual emptiness, for which only China had the cure. The Confucian principles of harmony, compromise, and intuition must be maintained, he thought, and social order should be upheld in the traditional manner through rituals and music, not by law and punishment. Accordingly, Liang Shuming called for a Confucianist revival. But, as far as both Liangs were concerned, Westerners, who had turned their backs on their ancestral culture, had more to learn from China than the other way round.

6 Keay, J., *China: A History*, Basic Books, New York, 2011, pp. 496–497.

7 Tanner, H. M., *China: A History*, v. 2: *From the Great Qing Empire through the People's Republic of China, 1644–2009*, Hackett Publishing Company, Indianapolis / Cambridge, 2010, p. 127.

8 Johnson, I., *The Souls of China: The Return of Religion after Mao*, Parthenon Books, New York, 2017, p. 281.

9 An, Y., 'Liang Shuming: Eastern and Western Cultures and Confucianism' in Cheng, C.-Y. / Bunnin, N. (eds), *Contemporary Chinese Philosophy*, Blackwell, London, 2002, pp. 147–164.

As Flaubert seemed to anticipate, some Westerners began to agree with this in the twentieth century. One of these was Bertrand Russell. In the 1920s, Russell suggested that the West could claim only a scientific advantage over China—an advantage which had been used chiefly for military ends amounting to little more than efficient methods of homicide.[10] Military matters aside, Russell believed that Chinese civilization was in no way inferior to its Western counterpart, and that we had much to learn from it. Nevertheless, Russell was not optimistic:

> Greece learnt from Egypt, Rome from Greece, the Arabs from the Roman Empire, mediaeval Europe from the Arabs, and Renaissance Europe from the Byzantines. In many of these cases, the pupils proved better than their masters. In the case of China, if we regard the Chinese as the pupils, this may be the case again. In fact, we have quite as much to learn from them as they from us, but there is far less chance of us learning it. If I treat the Chinese as our pupils, rather than vice versa, it is only because I fear we are unteachable.[11]

In other words, China would learn to imitate the West, but the West would learn nothing from China. As I see it, this is indeed what happened over the course of the twentieth century, albeit not exactly as Russell seemed to expect. China adopted the West's worst features: obsession with novelty, materialism, worship of progress, hostility to tradition, contempt of religion, and atomization of society. These problems became especially bad amidst Mao Zedong's Great

10 Russell, B. *The Problem of China*, George Allen and Unwin, London, 1922, p. 25; 41.

11 Russell, B. *The Problem of China*, George Allen and Unwin, London, 1922, p. 100.

Proletarian Cultural Revolution—an upheaval neither proletarian nor cultural. But they were worsened by the economic boom ushered in by market reforms under Chairman Deng Xiaoping and his successor Jiang Zemin. By the 1980s, Mao was out of favour, and his legacy was something of an embarrassment; but only Western materialism seemed likely to supersede it. A turning point came in 1987 when the Chinese state gave up the idea of demolishing the Mao Zedong Mausoleum in Tiananmen Square, and opened a Kentucky Fried Chicken immediately across from it instead.[12]

Now all the evils familiar from the capitalist West have appeared in supposedly Communist China.[13] But do not take my word for it. Instead, take the analysis of China's most powerful intellectual and political adviser: Wang Huning. He was *éminence grise* to Jiang Zemin, to Hu Jintao, and latterly to Xi Jinping, and is now one of the most senior leaders of the Chinese Communist Party. Wang's analysis of China's transformations after the death of Mao is somewhat understated. The change of 'an economy of production to an economy of consumption', Wang thought, meant a decline from 'a spiritually oriented culture to a materially oriented culture' and 'from a collectivist culture to an individualistic culture'. So far, so obvious. But then Wang says:

> . . . there are no core values in China's most recent structure. This lack has multiple meanings: it may mean that the value itself has yet to evolve; it may mean that the value exists but

12 *China: From the Long March to Tiananmen Square by the writers and photographers of The Associated Press*, A Donald Hutter Book, Henry Hold and Company, New York, 1990, p. 263.

13 Tanner, H. M., *China: A History*, v. 2: *From the Great Qing Empire through the People's Republic of China, 1644–2009*, Hackett Publishing Company, Indianapolis / Cambridge, 2010, pp. 256–264.

> has not universally entered political culture; and it may mean that we do not have vehicles to carry out the transmission of values. Since 1949, we have criticized the core values of the classical and modern structures, but have not paid enough attention to shaping our own core values. In and of itself, Marxism transcended the Western rule-based worldview, but in China, which never possessed that worldview, the results of the adoption of Marxism were not always positive.

Wang wrote that in 1988 in a long essay called *The Structure of China's Changing Political Culture.*[14] Much the same attitude to materialism appears in his 1992 memoir *America Against America.* It is an analysis of American society by an outsider, cast in the same mould as Alexis de Tocqueville's *Democracy in America.*[15] Wang sometimes seems to admire the dynamism of American society, but he is usually critical. He has a low opinion of American litigiousness, for instance, and he denounces the influence of lawyers and lobbyists on political processes. Constant use of credit cards, as far as Wang was concerned, was a serious moral flaw. Middle-class family life was insular and hedonistic. Social interaction was generally superficial. Children were indulged, while the elderly were neglected. Husbands and wives displayed affection in public but were privately cold to one another. And frequent divorces, declining family morality, and drug abuse were atomizing American society.

14 Wang Huning, *The Structure of China's Changing Political Culture*, 1988 (https://www.readingthechinadream.com/wang-huning-ldquothe-structure-of-chinarsquos-changing-political-culturerdquo.html). For a short analysis, see Horesh, N. / Lim, K. F., *An East Asian Challenge to Western Neo-Liberalism: Critical Perspectives on the 'China Model'*, Routledge, London, 2018, pp. 42–46.

15 An anonymous translation into English of *America Against America* can be found here: https://archive.org/details/america-against-america.

Many Americans acknowledged those flaws at the time of Wang's writing; but Wang noted that Americans tended to think of them not as social and cultural challenges, but rather as scientific and technological ones or, worse, as a matter of money.

There is much truth to Wang's criticisms of America. But I suspect that his book was also intended as a warning about trends which had taken hold in China also—trends which now threatened to produce a hollow society of disaggregated individuals cut off from their ancestral culture, without core values, and primed for dissolution. Accordingly, Wang and much of the senior leadership of the Communist Party picked up where Liang Shuming and Liang Qichao had left off. They resolved to halt the advance of Western liberalism and radical individualism, and the remedy that they settled on was to reconnect the present with the past. This is why contemporary Chinese propaganda glosses over the interruptions and false-starts of the nineteenth and twentieth centuries in favour of emphasizing '5,000 years of continuous civilization'—a chronology that is incidentally much longer and much less plausible than what is accepted by historians and archaeologists. It is why the early life of Xi Jinping is habitually linked with that of the mythical Yellow Emperor who supposedly established Chinese civilization.[16] It is why Xi regularly quotes from the Chinese Classics (notably from the Daodejing and the works of the Legalist scholar Han Feizi), among constant allusions to Western philosophy and world literature including the *Epic of Gilgamesh* and the Vedas.[17] Finally, it explains why such a banal matter as Chinese foreign investment

16 Bougon, F., *Inside the Mind of Xi Jinping*, translated by Vanessa Lee, C. Hurst & Co., London, 2018 (originally published in French in 2017), p . 61.

17 Bougon, F., *Inside the Mind of Xi Jinping*, translated by Vanessa Lee, C. Hurst & Co., London, 2018 (originally published in French in 2017), p . 7–9; 118–119; 120–121.

is surrounded by romantic references to the Silk Road and the cosmopolitanism of the Tang Dynasty (AD 618–907).[18]

But the centrepiece of all this is the revival of religion. Attitudes began to change after the destruction of the Cultural Revolution and the death of Mao, and in 1982 the Communist Party issued the famous *Document 19*.[19] That decree cautioned Party members against banning religious activity, directing them not to expect religion to disappear any time soon, to restore houses of worship that had been destroyed, and to rehabilitate the clergy. This was the context in which Jiang Zemin was rumoured to have been a Buddhist and to have considered making Christianity the official religion of China, or so it was said.[20] Wen Jiabao (premier under Hu Jintao) was suspected of being a Christian. And when he was governor of Zhejiang Province in the 2000s, a younger Xi Jinping developed a reputation as an admirer of Buddhism, encouraged the reconstruction of many local temples, and cultivated a close friendship with a Zen master.[21] Far below the top brass of the Communist Party, China pullulated with religious enthusiasm, but there was no centre to hold it all together.

When the State Administration for Religious Affairs was established in the 1990s, Ye Xiaowen was its first director. Though he

18 Frankopan, P., *The New Silk Roads: The Present and Future of the World*, Alfred A. Knopf, New York, 2018, pp. 62–112; Horesh, N. / Lim, K. F., *An East Asian Challenge to Western Neo-Liberalism: Critical Perspectives on the 'China Model'*, Routledge, London, 2018, pp. 12–36.

19 A translation of *Document 19* can be found here: https://www.globaleast.org/wp-content/uploads/2020/02/Document_no._19_1982.pdf. For some analysis, see Johnson, I., *The Souls of China: The Return of Religion after Mao*, Parthenon Books, New York, 2017, pp. 218–225.

20 Aikman, D., *Jesus in Beijing*, revised edition, Monarch Books, Oxford, 2006, pp. 31–32.

21 Johnson, I., *The Souls of China: The Return of Religion after Mao*, Parthenon Books, New York, 2017, p. 280.

claimed to be an atheist, he quickly resolved to restore that 'centre' to Chinese civilization. The missing piece, as Liang Shuming and Wang Huning would have agreed, was Confucianism. Mao had denounced Confucius as 'a regressive and feudal pedant' and had rejoiced at the Red Guard's desecration of Confucius' tomb. But popular adherence to Confucian principles had not been wholly eradicated. Ye Xiaowen and his ilk were, in a sense, pushing at an open door; but the rehabilitation of Confucius has been gradual and cautious. It began in 1979 with Deng Xiaoping's oft-repeated talking point about 'the moderately prosperous society', which he lifted directly from the *Book of Rites*, a core text among the Confucian classics. Hu Jintao later spoke of 'the harmonious society' and 'the eight honours and eight disgraces'—Confucian concepts which his audience would have recognized immediately.[22] In 2005, Ye presided over the opening of the Centre for the Study of Confucian Religion. At his prompting, scholars who had criticized Confucianism were ousted from public research institutes and replaced by those who favoured its revival. Universities and schools then fell into line, beginning to teach the Confucian classics once again. In 2011, late in the premiership of Hu, a statue of Confucius was erected in Tiananmen Square in Beijing. It must have aroused some ire within the Communist Party, because it was quietly taken down after a few months.[23] Open veneration of Confucius would have to wait for the leadership of Xi Jinping.

In 2013, Xi's first year in power, he made an official visit to Qufu, the hometown of Confucius. Xi toured the Research Institute

22 Bougon, F., *Inside the Mind of Xi Jinping*, translated by Vanessa Lee, C. Hurst & Co., London, 2018 (originally published in French in 2017), pp. 137–139.

23 Huang, S. *et al.*, 'Controversial Confucius Statue Vanishes from Tiananmen', *Reuters*, April 22, 2011 (https://www.reuters.com/article/us-china-conficius-idUSTRE73L0Y420110422).

of Confucianism there, and passed by a table covered in books, two of which caught his eye. They were *Interpretations on Family Teachings of Confucius* and *Explanations of the Analects*. 'I would like to read these two books thoroughly', Xi remarked to the surrounding journalists. The Chinese public broadcaster CCTV-13 instantly got the political message and began spreading the word that Confucius was back.[24] In 2014, Xi took part in Confucius' 2,565th birthday celebrations, and in the following year he gave a long encomium to the Venerable Sage at the Fifth Congress of the International Confucian Association.[25] Xi's repeated invocations of 'the spiritual world of the Chinese nation', 'spiritual pursuits', 'spiritual activities', 'spiritual progress', and so on sound odd coming from a Marxist, but there they are in Xi's speech nonetheless. And in the same address, Chinese communists of the twentieth century are reimagined not as the destroyers of old China as they certainly were, but as 'faithful inheritors and upholders of the country's fine cultural traditions'. This must have sounded odd to anyone who remembered the Cultural Revolution. But the overall message of the speech was sound. 'Fine traditional culture', Xi said, 'is the fountainhead of a country or nation's inheritance and development. Losing it will cut off the country or nation's spiritual lifeline'.

But the Chinese state's support for Confucianism does not extend to other religions—especially not to those deemed subversive, like the Falun Gong, or foreign, like Christianity. The Falun Gong is outlawed because it refuses to cooperate with the state in any way.

24 Liu, Q., 'President Xi Visits Hometown of Confucius', *China.org.cn*, November 27, 2013 (http://www.china.org.cn/china/2013-11/27/content_30722192.htm); Bougon, F., *Inside the Mind of Xi Jinping*, translated by Vanessa Lee, C. Hurst & Co., London, 2018 (originally published in French in 2017), p. 130.

25 A translation of the speech can be found here: http://library.chinausfocus.com/article-1534.html.

In contrast, all forms of Christianity are regulated by the State Administration for Religious Affairs. Or at least they are supposed to be. That body in theory monitors all officially registered churches, temples, and mosques. It approves the curriculum in seminaries, making sure that the political slogans of the day are included. And it determines who may be ordained. This would all be unconscionable in the West, but it is a substantial improvement on banning religion altogether and the horrors of the Cultural Revolution. There are, however, many 'underground' house churches—far too many for the state to spy on or control. Resources for this purpose are strained in any case, since the state already spends more on internal surveillance than on national defense. Anyway, the Chinese state's goal here is to 'Sinicise' Christianity: to appropriate it and assimilate it to Chinese civilization.[26] Ironically, this is exactly what has been happening since the first Christian missionaries appeared in China (from Persia, incidentally) in the seventh century, when Christianity was presented in terms reminiscent of Daoism.[27]

There is, of course, a dark side to this apparent revival. The reopening of China was punctuated by the protests in Tiananmen Square in 1989 and the violent crackdown that followed. The pro-democracy movement within China has been somewhat muted since then, but crackdowns of all kinds have continued. And China's policies in Xinjiang and Tibet have aroused revulsion and accusations of human rights abuses and genocide. The other crackdowns are different. Xi's disgust with the commercialization of society, China's nouveau riche, official corruption, and the moral evils of drugs and

26 Johnson, I., *The Souls of China: The Return of Religion after Mao*, Parthenon Books, New York, 2017, pp. 363–366.

27 Aikman, D., *Jesus in Beijing*, revised edition, Monarch Books, Oxford, 2006, pp. 34–37.

prostitution is surely genuine.[28] But all the latest public policy remedies are usually attributed to the influence of Wang Huning.[29] This is why we now see anti-monopoly and data-security measures directed at such Chinese tech and social media companies as Tencent, Alibaba, Weibo, and WeChat. It is why the Internet in general is censored in China, why tech IPOs are treated with such a heavy hand, and why algorithms are required to 'uphold mainstream values'.[30] It also explains the Chinese government's abolition of the private-tutoring sector, clearing cyberspace of content that promotes obsessional consumption of Korean pop music, and limiting children to no more than three hours of video games each week.[31] It is the motive for the enforced disappearances of online celebrities, influencers, billionaires, and athletes who are believed to undermine public morality.[32] And it has inspired increasingly stringent surveillance and the frightening 'social credit' system: a national credit rating and blacklist database now under development in China.[33]

And so, when I contemplate China, I have mixed feelings. China and the West now confront the same problems of hyper-materialism

28 Xi's feelings on those matters were reported in a Wikileaks cable of 2009 (https://wikileaks.org/plusd/cables/09BEIJING3128_a.html).

29 Lyons, N. S., 'The Triumph and Terror of Wang Huning', *Palladium*, October 11, 2021 (https://palladiummag.com/2021/10/11/the-triumph-and-terror-of-wang-huning/).

30 'China Has Become a Laboratory for the Regulation of Digital Technology', *The Economist*, September 11, 2021 (https://www.economist.com/china/2021/09/11/china-has-become-a-laboratory-for-the-regulation-of-digital-technology).

31 Lee, H. K., 'Chinese Government Cracking Down on K-pop Fandom', *ABC News*, September 13, 2021 (https://abcnews.go.com/International/chinese-government-cracking-pop-fandom/story?id=79987524).

32 Holmes, O., 'China's Disappeared: High-profile Figures Who Have Gone Missing in the Past Decade', *The Guardian*, November 19, 2021 (https://www.theguardian.com/world/2021/nov/19/china-disappeared-high-profile-figures-who-have-gone-missing-during-xi-jinpings-rule).

33 Dillon, M., *China in the Age of Xi Jinping*, Routledge, New York, 2021, 192–193.

amidst a degraded and deteriorating civilization. But only China seems to be in search of a solution. Unfortunately, much of the quest will amount only to an enlargement of the state's powers to surveil and control is citizens. Many, perhaps most, of those citizens will nevertheless accept that state of affairs on the ground that it preserves stability and unity.[34] As long as Chinese citizens immigrate in large numbers to the West, and not the reverse, no such trade-off will be embraced here, I think. As for Wang Huning's crackdowns, some of them may actually turn out to have wide appeal. We in the West may soon see the break-up of tech monopolies and heavy-handed control of the Internet. Western states may soon recover some of their former vigour and enforce public morality. Nevertheless, it is hard to see spiritual and cultural renewal emerging from purely negative forces.

The rehabilitation of Confucianism is much more obviously good. If ostensible atheists like Ye Xiaowen can recognize the spiritual emptiness of contemporary China, and attempt to correct it, what excuse have we in the West for not doing likewise? And so, like the fictional Bouvard, I would like to think that the Chinese revival of their intellectual, philosophical, and spiritual patrimony is an example for us to imitate. We may soon find, as Ian Johnson has predicted, that China is no longer the 'hyper-mercantilist, fragile superpower' that we now know. China may be at the forefront of a worldwide quest to restore stability, solidarity, and values to dislocated and deracinated societies in which economics has become the only measure of culture.[35] This would constitute a

34 Wood, M., *The Story of China: The Epic History of a World Power from the Middle Kingdom to Mao and the China Dream*, St. Martin's Press, New York, 2020, pp. 529–530.

35 Johnson, I., *The Souls of China: The Return of Religion after Mao*, Parthenon Books, New York, 2017, p. 400.

serious ideological challenge to us, more formidable in my view than the still-distant possibility of China's economic and military supremacy over America. Unless we get our act together, there may be a greater sense of continuity with the past in a supposedly Maoist surveillance state than anywhere in the West. Abandoning this ideological struggle would mean a world in which the greatest achievements of Western civilization (to say nothing of any other kind of civilization) are more readily venerated in Beijing and Shanghai than in Washington, London, or Paris. So, on that grim note, I would urge us here in the West to pursue the same goal of renewal as China without imitating all the same means. And yet, like Bertrand Russell, I too fear that we in the West will turn out to be unteachable, doomed by an obsession with novelty. Then again, to quote Chou Enlai, it may be too soon to tell.

Afterword

. . . A people without history
Is not redeemed from time, for history is a pattern
Of timeless moments. So, while the light fails
On a winter's afternoon, in a secluded chapel
History is now and England.

T. S. Eliot, 'Little Gidding'

KENNETH CLARK ENDED HIS documentary *Civilisation* with a short description of his personal views—beliefs which had been 'repudiated by the liveliest intellects of our time':

> I believe that order is better than chaos, creation better than destruction. I prefer gentleness to violence, forgiveness to vendetta. On the whole I think that knowledge is preferable to ignorance, and I am sure that human sympathy is more valuable than ideology. I believe that, in spite of the recent triumphs of science, men haven't changed much in the last 2,000 years; and in consequence we must still try to learn from history. History is ourselves.[1]

1 Clark, K., *Civilisation*, 1969, pp. 346–347.

This message is more urgent now than it was in 1969. When I was growing up in the 1990s, it was still widely believed that history was a story of progress, and people scoffed at the idea that decline was even possible. Everyone seemed to think that the present state of the world was better than at any former time, and that it could only continue to improve. Even human nature itself would improve. This outlook was reinforced by a perception of relative calm after a century of chaos and upheaval; and the collapse of the USSR seemed to suggest that a new age of peace and stability had opened. The mood of the time is captured in the near-universal misunderstanding of Francis Fukuyama's thesis about the 'end of history', as well as the Disney cartoon *Aladdin*'s invitation to imagine 'a whole new world'—both of which appeared in 1992.[2] It was not a golden age everywhere, of course. Many in the West seemed to ignore all evidence of calamity and disaster in places like Iraq, Rwanda, and the Balkans. The 1990s also saw the rise of the Taleban, and the following century opened with the destruction of the Buddhas of Bamyan in Afghanistan and the attacks of 9/11 in America. Since then we have lurched from one crisis to another: warfare and humiliation, financial collapse, terrorism, pandemic, supply chain problems, inflation, and so on.

The 'whole new world' is much like the old one, only worse. History has not ended. Declinism no longer elicits scoffing as it once did. Peter Frankopan's *New Silk Roads*, for instance, appeared in 2018, and it is a tale of Western decline and the rise of Asia. Canadian academic Andrew Potter's 2021 book *On Decline* determines that 2016 was the year that decline set in for good.[3]

2 Frankopan, P., *The New Silk Roads: The Present and Future of the World*, Alfred A. Knopf, New York, 2018, p. 25; Fukuyama, F., *The End of History*, with a new afterword, Free Press, New York, (originally published 1992), 2006.

3 Potter, A., *On Decline: Stagnation, Nostalgia, and Why Every Year Is the Worst One Ever,* Biblioasis, Windsor, Ontario, 2021.

Books with such titles as *Disorder* and *The End of the World Is Just the Beginning*, and *Doom* have begun to appear, predicting—without hyperbole—looming catastrophes comparable to the Bronze Age Collapse.[4] And, of course, Donald Trump still speaks incessantly of American decay and Western stagnation, while Greta Thunberg prophesies imminent and irreversible calamity. Many agree with them, and we will hear more such talk for some time, I am sure. Civilization is indeed in decline, the rot set in long ago, and we in the West are still looking for renewal in the wrong place.

Orientation toward the future means hostility to the past, as well as an absence of rootedness, permanence, and stability. What emerges from this outlook are conditions in which civilization is not possible. Nevertheless, if we think of the matter at all, most of us in the West probably imagine ourselves as living in a civilization and an *advanced* one at that. We could cite our constant abolition of what is old and our ever-improving technology as the proof. But this would be the wrong way to think about it. A never-ending quest for novelty cannot possibly be a feature of an advanced civilization. On the contrary, the defining feature of an advanced people would be a long list of past accomplishments, just as we would say that someone who is advanced in his trade is a person who has a long record of prior accomplishment. But people who are forgetful of history, ignorant of former achievements, fixated on whatever new things might appear in the future cannot be thought of in this way. This is what Jean Baudrillard meant when he described America, whence most radical innovations originate, as 'the only remaining

4 Thompson, H., *Disorder: Hard Times in the 21st Century*, Oxford University Press, Oxford, 2022; Zeihan, P., *The End of the World Is Just the Beginning: Mapping the Collapse of Globalization*, Harper Business, New York, 2022; Ferguson, N., *Doom: The Politics of Catastrophe*, Penguin Press, New York, 2021.

primitive society'.[5] One does not need to be a postmodernist to understand that there is truth to that description.

The remedy that I propose is not to abandon hope for the future, but to reconnect ourselves with the past. I hope that we shall have the courage to do it voluntarily. But, unless we destroy ourselves first through the endless pursuit of revolutionary newness, as we have almost done many times already, sooner or later we shall be *forced* to make our peace with the past. I believe this for three reasons. First, if there is a single lesson to take from the twentieth century, it is that most new ideas are bad and many are evil. There should be enough cultural maturity in the West to understand this now. Second, the cultural exchanges and mutual influence occasioned by globalization may soon be impossible.[6] The paradoxical outcome of globalization is to erode differences and to make people more and more similar to one another. And so, looking to the past may eventually be the only way for one culture to influence another. If globalization has already reached its peak and is now reversing itself, as Peter Zeihan argues,[7] this looking to the past will be the only source of cultural renewal available to us. Third, the universal imitation of older models suggests to me that there is something about human nature that predisposes us to do it. I am tempted to think that such imitation is really vital to us, it was a mistake to halt it, and as long as our species continues, it will not be possible to keep it down forever. The Confucian revival in China seems to be an example of this.

5 Baudrillard, J., *America*, translated by Chris Turner, Verso, New York, 1988 (originally published 1986), p. 7.

6 Fernández-Armesto, F., *Out of Our Minds: What We Think and How We Came to Think It*, London, One World Books, 2019, pp. 399–402.

7 Zeihan, P., *The End of the World Is Just the Beginning: Mapping the Collapse of Globalization*, Harper Business, New York, 2022.

If I am right, some of our attitudes will have to change. No participant in any civilizing epoch shared, for instance, the contemporary elite fear of 'cultural appropriation' which now stands in the way of imitation and learning. It would be absurd to suggest that human differences had never provoked tension or violence in the past, but differences in religion, language, or ethnicity were not normally barriers to the spread of civilization. It seems tragic to me that, in our own time, we are torn between two antithetical doctrines of multiculturalism: one holding that differences between people are superficial and insignificant; and the other that differences are so great that every person's 'lived experience' is unique and inaccessible to others. Accordingly, imitation would be either a shallow affectation or an imaginary pretence. This dichotomy is fundamentally wrong, and we must abandon it.

And what about our attitudes to science and technology? Francis Bacon foresaw only increased wealth and happiness from those sources. Was he right to do so? Most of us will acknowledge the convenience brought about by the car, the telephone, the computer, and the Internet because we simply cannot do without them. Those things may have made some of us wealthy, and some people may believe that they have promoted happiness. Few now seem willing to confront the dark side of technology, though. In the last century, it was represented above all by the atom bomb which is still with us, though the threat of nuclear war seems smaller now, Russian threats against Ukraine notwithstanding. At the present moment, we might reflect that one branch of medical science has been mobilized to confront a problem which may have arisen in another branch of it. The victory of vaccines seems unambiguous to me, but the utility of gain-of-function research on deadly viruses may not always be worth the risk. On a less calamitous note, I fear that science and technology have long ceased to promote either ease or happiness. Instead of adapting technology to serve our needs, we now adapt ourselves to technology, as anyone dependent upon a smartphone and the Internet must realize. An especially sad consequence of technology is embodied in hook-up and dating apps which have fragmented and abridged courtship and romance, and thereby made many people miserable. Far more grim are the implications of video games and online pornography. I do not know what Francis Bacon would have made of this state of affairs. But happiness is not so much the heart of the matter as the fact that science and technology cannot teach us to be virtuous. They cannot make us civilized. Nor do they even inform us what it means to be human. So, the sort of technological society that I fear most is *not* one in which machines become more human, but one in which men and women become more like machines.

Instead of promoting the 'passive and vicarious amusement' of the online world, science and technology should enhance communal life.[8] They should make our communities more orderly and more beautiful. They should allow us more time for friends and family. But I fear this is all another fond hope of mine. Every day we awaken, like the Seven Sleepers of Ephesus or (as Fernández-Armesto says) Rip van Winkle, to a strange world of new things, as the pace of technological change continues to accelerate.[9] Virtual socialization in an imaginary online universe, 3D-printed fake meat, colonizing space, artificial wombs, robot sex dolls, genetically engineered immortality, suicide pods, transhumanism, and downloading human consciousness into machines are only a few of the more recent ideas which are supposed to inspire optimism and excitement. If Flaubert were writing now, they would no doubt

8 Sixsmith, B., 'The American Dream Is Starting to Look Like a Creepy Carnival', *The Daily Caller*, January 27, 2022 (https://dailycaller.com/2022/01/27/sixsmith-the-american-dream-is-starting-to-look-like-a-creepy-carnival/).

9 Fernández-Armesto, F., *Out of Our Minds: What We Think and How We Came to Think It*, One World Books, London, 2019, p. 356.

all be investigated and discussed by the two idiots Bouvard and Pécuchet. Sooner or later they will take their place in the ever-expanding encyclopaedia of evil ideas, and it will be proved, once again, that we are wrong to emphasize constant innovation over keeping civilization alive. And so let us hope, and pray, that one day soon we may remember that we got some things right the first time.

If we want a practical example of what imitation of the past might mean in the West, we should look to music. Despite some people's best efforts, revolutionary change never really took hold in music. The works of Schoenberg, Berg, and Webern, for instance, were supposed to mark a permanent break with the past by abandoning traditional harmonies and keys.[10] But none of it caught on, and the chord progressions, scales, and modes of contemporary pop music or movie scores have more in common with those of the sixteenth-century masters than with Schoenberg and his ilk. No less importantly, music is the only art for which no one now questions the idea of execution according to the artist's original intentions. This had not always been the case. Until the mid-twentieth century or so, it was common to hear all sorts of orchestral music performed according to Romantic practices laid down in the late nineteenth century. This tended to mean slow and heavy phrases and warbling bel canto singing. But now a 'modern' performance of a piece of music is a paradox, since it implies that you will hear the piece according to an older standard as elucidated by the best of contemporary knowledge. And it is not just the apostles of the 'early music' movement who do this. Vintage instruments, as well as original performance practices, are preferred for blues and rock music

10 Conrad, P., *Modern Times, Modern Places: How Life and Art Were Transformed in a Century of Revolution, Innovation and Radical Change*, New York, Alfred A. Knopf, 1999, pp. 173–201.

as well as for the high baroque. Musicians and fans alike will also study original performance practices down to the minutest details of the costumes and stage antics of Chuck Berry or Jimmy Page, just as *they* had imitated Muddy Waters and the great Blues players of Chicago and the Mississippi Delta.[11] Nobody questions any of this in the way that, say, elites consider a preference for classical art to be boring and unimaginative, or performing Shakespearian plays with seventeenth-century pronunciation is thought to be unusual.

So will the likes of Jordi Savall, Paul McCreesh, and Christina Pluhar, as well as the huge proliferation of classical and baroque music festivals point the way to a general renewal? Will Keith Richards or Jimmy Page do so? Unlikely, it would seem. Nevertheless, when I think about the influence of the image over the word or of physics over visual art, anything seems possible.

'History is now', said T. S. Eliot in the epigraph above. 'History is ourselves', says Kenneth Clark. Each generation must seek facts, narrative, and truth in the past. The feeling that one is a part of history is mankind's proper orientation in space and time: it civilizes us and, I daresay, makes us fully human. This is what the postmodernists would rightly call a 'grand narrative', but we should not be deterred by this label. The promise of relativism and subjectivity to usher in a new and better world has been exposed as a confidence trick or a quack cure. There are still many true believers, of course, but their old enthusiasm seems to have turned to bitterness and resentment. Yet, for those of us who were never deceived, this is not a crisis, but an opportunity to rediscover who we really are and to tell truths again that have been forgotten.[12]

11 In some notable cases there was outright theft, of course, but that is another matter.

12 I am grateful to Henry Hopwood-Phillips and Lola Salem who helped me form this conclusion in many a Twitter exchange and direct message.